THE NEOLIBERAL CITY

THE NEOLIBERAL CITY

Governance, Ideology, and Development in American Urbanism

JASON HACKWORTH

Cornell University Press
Ithaca and London

First published 2007 by Cornell University Press
First printing, Cornell Paperbacks, 2007

Printed in the United States of America

Library of Congress Cataloging-in-Publication Data

Hackworth, Jason R.
    The neoliberal city : governance, ideology, and develop-
ment in American urbanism / Jason Hackworth.
        p.   cm.
    Includes bibliographical references and index.
    ISBN-13: 978-0-8014-4488-3 (cloth : alk. paper)
    ISBN-10: 0-8014-4488-8 (cloth : alk. paper)
    ISBN-13: 978-0-8014-7303-6 (pbk. : alk. paper)
    ISBN-10: 0-8014-7303-9 (pbk. : alk. paper)
    1. Urban policy—United States.   2. Municipal govern-
ment—United States.   3. City planning—Political aspects
—United States.   4. Neo-liberalism—United States.
I. Title.
HT123.H245   2006
307.760973—dc22   2006023306

Cornell University Press strives to use environmentally responsible suppliers and materials to the fullest extent possible in the publishing of its books. Such materials include vegetable-based, low-VOC inks and acid-free papers that are recycled, totally chlorine-free, or partly composed of nonwood fibers. For further information, visit our website at www.cornellpress.cornell.edu.

Cloth printing   10 9 8 7 6 5 4 3 2 1
Paperback printing   10 9 8 7 6 5 4 3 2 1

CONTENTS

TABLES AND FIGURES

Tables

Figures

PREFACE

A few years ago, United Nations Habitat produced a textbook on cities that I still use as a teaching reference (Habitat, 2001). One of my favorite graphs in the book occurs in the prologue, where the authors plot the increase in the frequency of the word *globalization* in academic articles during the 1990s to demonstrate the increasing salience of global interconnections. Not surprisingly, the number of articles in 1990 that used the word in their title was very small, but the frequency increased at an almost exponential rate during the ensuing decade. They explained the rise as an expression of the growing social importance of global connections in today's political economy. Though this explanation is undoubtedly true, the example always makes me think about the ways that ideas gain a certain popularity within the social sciences and begin to take on a life independent of their social importance or empirical frequency. While globalization is indeed real, it was neither so absent in 1990 nor so prevalent in 2000 to justify its rise in the social science literature. Its rise had as much to do with its popularity as a concept as it did to its salience to contemporary society.

I've begun recently to think that *neoliberalism* is poised to replace *globalization* as the next popular metaconcept in the social sciences. The literature on neoliberalism as a concept has exploded in recent years, for reasons broadly similar to those that led to the rise of globalization. States, provinces, policies, eras, people, countries, and institutions have all been deemed "neoliberal" or "neoliberalizing" by various commentators in recent years. It is used broadly to characterize the right wing; to mean the guiding light for the "Washington Consensus"; to mean anything related to business; to mean anything related to capitalism; to mean anything related to liberals in the United States. Neoliberalism is everywhere and, apparently, everything.

Unlike globalization, neoliberalism is rooted in a very specific set of ideas, so the diffusion of the label as though it were new, uncontested, or unrooted to a long line of scholarship is much more problematic. I see the unmoored expansion of neoliberalism as a serious conceptual and political problem. Much of the current writing on neoliberalism does not adequately link itself to the broad set of ideas underlying the liberal tradition. Worse yet, many writings about neoliberalism rely on almost paraphrased versions of classical readings of the liberal tradition—Marx, Foucault, Polanyi, and Hayek, among others. Very few authors have bothered to explore the ideas in their original form or to think about contextual issues that might have influenced their inception. I think that this makes for a very shaky foundation for understanding why these ideas are important to contemporary political economy. More to the point, it makes a serious critique of neoliberalism nearly impossible.

I wrote this book, in part, to "ground" the literature on neoliberalism, a task that has at least two dimensions. First, I think that neoliberalism derives from a very specific and historically rooted set of ideas. It is not everything related to business or capitalism, but it is changing the way that both work. Too little of the literature on neoliberalism provides any basic philosophical or historical background to the idea. This book sets out to do precisely this. Second, much of the historical literature on neoliberalism is placeless. It does not recognize the geographically rooted nature of the process. This book attempts to ground neoliberalism in this way by focusing on one particular form of settlement (cities) in one country (the United States). Cities are the sites of both the most acute articulation of neoliberalism and of its most acute opposition. This book explores how and why this is the case.

I have a great number of people to thank for their help in conceiving, developing, and finishing this project. Peter Wissoker of Cornell University Press has been a fantastic person to work with on this project, giving me the freedom and time to develop the project while also keeping me to a schedule. Karen Laun and Martin Schneider, also at CUP, did a very careful and thoughtful edit of the manuscript. Tenley Conway, my wife, read the entire manuscript and has helped me immeasurably with the content and also by providing me with the confidence and patience I needed to finish it. Katharine Rankin, Meric Gertler, David Ranney, and Jamie Peck all provided a great deal of guidance with navigating the book publishing process for me. A number of people have read portions of the manuscript in some form, and I thank them for their help: Larry Bourne, Neil Brenner, Elizabeth Burns, Gunter Gad, Kanishka Goonewardena, Briavel Holcomb, Bob Lake, Robin Leichenko, Debby Leslie, Robert Lewis, Jamie Peck, Katharine Rankin, Neil Smith, Phil Steinberg, Frederick Steiner, Barney Warf, and Elvin Wyly. A number of others have been helpful at pushing me to develop certain themes during academic presentations or informal conversations about this work. They include: Alana Boland, Deb Cowan, Cheryl Gowar, Noriko Ishiyama, Andy Jonas, Stephan Kipfer, David Ley, Eugene McCann, Roger Picton, Norma Rantisi, Jen Ridgley, Sue Ruddick, Amy Siciliano, Bansuri Taneja, Jeff Ueland, Andy Walter, and Jill Wigle. I also thank Chin-fan Chang, Winnie Man, Brian Yeitz, and particularly Bobby Ramsay (who read the entire manuscript) for their research assistance and Tony Stallins, Andy Walter, Jeff Ueland, and Barb Trapido-Lurie for providing help along the way with various empirical tasks. Finally, several research grants helped in various ways to develop this project. These include grants from the U.S. National Science Foundation, Florida State University, the U.S. Department of Housing and Urban Development, the University of Toronto, and the Canadian Social Science and Humanities Research Council.

Some of the material in this book draws on work of mine published elsewhere in a more detailed form. Where applicable, I gratefully acknowledge the permission of each respective publisher to reprint passages from this earlier material. If the reader is interested in exploring these materials further, please consult the following: "Emergent Urban Forms, or Emergent Post-Modernisms? A Comparison of Large U.S. Metropolitan Areas," *Urban Geography*. 26, no. 6 (2005): 484–519 (© V.H. Winston and Sons); "Public Housing and the Re-Scaling of Regulation in the U.S.," *Environment and Planning A* 35, no. 3(2003): 531–49 (© Pion Limited); "Local Autonomy, Bond-Rating Agencies and Neoliberal Urbanism in the U.S.," *International Journal of Urban and Regional Research* 26, no. 4 (2002): 707–25 (© Blackwell Publishing); "Post Recession Gentrification in New York City," *Urban Affairs Review* 37, no. 6 (2002): 815–43 (© Sage Publications); "Inner City Real Estate Investment, Gentrification, and Economic Recession in New York City," *Environment and Planning A* 33, no. 5 (2001): 863–80 (© Pion Limited); "State Devolution, Urban Regimes, and the Production of Geographic Scale: The Case of New Brunswick, NJ," *Urban Geography* 21, no. 5 (2000): 450–58 (© V.H. Winston and Sons); "Local Planning and Economic Restructuring: A Synthetic Interpretation of

Urban Redevelopment," *Journal of Planning Education and Research* 18, no. 4 (1999): 293–306 (© Sage Publications).

Friedrich Hayek, the father of neoliberalism, dedicated his 1944 classic, *The Road to Serfdom*, to "socialists of all parties." He clearly meant it as a smug jab at what he saw as the misguided masses who felt that socialism, benevolent or not, was capable of something more humane than Stalin. To him, socialism—no matter what its variant—was and always would be a road to serfdom. Liberal individualism was the only path toward social justice. A lot has changed since 1944. Most of the regimes that troubled Hayek are now a distant memory, and economic liberalism is not the marginal discourse that it was when he was alive. But one thing that hasn't changed, apparently, is the myopic inertia that can develop around an all-encompassing political ideal. In Hayek's time, that inertia could turn a blind eye to the brutal excesses of Stalin, Pol Pot, and the Cultural Revolution as long as the wheels of socialism were in motion. In our time, that inertia turns a blind eye to the excesses of Pinochet, the IMF, unjustified wars, and the "Washington Consensus" as long as the wheels of unregulated capitalism are in motion. With this in mind, I dedicate this book to liberals of all parties.

THE NEOLIBERAL CITY

Chapter 1

The Place, Time, and Process
of Neoliberal Urbanism

During his largely symbolic quest for the 2004 Democratic Party presidential nomination, Dennis Kucinich became an iconoclast for the economic justice Left in the United States. After entering the race, he immediately separated himself from the rest of the candidates by calling for the abolition of the North American Free Trade Agreement (NAFTA), the unilateral withdrawal of troops in Iraq, and the creation of universal health care. Soon he became featured in *Mother Jones* and *The Nation* and began appearing at fundraising outings in Hollywood that were remarkably successful—at least compared to other candidates with his politics. One of the central narratives he used to promote his candidacy was an experience that he had as the youngest mayor in the history of Cleveland, Ohio, nearly thirty years earlier. Already known for his confrontational style after a few months in office, Kucinich faced a financial crisis that threatened to bankrupt the city. Banks were willing to continue extending credit to the beleaguered city on the important condition that Kucinich privatize the city's electricity provider, Muni Light. When he refused to agree to this condition, the banks cut off the city's credit, and Kucinich was ignominiously recalled, ironically for doing what he was elected to do in the first place. Largely because of this episode, many considered Cleveland the classic prototype of municipal mismanagement in the United States. The city's industrial base was eroding, its coffers empty, and, for a brief while, its river ablaze. Kucinich took the fall for most of it. The local press deemed him a "vain, yappy, little demagogue," and a panel of historians later rated him the seventh worst mayor in the history of the country (Bowden 2003).

Considering such bad publicity, it is initially difficult to understand why someone running for political office would advertise his involvement in the affair. After all, his political career was sidelined for nearly a decade because of it, and Cleveland still lives with the stigma of being a mismanaged city. But, as Kucinich points out in the denouement of his vignette, the city's power supply is still publicly owned, and service is more widely available than would be the case had he acquiesced. He had won a small battle against the reckless rollback of public subsidies but was simply underappreciated for it at the time. Yet while vindicated enough to use the experience to garner votes now, it is unlikely that he (or anyone in his situation) would be treated any differently if the same situation were to occur today. The notion that city officials should do everything in their power to placate corporate financial interests that threaten to leave or penalize the locality has become so unquestioned that it is considered common sense by public administrators and the popular press. Though the collectivization of public resources was once held sacrosanct in American cities, Kucinich was judged a fool by critics for trying to apply such principles in such an ostensibly different era.

What changed to make the privatization of erstwhile public resources so axiomatic? Was it something structural or a simple matter of populist backlash? Is it long-lasting or more ephemeral? This book attempts to answer some of these questions by exploring the physical, political, and economic changes experienced by large American cities in the past thirty years. The book is titled *The Neoliberal City* because it is my contention that much of the shift reflected in the vignette above can be traced to the utterly astonishing rise and reproduction of "neoliberalism" as an ideology, mode of city governance, and driver of urban change. As Anderson points out, the scope, power and extent of what was as recently as the 1960s considered little more than the workings of a "lunatic right fringe" (Girvetz 1963) is nothing short of remarkable:

> For the first time since the Reformation there are no longer any significant oppositions—that is, systematic rival outlooks—within the thought-world of the West; and scarcely any on a world scale either, if we discount religious doctrines as largely inoperative archaisms, as the experiences of Poland or Iran indicate we may. Whatever limitations persist to its practice, neo-liberalism as a set of principles rules undivided across the globe: the most successful ideology in world his-

tory. . . . Virtually the entire horizon of reference in which the generation of the sixties grew up has been wiped away—the landmarks of reformist and revolutionary socialism in equal measure. (2000, p. 17)

But just what is neoliberalism and what does it have to do with American cities? This chapter attempts to address this question in order to better situate the exploration of examples of "actually existing" neoliberalism in American cities.[1]

The Time and Place of Neoliberalism

Genealogy of an idea

The language of neoliberalism is quite common within contemporary social theory, but because so little time is spent defining the term and associated terms, the meaning of the ideas tends to be unmoored and somewhat variable. This section attempts to clarify the way that liberalism and neoliberalism have recently been conceptualized by briefly revisiting the evolution of both ideas. Understanding the evolution of the wider liberal tradition (see Girvetz 1963) is the first step toward a workable definition of late twentieth-century *neo*liberalism and its policy framework, the "New Political Economy" (Chang 1997; Meier 1993). Though the ideas underlying liberalism as a general concept are evident in Greek, Roman, and reformist Christian writings, the most commonly cited root to the project is the classical liberalism of the eighteenth and nineteenth centuries. Classical liberals varied in their politics, method, and purpose (see Gray 1989) but were relatively unified on several counts. First, there was an intense focus on the individual within liberal political thought. Following Hume, Paley, Bentham, and James Mill in particular, classical liberalism asserted that the highest virtue of a society is the degree to which its individuals are allowed to pursue pleasure. Individuals themselves are seen as the most qualified at understanding their needs and wants, so society should be structured around lowering barriers to the individual realization of this pleasure. Classical liberals varied on whether the right to pursue pleasure was "natural" (Hume) or part of a "social contract" (Locke), but virtually every classical liberal thinker believed that individual autonomy should be

---

1. The phrase "actually existing neoliberalism" is borrowed from Brenner and Theodore (2002) and explained later in the chapter.

venerated above all else. The second major tenet of classical liberalism, following largely from Adam Smith (and the classical school of economics that he inspired), is that an unfettered market is the most efficient and effective means for encouraging individual autonomy and assuring that the simultaneous pursuit of individual pleasure did not devolve into anarchy. Within this frame, society is best served when individuals are able to pursue their needs and wants through the mechanism of price; producers, moreover, are servants of consumers, who demand certain goods from these producers based on their wants. The third major tenet of classical liberalism is a non-interventionist state. Classical liberals—in particular Smith, Bentham, and Acton—argued that the most effective way to achieve the aforementioned society of pleasure-seeking, market-oriented individuals is for the nation-state to be minimalist or "laissez-faire." According to classical liberals, the state should focus only on the pursuit of safety, competitive (unfettered and nonmonopolistic) markets, and a constitution guaranteeing individual rights, particularly the right to retain property (Sally 1998).

Though never fully implemented in any society, the ideas of liberalism took one of their strongest institutional forms in the founding documents of the United States—the Federalist Papers, the Constitution, and the Declaration of Independence in particular. Though all of these documents were the result of complicated political leanings at least a century old at the time, they institutionalized what Isaiah Berlin would much later characterize as "negative liberty" (1969). "Negative liberty" is freedom from state interference in one's daily life and is contrasted with "positive liberty," which is simply a vision for how the current power structure should be replaced. The formal separation of powers, the electoral college, and the separation of church and state, for example, were all designed to "protect" people from imposing a deleterious form of "positive liberty" upon themselves. "Negative liberty," in essence, was seen as the highest form of liberalism, and the founding documents of American statehood, superficially at least, defended its virtues. Actually existing negative liberty, however, was far more elusive than its initial institutional form in the United States. Early liberal idealism in the United States was also counterbalanced by strong residual feudalisms: legalized slavery, highly selective suffrage, debtor's prisons, and genocide of native peoples, to name but a few examples.

Obvious on-the-ground contradictions like these (and the various social movements that they inspired) were part of the reason that prominent fissures within the classical liberal project began to emerge by the late nineteenth century. Social movements critical of liberalism were paralleled by like-minded intellectual movements. Though much of the academy favored classical liberalism, not all mid-nineteenth century scholars—particularly socialists—were convinced of the liberal idea that capitalism was intrinsically neutral. The middle part of the nineteenth century saw the rise of the first progressive counterresponse to classical liberalism, its most famous advocates being Marx and Engels. To Marx in particular, classical liberalism represented little more than an elaborate justification for capitalist exploitation. He was critical of the seamless apology for capitalism that liberals like Bentham had constructed. In one memorable passage from *Capital*, Marx mockingly paraphrases the simplistic appeal of liberal thought:

> This sphere that we are deserting, within whose boundaries the sale and purchase of labour-power goes on, is in fact a very Eden of the innate rights of man. There alone rule Freedom, Equality, Property and Bentham. Freedom, because both buyer and seller of a commodity, say of labour-power, are constrained only by their own free will. They contract as free agents, and the agreement they come to, is but the form in which they give legal expression to their common will. Equality, because each enters into relation with the other, as with a simple owner of commodities, and they exchange equivalent for equivalent. Property, because each disposes only of what is his own. And Bentham, because each looks only to himself. The only force that brings them together and puts them in relation with each other, is the selfishness, the gain and the private interests of each. Each looks to himself only, and no one troubles himself about the rest, and just because they do so, do they all, in accordance with the pre-established harmony of things, or under the auspice of an all-shrewd providence, work together to their mutual advantage, for the common weal and in the interest of all. (1996, p. 172)

Marx goes on, of course, to argue that the capitalist economic system produces a series of institutions that actually perpetuate (rather than overcome) social inequality. Far from being a system that could, if left alone, produce the greatest good for the greatest number, capitalism, Marx argued, was a system premised on exploiting some for the benefit of others.

It is difficult to assess the influence of Marx and Engels on late nineteenth-century *American* political thought, but at a minimum their appeals in the widely distributed *Communist Manifesto* (1848) and periodic columns in the *New York Daily Tribune* inspired a consciousness that had been lacking in America's urban working class until that point. This consciousness was enhanced by deplorable working-class living conditions in many cities and the origin countries of new immigrants, many of which were more hospitable to "anti-liberal" political thought. Sympathy for such ideas congealed into radical labor movements in New York, Philadelphia, Chicago, and Milwaukee first, then spread to smaller, less militant cities by the end of the century. Workers demanded better conditions (at home and at work) and increasingly came to reject the ideology of laissez-faire.

Other scholars less skeptical than Marx were no less insistent that the ideals of classical liberalism could not be enjoyed by a significant number without some redress of economic conditions. Following John Stuart Mill in particular, an increasingly egalitarian strand of liberalism began to argue that the tenets of classical liberalism were neither being attained nor even attainable without a strong secular state that redistributed wealth among the populace. Mill's calls for a strong estate tax and compulsory education are among the suggestions for intervention that this variant of liberalism began to inspire. Partially in response to the negative material outcomes of classical liberalism, an egalitarian liberal movement emerged (Kekes 1997).

Egalitarian liberalism is a loose assemblage of ideas with fewer foundational thinkers than classical liberalism, but the work of John Stuart Mill, Keynes, and much later Rawls (1971; 1993), Dworkin (1985), and Nagel (1978) became inspirational works for this line of reasoning. Egalitarian liberalism took root most firmly in places where anti-socialism was strongest—the United States being the most acute example (N. Smith 2002)—and became increasingly widespread after Keynes (1936; see also 1926), and the American New Deal demonstrated that such an approach could actually promote (rather than impede) economic growth.[2] Egalitarian liberalism combined several basic tenets of classical liberalism—particularly the focus on the individual and the elegance of the market—with a redistributive nation-state that would more aggressively intervene to provide some of the basic economic conditions necessary for experiencing the putative political freedoms of classical liberalism (Girvetz 1963). As Kekes explains,

> The core of egalitarian liberalism continues to be autonomy. The autonomous life, however, is seen as requiring both freedom and welfare rights. It requires that individuals should be guaranteed certain

2. Outside of North America, such political thought more often than not congealed into "democratic socialism," which shares many ideas with egalitarian liberalism but is nonetheless a different project.

basic goods that are needed for living according to any conception of a good life. The role of government, therefore, is to protect not merely freedom rights but also welfare rights. (1997, p. 13)

Justifiable interventions included but were not limited to public housing, corporate antitrust laws, food stamps, and basic income redistribution. Twentieth-century classical liberals generally loathed this turn in liberal thought and rejected it (see Hayek 1944; 1960; Friedman 1962). Hayek in particular argued that egalitarian liberalism was not liberal at all, and he worked both to discredit it and distance himself from it. Incidentally, he was just as keen to distance himself from the American conservative movement. Though neoconservatism and neoliberalism are now part of a complicated political amalgam in the United States, Hayek argued that true liberals did not share the conservative desire for the status quo, much less its ideas of racial and gender exclusivity. Both Friedman and Hayek argued that liberalism was progressive and transformative in nature and that the practices of egalitarian liberals (welfare, regulation, and so on) would eventually lead to the erosion of personal freedom. Their belief, however, was relatively marginal until the 1970s, as the basic ideas of egalitarian liberalism (particularly Keynesianism) inspired (and were in turn inspired by) a massive shift in governance during the mid–twentieth century toward a stronger, openly regulatory nation-state.

Interventions were justified on several counts. First, a foundational governance principle of Keynesianism, among other ideologies, is that markets are far from perfectly self-regulating; rather, they can self-destruct without targeted intervention by various levels of government. The central principle upon which this form of governance rests is the maintenance of effective demand. By providing some forms of income redistribution, government was able to assist growth in the collective ability to consume more commodities. It was felt, furthermore, that such government expenditures would not be a net weight on the economy because of the "multiplier effect." The multiplier effect suggests that if the conditions for circulation are protected and the populace saves some portion of its income, government expenditures can generate economic value greater than the original investment. Though the idea actually preceded Keynes (see Canterbery 1995), the multiplier effect transformed the way that government expenditures under capitalism were viewed.

But Keynesian policy intervention was not limited to a demand-side cover for capitalism. There were also a set of theoretical market failures that justified regulatory and redistributory interventions. Four such theorized failures emerged as justifications for intervention. First, markets would fail when there was "imperfect competition"—industries, if left alone, would actually tend toward a limited number of firms, a pure monopoly being the most extreme case. Without adequate competition, output would be lower and prices higher than under "perfect competition." The most tangible institutional manifestation of this idea is the anti-monopoly wave of regulations that emerged to varying extents in North America and Western Europe in the late nineteenth and early twentieth centuries. Second, some goods were considered "public" or "social" to the extent that they are collectively consumed and very difficult to price on an individual basis. The most commonly used example of this type of good is national defense, but infrastructure and transportation networks have been financed using a similar justification. Third, the presence of "externalities" (primarily negative) could induce a form of market failure that would necessitate government intervention. Many firms do not factor the full (external) cost of production into their price, so it was acceptable for governments to intervene through taxation and regulation to make sure that the firms that generate such externalities have to pay at least a portion of their costs, whether directly or indirectly. The pollution generated in the production of an automobile, for example, is not directly factored into its price even though it is a tangible cost that often gets transferred to a city, state, or province. Finally, mainstream economists considered "imperfect information" a source of market failure, because ideal markets cannot work properly without full or near full information on product prices, characteristics, and so on.

Though most Keynesian economists never intended for non-market forms of failure to serve as justifications for intervention, one could also add a fifth type of failure to this typology, because of its importance for justifying government expenditures in cities. Specifically, some state intervention was justified because markets tended not to protect minimum socially acceptable standards for important commodities like housing and workplace conditions. Many economists never considered such failures to be the responsibility of the market, but the transparent inability of stand-alone markets to generate housing, health care, safe working conditions, and infrastructure served as a powerful social justification within the egalitarian liberal frame. Collectively, the egalitarian liberal architecture of governance justified and led to a very different set of government interventions than are acceptable today. At the municipal level, these ideas helped to justify regulations like Euclidean zoning, property taxes, and building codes, not to mention (federally funded, locally managed) redistributions such as public housing, unemployment insurance, and food stamps. These were justifiable in part because they fit within the ideological bounds of Keynesian managerialism in particular and egalitarian liberalism in general (see Harvey 1989b).

The federal government, newly educated to the ways of such intervention, also did their part in this agreement by facilitating and protecting the conditions for urban growth. A "spatial fix" to the Great Depression emerged in which the federal government targeted massive outlays for defense, freeway construction, and suburban real estate (Harvey 1989a). The synergy was very powerful. The defense industry produced jobs; the freeway system allowed for suburban living; suburban living required automobile usage. In the process, real estate capital was revived via a transfer to the urban fringe, but the inner city was left to disinvest for several decades in the mid–twentieth century (see N. Smith 1990). It would not be until the early 1970s that this bundle of political and economic forces would begin to unravel.

Neoliberalism increasingly came to be seen as a salve for the economic crisis that had emerged with this unraveling. Neoliberalism, simply defined, is an ideological rejection of egalitarian liberalism in general and the Keynesian welfare state in particular, combined with a selective return to the ideas of classical liberalism, most strongly articulated by Hayek (1944; 1960) and Friedman (1984; 1962). Both Hayek and Friedman argued that government should be used only sparingly and in very specific circumstances, rather than interfering within the marketplace. They revived classical notions of liberalism (particularly from Smith, Bentham, and James Mill) by arguing that the greatest good would be encouraged by using government only as a protector of free exchange. Hayek and Friedman were deeply troubled by the results of government intervention in the Soviet Union, Nazi Germany, and Fascist Italy, and argued that such atrocities could happen anywhere if personal political freedoms were not protected above all else. Hayek's firsthand experience as an Austrian exile gave his work an unusual passion, but his ideas would not be widely accepted by governments until the very end of his life (he died in 1992).

By the 1990s, neoliberalism had become naturalized as the proper mode of governance for a variety of geo-institutional contexts. In the United States, neoliberalism became tenuously connected to an equally pervasive form of social conservatism. It would be a mistake, however, to group neoconservatism and neoliberalism into one monolithic whole. As Hayek (1961) argued, the two projects have different roots and distinguishable characteristics. Neoliberalism is rooted in the aforementioned trilogy of the individual, the market, and the noninterventionist state. Neoconservatism, by contrast, is fundamentally rooted in an effort to resurrect a past set of social conditions. Though the two can often seem indistinguishable in American politics, it is important to point out that their union is neither naturally compatible nor consistently replicated elsewhere in the world.[3]

In either case, neoliberalism achieved hegemonic status through a number of important channels, including the Thatcher and Reagan administrations of the 1980s, both of which openly sought to roll back many elements of the Keynesian state, such as public housing, income supplements, and medical subsidies. "Libertarian" think tanks such as the Cato Institute also served to promote and reproduce neoliberalism, as did large global institutions like the International Monetary Fund, the World Bank, and bond rating agencies (see Gill 1995; Sassen 1996; Hackworth 2002a). The boundaries of urban governance have shifted dramatically in the past thirty years, partially because of structural constraints to governments (municipal or otherwise) in the capitalist world (see Harvey 1989b) but also because of a related ideological shift toward neoliberal governing practices (Goonewardena 2003). As Meier (1993) and Chang (1997), among others, point out, the ideology of market failures has given way to a generalized set of government failures. According to this logic, whatever failures typical of markets are eclipsed by the inefficiency, inequity, and corruption of governments that try to regulate outside of a market mechanism. Moreover, generalized redistribution is now seen as an impediment to international competitiveness (Jessop 2002), labor "flexibility" is seen as crucial for a working economy (Peck 2001a; Moody 1997), and monetarism is seen as the only proper macroeconomic intervention for the nation-state (Canterbery 1995). Government failures are the central justification for the rollback of intervention, while the notion of market failures has virtually disappeared from the policy (urban or otherwise) dialogue (Chang 1997). "Good" governance at the municipal level is now largely defined by the ability of formal government to assist (Harvey 1989b; Leitner 1990), collaborate with (Elkin 1987; Stone 1989), or function like (Box 1999) the corporate community. Extant regulatory powers such as land-use zoning have

---

3. The recent rift in the U.S. Republican Party over federal intervention in the case of Terry Schiavo—a brain-dead Florida woman whose husband had decided to remove her from life support after 10 years—partially revealed the natural *incompatibility* of these two political projects. Many neoliberals (deeming themselves "process conservatives") were publicly disturbed by such a use of state intervention, while most neoconservatives were aggressively supportive of the action.

been weakened, as have redistributive impulses in the area of social services and housing. Neoliberalism has become naturalized as the "only" choice available to cities in the United States and elsewhere.

Locating Neoliberalism

It would be easy to end with this relatively linear, aspatial genealogy of neoliberalism. It might also be possible to end by suggesting that cities, as complex manifestations of a wider politico-economic sphere, have somehow organically absorbed this turn in ideology. But as an increasingly large number of geographers and social scientists have argued, this would be mistake. Neoliberalism, like many other "–isms," is a highly contingent process that manifests itself, and is experienced differently, across space. The geography of neoliberalism is much more complicated than the idea of neoliberalism. There are several dimensions to this point.

First, neoliberalism is not a thing as much as a process—one that occurs alongside and in combination with many other processes that affect urbanization (see Jessop 2002). Some of these parallel processes are complimentary or supportive (like neocorporatism), while others are blatant contestations of neoliberalism (like neo-communitarianism). A segment of critical scholarship on neoliberalism is particularly concerned with understanding the "actually existing" nature of the ideology—that is, less the intellectual lineage of liberal thought than the way that such ideas permeate, and are experienced at various geographical scales. One particularly useful concept in this literature is the notion that actually existing neoliberalism is a more highly contingent process than the pure end-state it is often framed to be within neoliberal ideology (Brenner and Theodore 2002; Peck and Tickell 2002; Tickell and Peck 1995; Mitchell 2001; Larner 2003, 2000). Brenner and Theodore (2002) have described this process as a dialectical one, composed of the conflicting tendencies toward destruction and creation. Neoliberal destruction consists of the removal of Keynesian artifacts (public housing, public space), policies (redistributive welfare, food stamps), institutions (labor unions, U.S. Department of Housing and Urban Development), and agreements (Fordist labor arrangements, federal government redistribution to states and cities), while neoliberal creation consists of the establishment of new, or cooptation of extant, institutions and practices to reproduce neoliberalism in the future (government-business consortia, workfare policies). Peck and Tickell (2002) have depicted this evolution in a slightly more linear way, arguing that ne-oliberalism consists of an initial "roll-back" phase, which is followed by a "roll-out" phase. In this process, Keynesian policies and artifacts are de-stroyed to make way for a roll-out of more proactively neoliberal practices and ideas. Globally, some have suggested that the restructuring of Keynes-ian urban policy has had the aggregate effect of "hollowing out" the na-tion-state—decreasing its role as an institutional buffer between localities and the machinations of the global economy (Jessop 2002). Because of the reduction of national interventions in housing, local infrastructure, wel-fare, and the like, localities are forced either to finance such areas them-selves or to abandon them entirely. Swyngedouw (1997) has deemed this larger process "glocalization," as it involves a simultaneous upward (to the global economy and its institutions) and downward (to the locality and its governance structures) propulsion of regulatory power previously held or exercised by the nation-state.

Given its geographically and temporally contingent nature, however, this process has affected different national contexts in different ways. The aggressive rollback of the welfare state in the United States, for example, preceded that in Canada, and in both countries one can think of examples where the rollback has been incomplete for some sectors and more com-plete for others. The rollback/destruction of Keynesian interventions and the roll-out/creation of more proactively neoliberal policies are thus highly contingent, incremental, uneven, and largely incomplete. The resultant policy landscape is highly segmented—geographically and socially—and almost randomly strewn with concentrations of Keynesian artifacts (such as public housing) alongside roll-out neoliberal policies (such as workfare) in different places and in different stages of creation or destruction. Thus, while it is useful to suggest that policy ideas in North America and Europe are increasingly dominated by a unified, relatively simple set of ideas (ne-oliberalism), it is just as clear that the institutional manifestation (mainly through policy) of these ideas is highly uneven across and within countries.

Given all of this geographical specificity, it is reasonable to ask why the inner city—particularly the *American* inner city—is a useful space through which to evaluate the process of neoliberalism. After all, much of the liter-ature on neoliberalism is neither particularly urban nor particularly Amer-ican-oriented in nature. Much of the work that uses this concept looks at the impacts of neoliberalism on developing countries, particularly those with a large agricultural sector that has been absorbed by the capitalist economy. Furthermore, the meaning of liberalism is complicated in the

American context, where the egalitarian variant of liberalism became associated with the putative left wing of the U.S. polity, while the right wing became associated with the ideals of classical liberalism. The United States is, moreover, the most thoroughly liberalized environment in the developed world. What then would be novel or useful about identifying the influence of neoliberalism in already-liberalized spaces?

This book takes the position that precisely *because* the United States is such a thoroughly liberalized environment, the identification of changes within this context could very likely be harbingers of changes globally. That is, while the transition to neoliberalism in agriculture-oriented developing countries is easier to identify, documenting the influence of neoliberalism on American cities likely portends similar changes in other parts of the world. Furthermore, the inner city—seen widely as a vestige of the Keynesian national welfare state (Jessop 2002)—is an area of extreme transition. It has served as the focus of high-profile real estate investment, neoliberal policy experiments, and governance changes; Marcuse and van Kempen (2000) have deemed the inner city a "soft spot" for the implementation of neoliberal ideals. The intent of this book is to use the physical, political, and discursive space of the American inner city as a vehicle for understanding the nature of neoliberalism as it actually exists.

Organization of the Book

The variability of actually existing neoliberal urbanism is impressive, in progress, and not very linear. However, we can begin the journey of understanding both the nature of contemporary urbanism and the nature of contemporary neoliberalism by examining the various empirical fragments that exist today. This book is divided into three sections to shed light on the larger issue at hand. Part 1 (chapters 2 through 4) deals explicitly with the neoliberalization of local governance. It address why cities "choose" a neoliberal path and some of the material consequences for doing so. Part 2 (chapters 5 through 8) deals with the landscape changes associated with the neoliberal city. It seeks to document the impact of massive changes in real estate investment during the past thirty years—much of which is attributable to changes in the local state. It does so by focusing on changes occurring at four different levels: metropolitan areas, individual cities, neighborhoods, and single-site mega-projects. Examining changes at each scale helps to shed light on how the ideological changes of neoliberalism manifest themselves as material landscape changes. Part 3 (chapters 9 and 10) deals with the various efforts afoot to replace neoliberalism—either in a discursive or material sense. The consequences of neoliberalism have been fairly negative for the urban poor in the United States, and there are various projects attempting to either carve out an entirely new policy space or to dramatically reform the current one. The book ends with a consideration of such efforts.

PART 1

GOVERNING THE NEOLIBERAL CITY

Competition between local authorities or between larger entities within an area where there is freedom of movement provides in a large measure that opportunity for experimentation with alternative methods which will secure most of the advantages of free growth. Though the majority of residents may never contemplate a change of residence, there will usually be enough people, especially among the young and more enterprising, to make it necessary for the local authorities to provide as good services at as reasonable costs as their competitors.

F. Hayek in *Constitution of Liberty* (1960, p. 263–64)

It has taken several decades since Hayek penned his famous paean to neoliberalism to become evident, but his dream of decentralized and entrepreneurial urban governance reads as though it were a contemporary guide to "best practices" in American local government. The relatively regulatory Keynesian local state of the mid–twentieth century has been supplanted by a neoliberal version that seems itself to be regulated by local capital. The 1990s were a particularly important phase in the transition toward neoliberal urban governance.[1] As Robert Lake recently remarked, "in the turbulent politics of the 1990s, the major parties agree on perhaps only one thing: that the era of 'big government' [is] over" (1997, p. 3). Local authorities—cities, states, provinces, special districts—now have more re-

---

1. Arguably the iconic document of this transition was the Republican-led *Contract with America* that was drafted before, and enacted after, the Republicans were elected to majority status in the U.S. House of Representatives in 1994. In that document, the Republicans promised to legislate according to five key principles: individual liberty, economic opportunity, limited government, personal responsibility, and national security (Gillespie and Schellhas 1994, p. 4). The specific policy agenda entailed a massive rollback of mid–twentieth century social programs and a return of "power" to localities.

sponsibilities and, some would argue, more ability to act independently of the larger bodies of government above them. But given the ostensible latitude for local governing autonomy in the United States right now, it is interesting that such a diverse array of municipalities have "chosen" such a common path. The path is characterized by the reduction of public subsidies and regulations, the aggressive promotion of real estate development (particularly spaces of consumption), and the privatization of previously public services. The following section attempts to probe this paradox by looking at various aspects of the neoliberal turn in local governance.

Chapter 2 begins the overall project by questioning the very notion of autonomy and considering the institutions that might affect the choices of ostensibly independent local governments. Chapter 3 considers the impact of "glocalization" on the governing institutions that were established under the Keynesian managerialist state by exploring the recent travails of public housing authorities in the United States. Chapter 4 considers the administrative potential of the much vaunted public-private partnership by exploring a case of downtown redevelopment in New Brunswick, New Jersey. The intent of this section is threefold. First, the chapters attempt to demonstrate that local governance is not an entirely local affair. The geo-institutional context within which local decisions are made is complex and multiscalar. Second, the neoliberal turn is not an organic (or populist) shift in policies but rather one that is highly engineered by external institutions that have no formal governing role in any municipality. Third, the neoliberal turn, in contrast to the narrative put forth by its localist promoters, has created enormous challenges to the capacity of municipalities to facilitate collective consumption or, more generally, social reproduction.

Chapter 2

Choosing a Neoliberal Path

As Molotch (1976) and many others have argued, the political and institutional inertia around the goal of economic growth can be extremely powerful, eclipsing most other concerns about progressive reform. The "choice" of officials in Mayor Kucinich's position is often heavily influenced by this imperative for growth and the institutions that support it. Despite generalized agreement around this point, however, a highly problematic, localized notion of autonomy is still found within the urban politics literature—regime theory in particular, but also, more surprisingly, in radical accounts of urban politics as well (see, for example, Cox 1993). Much of this literature is the result of an (understandable) attempt to distance urban political analysis from the economism of past state theory. In the process, however, a nearly unanimous but empirically problematic notion of autonomy and choice in urban decision-making has emerged. This chapter interrogates the notion of choice in municipal decision-making to understand why cities with such different constituencies have "chosen" to pursue a neoliberal path of governance. Following in part Harvey (1989b), the central argument is that the choices available to cities are highly constrained even for the most powerful municipalities. Deviating then somewhat from the likes of Harvey, I argue that the shift to entrepreneurial or neoliberal urban governance is less the result of an organic shift to the right made in the face of capital flight than it is the result of an institutionally regulated (and policed) disciplining of localities. That is, the central justifications of Keynesian managerialism have disappeared less because of the political popularity of neoliberalism or even because of the intrinsic risk of capital flight (as important as that is) than because of an institutionally rigid set of ideological constraints imposed by finance capital. For cities in the "developing world" (and for many that are not), the International Monetary Fund (IMF) and the World Bank serve as policing institutions in this regard, rewarding cities that adhere to a particular order and penalizing those that do not (Gill 1995). In the "developed world," particularly though not exclusively in the United States, bond-rating agencies increasingly serve in this capacity. Bond-rating agencies are arguably the most directly influential "police officers" of neoliberal urban governance for cities in wealthy countries like the United States, Canada, and Japan.[1] This chapter explores the policing activities of such institutions to shed some light on how external institutions can steer cities toward neoliberalism.

"Choice" and Autonomy in the Urban Governance Literature

Recent discussions of urban governance have focused on the difficulty of providing municipal services in the context of heightened capital mobility. Despite vast normative and epistemological differences, almost all of this work has dealt with the issue of autonomy or governing choice. Some have argued that cities possess significant autonomy, that their fates are determined as much by governing strategy as by changes to the larger economy or federal government (Stone 1989; Clarke and Kirby 1990; Goetz and Clarke 1993; Jones and Bachelor 1993; Eisinger 1998). Others argue, following Peterson (1981), that cities are virtually powerless at determining their economic fate (Kennedy 1984; Logan and Molotch 1987; see also O'Connor 1973), with some going so far as to argue that local politics have completely "died" (Gottdiener 1987). Still others fall somewhere in between, arguing that certain factions of capital are locally dependent and that while capital might have the upper hand overall, localities have some autonomy (Cox and Mair 1988; Cox 1993). Consistent throughout much of this literature is the notion that autonomy is a mindset or a skill to be realized (for a critique of this, see Defilippis 2003). City officials either "re-

---

1. It should be noted that among wealthy countries in the world, the United States has the most dispersed form of infrastructure finance. Throughout Western Europe and to a lesser extent Canada, local infrastructure projects are financed through the national state. However, many of the lessons learned from the American case are applicable to more politically centralized cases, as the latter are often still financed and regulated through the bond market. The chief difference is that the resources are routed through a national development authority before going to local infrastructure projects.

alize" that capital flight is too powerful for them to contest meaningfully (Peterson 1981; Kennedy 1984; Logan and Molotch 1987; Gottdiener 1987) or they have "overstated" or "misinterpreted" these risks in their decision-making (Stone 1989; Clarke and Kirby 1990; Goetz and Clarke 1993; Jones and Bachelor 1993; Eisinger 1998; Cox and Mair 1988; Cox 1993). Though it is undoubtedly true that much of the shift in "good governance" is rooted in a perception of the risk of capital flight on the part of city officials, few authors delineate the specific institutional mechanisms that carefully socialize and discipline such decision-makers into a neoliberal mindset (for a notable exception, see Sbragia 1996)

Also consistent throughout most of this literature is the notion that autonomy is the degree of separation that a city has with the wider political economy—a particular quality, to be obtained to greater or lesser degree (Clark 1984). As the degree of separation increases, the assumption goes, so increases the number of choices a city has in determining its political and economic future. More recent scholarship has argued, by contrast, that this notion of autonomy is neither politically nor conceptually useful within the capitalist world economy, where spatio-economic connections are a given (see Brown 1992; Lake 1994; Defilippis 1999). These researchers argue, in part following Foucault, that autonomy is not about the degree of separation from the wider economic sphere but is rather about the degree of control over the social construction of place. Autonomy from this perspective refers not to the degree of separation but rather to the degree of control over an assumed connection. It is a subtle but important difference. An emphasis on the connection is important because it replaces the burden of showing how local politics are extra-economic (a preoccupation with much of the aforementioned local politics literature) with the imperative of understanding how institutions and processes regulate the *interaction* with wider processes such as globalization.

Current research indicates that autonomy, defined as the social construction of place—or, we might say, defined relationally—has less to do with "natural" comparative advantage, agglomeration economies, or central government redistribution than with a growing suite of intermediary institutions—such as the IMF and the World Bank—that increasingly determine where, when, and how capital gets invested throughout the world (Gill 1995; Sassen 1996; Hewson and Sinclair 1999). Though less frequently cited in this regard, bond-rating firms, such as Moody's Investors Service and Standard and Poor's (S&P), are perhaps the single most influential institutional force in determining the quantity, quality, and geography of local investment in the developed world (Sinclair 1994a, b, 1999).

Cities, towns, counties, states, and sovereign governments depend on the bond market for the provision of basic infrastructure, services, and economic development (Sbragia 1996). Their ability to enter this market is determined almost entirely by three multinational bond-rating agencies that draft credit reports for investors. Localities can be summarily redlined from credit if bond-rating agencies judge them fiscally or economically "inept." Unlike interstate organizations, bond-rating agencies are functionally separate from the governments that they evaluate and thus more immune than, say, the IMF to state-based political pressure. Recent evidence suggests that rating agencies have become even more influential in the last thirty years because of several key urban-economic changes. Though past work has addressed some of the institutional constraints posed by rating agencies (see Elkin 1987; Glasberg 1988), comparatively little work has addressed how these constraints are subject to historical change (for a notable exception, see Sbragia 1996). Understanding the practices and shifting institutional power of rating agencies is an important step toward unpacking the boundaries of choice in contemporary urban governance. This chapter challenges the traditional conception of governing autonomy by exploring the activities of a set of institutions that place powerful limitations on the choices that city officials can and cannot make. A central premise is that the competition for capital and the institutional fear of capital flight are far from nebulous forces acting on cities. Rather they are institutionally reinforced in such a way as to challenge the prevailing notion of autonomy.

Background on Municipal Debt and Rating Agencies

Cities in the United States are permitted by state law to issue debt to build and repair infrastructure, offset shortfalls in cash flow, and attract business (for the most comprehensive treatment of this issue, see ibid.). Short-term debt,[2] usually acquired through commercial banks, is typically used to cover general budgetary shortfalls, while long-term debt is more often used to purchase or repair capital infrastructure. There are two types of long-term municipal debt: general obligation bonds and revenue bonds. General obligation (GO) bonds are backed with the "full faith and credit" of a

---

2. Short-term loans are also known as notes. Under most arrangements, notes are to be repaid within one year.

municipality's tax base.[3] That tax base functions as collateral, since most states prohibit localities from using their physical property (real estate, equipment, etc.) for such collateral. Because of the commitment, most states require that cities and counties hold a formal referendum to issue GO bonds. Revenue bonds, by contrast, can be issued without a formal vote. They are repaid with a specific revenue stream, such as electricity remittance or airport user fees, and are issued twice as often as general obligation bonds (Lipnick et al. 1999, p. 38). There has been a recent growth of bond-issuing special districts (e.g. an airport authority, water treatment service area) that are organized around a particular revenue stream (Sbragia 1983, 1996). This tends especially to be the case with larger municipalities whose sewage system, airport traffic, or bridge system is too complicated and expensive to be run by city hall. The creation of districts alleviates the responsibility for certain expected services and allows for quasi-public entities such as housing authorities, sewage districts, and airport authorities—often led by unelected decision-makers—to issue debt without a formal referendum (Monkkonen 1995). In addition, such authorities provide a mechanism to circumvent state-imposed debt limitations (Monkkonen 1995; Sbragia 1996).

Bond-rating agencies evaluate the creditworthiness of municipalities and other public authorities trying to issue long-term debt.[4] The bond-issuing municipality hires an agency as soon as the decision to issue debt is made. After being contacted, the agency will request an internal financial statement from the issuing city and combine this information with its own databases and independent research to arrive at a rating. The ratings are based on the municipality's financial history (past and current debt), its economic outlook (whether growth is going to occur), and its administrative structure and history (whether there is a history of mismanagement). The final rating is meant to be a reflection of how likely a given municipality is to repay its debt in a timely manner. All three recognized agencies— Moody's, S&P, and Fitch (the third-largest firm in the industry)—use a similar rating nomenclature (see table 2.1) to summarize their research. Though there are several gradations, the meaningful threshold that rating agencies police is whether a bond is rated as "speculative-grade" (a "junk bond") or "investment-grade." Speculative-grade bonds are about ten

3. The tax base usually, though not exclusively, consists of property taxes. User fees and sales taxes are sometimes used to guarantee "full faith and credit."
4. Bond-rating agencies also, of course, rate corporate debt, which is not a direct concern of this chapter.

TABLE 2.1
Categories for major bond-rating agencies

Status	Moody's	Standard and Poor's	Fitch
Investment grade	Aaa	AAA	AAA
	Aa	AA	AA
	A	A	A
	Baa	BBB	BBB
Speculative grade	Ba	BB	BB
	B	B	B
	Caa	CCC	CCC
	Ca	CC	CC
	C	C	C
Defaulted issues		D	DDD, DD, D

Note: Intermediate S&P ratings are created with a plus or a minus sign (e.g., AAA−). Intermediate Moody's ratings are created with a number from 1 to 3 (e.g., Aa2).

times as likely as investment-grade bonds to default (Litvack 1999) and are very difficult to sell to investment banks or investors. In such cases where a sale can be arranged, the interest rate for speculative-grade bonds is significantly higher than that for investment-grade bonds. City managers are compelled to keep expenses low and revenues high to maintain a positive rating. Even those services that are not usually funded through municipal bonds (such as payroll) are affected by the decision of bond-rating agencies, because credit reports are based on overall patterns of fiscal decision-making and economic health. Bond-rating agencies thus not only determine how expensive a city's loan will be but also have an impact on the overall scope of local government.

Municipal debt rating evolved indirectly from the highly volatile corporate debt markets of the mid–nineteenth century (Cantor and Packer 1995). Small rating agencies began evaluating corporate debtors for interested investors after the century's multiple recessions drove indebted companies into default with increasing regularity. Municipal debt markets were similarly volatile, but the volume of bond issuance was kept low by state-imposed limitations (Monkkonen 1995) and the more general limitations on the scope of services provided by local government during the nineteenth century. Though the scope of local government expanded in the early twentieth century, municipal debt markets still remained relatively small and stable compared to corporate debt. The allocation of credit, whether from banks or individuals, remained relatively informal.[5]

5. Moody's Investor Service started rating municipal bonds in 1918, but it was a very small part of their total operations at the time.

The Great Depression, however, introduced widespread uncertainty into municipal debt markets, as hundreds of American cities went into default. Banks and investors clamored for more certainty, and commercial rating agencies rushed to fill the void. Their legitimacy among municipal investors was strengthened during the immediate postwar years as they presided over a market of unprecedented safety and growth (ibid.).

Until 1997, there were five rating agencies recognized by the U.S. Securities and Exchange Commission (SEC): Moody's, S&P, Fitch, Duff and Phelps, and IBCA. In 1997, Fitch and IBCA merged and then merged again in 2000 with Duff and Phelps (Fitch IBCA Investors Corporation 2000). There are now only three major firms, each of which is a highly capitalized transnational corporation. Confined as recently as the 1970s to their New York headquarters and a few regional (U.S.) offices, S&P, Moody's, and Fitch IBCA now have offices in most of the world's major cities. Moody's now rates 85,000 corporate and government securities, 68,000 public finance obligations, and 100 sovereign nations (Moody's Investors Service 2004). Standard and Poor's now has offices worldwide and achieved a profit of $370 million in 1999 (Standard and Poor's 2000). Even the smallest, Fitch IBCA, now employs 600 analysts (the equivalent of mid-level management) and has twenty-one offices worldwide. Though the bond-rating industry began humbly, it has evolved into a highly consolidated, transnational handful of companies that now serve as the primary gatekeepers for corporate and municipal debt markets.

The Growing Influence of Bond-Rating Agencies

Though bond-rating agencies have rated U.S. municipals since the early twentieth century, a central argument of this chapter is that their influence on local governance has grown in the last thirty years because of three interrelated changes to the global political economy. First, the general shift away from the federal maintenance of collective consumption in the United States has accelerated in recent years. Cities now receive fewer dollars per capita than before, even though their responsibilities often remain high. Municipal lending has partially covered extant housing, welfare, and general assistance demands as well as more recently intensified pressures, such as prison construction and law enforcement. Cities are more vulnerable to the decisions of capital market gatekeepers, in part because they are more dependent on debt. Second, because of demographic changes and the generalized shift toward generating wealth through finance capital, institutions such as pension funds, money market funds, and insurance firms now constitute a greater share of the securities industry than before. Several new and existing federal laws in the United States and abroad place limits on the amount of speculative-grade debt institutions can hold. Given the increased presence of funds with such limitations, the judgments of rating agencies have ipso facto become more important because there are fewer bond buyers willing and legally able to ignore their assessments. Third, less municipal lending takes place through traditional banking institutions than before. The relative security of this form of lending and investment has been replaced by a more volatile system of direct lending. The remaining investors (households and funds) are more reliant on "professional" assessments than before because the banking intermediary has disappeared. The following section considers each of these shifts in some detail.

Entrepreneurial Urbanism

After nearly four decades of targeted military and social program expenditures, the American federal government was fundamentally restructured starting in the early 1970s. Maintaining collective consumption levels—the raison d'être of Keynesian economic regulation—was supplanted by the pursuit of unregulated economic growth, somewhat reminiscent of the late nineteenth century. Popular support for the welfare state was replaced by anti-statist politics. The American inner city, long abandoned by the de facto federal urban policy of suburbanization (Mills 1987), became increasingly removed from the economic mainstream with an enormous concentration of the working and workless poor (Wilson 1987). Direct outlays to localities were slashed during the 1980s behind the neo-federalist rhetoric of returning power to the local. Cities became more entrepreneurial in part to cover the budgetary shortfalls that accompanied this transition (Harvey 1989b; Leitner 1990).

Not as commonly acknowledged in this literature is the increasing reliance of cities on debt for social service and capital infrastructure. As figure 2.1 shows, the decline in federal support for urban development[6] has been almost perfectly counterposed by an increase in municipal debt, as localities are increasingly left to fend for themselves in an internecine competition for more investment (see also Gottdiener 1987, pp. 80–84). As

---

6. Urban development outlays are only one form of federal redistribution, but since they assist the construction of physical infrastructure that would otherwise be financed with debt, they provide a more useful comparison than, say, social service expenditures.

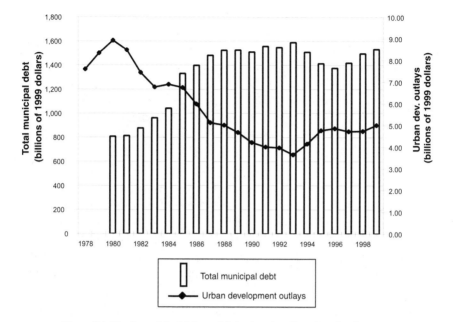

Figure 2.1: Total municipal debt and federal outlays for urban development

Source: U.S. Office of Management and Budget, Bond Market Association

Sbragia (1996) points out, the rising proclivity to incur public debt has also been driven by the local desire to circumvent restrictive state-level debt limitations through the mechanism of special districts. Ironically, this desire to achieve "autonomy" (in a *non*-relational sense) from state government has undermined municipal autonomy (relationally defined) vis-à-vis the rating agencies. Borrowing money to cover expenditures previously dealt with at the federal or state level comes with consequences, albeit different ones than those imposed by state governments. Entrepreneurial governance is a de facto requirement of increasing a city's exposure to capital markets.

Compounding the desire to circumvent state law and the decrease in federal outlays to cities, there has been a very specific *increase* in federal mandates to deal with social problems. Policies to encourage the construction of prisons and the employment of more police officers have been among the most significant (Gilmore 1998; Schlosser 1998). Schlosser (1998) points out that of the 1.8 million people currently in prison in the United States, 600,000 are housed in local jails; with increased pressure to impose mandatory-minimum sentences and to relieve overcrowding, the imperative to build more prisons only figures to increase. Moreover, the highly publicized increase in federal funding for new police officers in the mid-1990s came with a less publicized caveat that after a specific span of time (usually two years), localities were required to finance police officer salaries, thus increasing pressure on their budget.[7] The net effect of these changes is that local governments are increasingly forced to respond to unfunded federal decrees—particularly social control mandates—by incurring debt. Bond market gatekeepers, as a consequence, become more influential.

The less immediate result of the decline of traditional Keynesianism has been the successful "naturalization" of public-private cooperation at the local level. Though American municipalities have always facilitated the conditions for growth, local governance under Keynesianism was more precarious. In the immediate postwar period, local government also functioned as an arbiter between capital and labor. Urban policy reflected this tenuous balance between local-state-as-arbiter and local-state-as-entrepreneur. In New York, for example, the city during the 1960s enacted anti-gentrification measures in Hell's Kitchen at the same time that it was actively encouraging the process in SoHo. The imperative to facilitate growth was counterbalanced with the need to facilitate social reproduction. But as the cycle of economic growth upon which the state-as-arbiter model was based began to unravel in the mid-1970s, so went the tendency of local planning and policy to regulate and redistribute. Even the most socially progressive municipalities were forced to follow the federal government's anti-Keynesian lead by cutting back social welfare expenditures and regulations during downturns. Local governments are now not only expected to ally with business to improve its plight (see Peterson 1981), they are also increasingly expected *to behave* as businesses as well. In addition to shrinking during recessions (as opposed to the Keynesian tendency to expand during such episodes), local governments are more keenly pressured to produce tax revenue generators than before. By the late 1970s municipalities had begun using their sub–market rate debt-raising capacity to secure low-cost loans for middle-class homeowners, highly capitalized developers, and corporations (Sbragia 1986). The use of public debt for private gain became widespread enough for the federal government to intervene in the

7. This is not to imply that cities can use long-term debt to pay for police salaries in any direct way. Rather, the point is that the increased pressure to finance such expenditures has generally reduced the amount of revenue that cities can devote to debt service for items that can be financed with bonds.

1980s. The Tax Equity and Responsibility Act of 1982 and the Tax Reform Act of 1986 were established in part to curb the most egregious uses of this privilege (ibid.), but it is still routine for American localities (usually special districts) to raise debt for private pursuits such as mortgages, sports stadiums, and miscellaneous commercial redevelopment projects. Doing so has become nothing less than an axiom of good governance. The increasingly heavy-handed analyses of bond-rating agencies are thus not only uncontested, they are often enthusiastically *supported* as the roadmap toward economic sustainability.

Institutional Investing and Legal Constraints

While households—particularly wealthy households that can take advantage of the tax-free status of municipal bonds—remain a large segment of municipal bond owners, the most interesting aspect of recent ownership has been the simultaneous growth of institutional investors (mutual funds, pension funds, insurance companies, and so on) and decline of commercial banks during the last twenty years, as shown in figure 2.2 (see also Useem 1996; Harmes 1998). Mutual funds, insurance companies, and money market funds in particular were either non-existent or insignificant investors in 1980 but had collectively come to assume a significant portion of the mar-

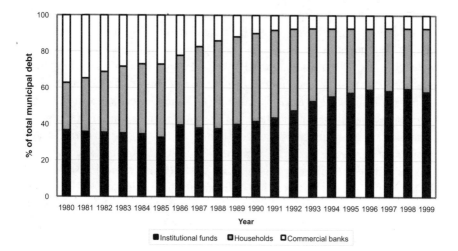

Figure 2.2: Ownership of municipal debt in the United States, 1980–1999

Source: Bond Market Association

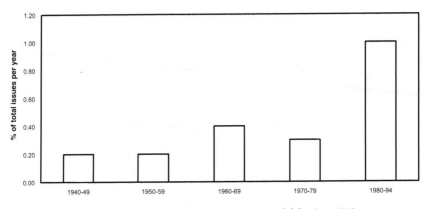

Figure 2.3: Default rates for long-term municipal debt since 1940

Source: Bond Market Association

ket by the end of the 1990s. Growth in this industry mirrors a larger pattern of institutional fund growth and commercial bank savings decline. The proportion of American household assets contained in commercial savings accounts fell from 46 to 37 percent between 1980 and 1990, while the proportion of households that owned a mutual fund grew from 6 to 28 percent between 1980 and 1994 (*Economist* 1994). This trend continued throughout the 1990s as stock market returns outstripped basic savings account returns.

The shift has had important implications for municipal finance because most institutional investors are prohibited by the federal government (in the United States and elsewhere) from owning too much speculative-grade debt (Sinclair 1994b; Cantor and Packer 1995). The earliest regulations of this sort—those that evolved out of the credit crisis of the Great Depression—prohibited or strictly discouraged commercial banks from purchasing speculative debt (see table 2.2).[8] In 1931, for example, the Federal Reserve required banks to downgrade their appraisal of speculative-grade bonds. By 1936, the federal government prohibited outright the purchase of speculative securities by commercial banks (Cantor and Packer 1995). In 1951, the National Association of Insurance Commissioners (NAIC) required insurance companies to hold a greater proportion of liquid assets if they invest in speculative-grade bonds (Cantor and Packer 1995; *Wall Street Journal* 1996a). The scope of these regulations expanded during the 1970s and 1980s. Among the most influential was the Employee Retirement In-

8. Early regulations required at least one rating agency decision, sometimes two.

come Security Act of 1974, which prohibits pension funds and other institutional investors from purchasing speculative-grade bonds as part of their portfolio (Sinclair 1994b). Other regulations required speculative-grade issuers to disclose more information about their financial history than investment-grade issuers. Still others limited the number of speculative-grade securities that money market mutual funds could own (Cantor and Packer 1995). Such regulations are not limited to the United States. Other countries have followed suit by placing limitations on the sale of speculative-grade bonds. The Japanese government, for example, now requires American corporate or municipal debtors to achieve an investment-grade rating in order to sell there, and British regulators use the ratings to determine the percentage of capital reserves that a company must keep on hand (*Economist* 1996b). The net result of these disparate regulations is that the judgments of three rating firms now determine the buying decisions of the fastest-growing segment of the municipal bond market. With their creditors increasingly limited in what they can purchase, city managers must now, by default, be more compliant with rating agencies. The opportunities for swaying wealthy local residents or banks to "rescue" the city are evaporating as such investors—now *less* burdened by regulation than before—pursue opportunities elsewhere. Speculative-grade bonds have, moreover, become more expensive to sell, and, as O'Barr and Conley (1992) point out, fund managers are discouraged from investing in socially useful endeavors—low-return projects to create jobs or build needed housing or infrastructure.

The top agencies are given further market legitimacy by the SEC's "Nationally Recognized Statistical Rating Organization" (NRSRO) designation—a label that the commission instituted in 1975. NRSRO status is very difficult for smaller firms to achieve because the litmus test for entry is for a firm to have "market recognition"—to be seen by investors as a reputable source. But the status is ultimately based on a tautology, as most municipal bond laws recognize only those agencies with NRSRO status. Though the SEC recognizes the self-fulfilling monopoly status of requiring market recognition before agencies can become an NRSRO (U.S. Justice Department 1998), efforts to change the structure have been ineffective. Some cities with marginal ratings have attempted to break the NRSRO juggernaut by soliciting an outside rating, but to little avail. The web of legal supports for NRSRO decisions is often too strong for even the most determined municipality to overcome alone.

Disintermediation and the Investment Knowledge Vacuum

As the previous section showed, a greater percentage of corporate and municipal debt was handled by traditional lending institutions during the immediate postwar years than is the case today (Sinclair 1994b). Federally insured commercial banks would provide short-term notes for budgetary shortfalls and buy small issues of long-term bonds as well.[9] Often, the lending institution was locally based, making it deeply interested in the fate of the city. Though they did thorough analyses of city finances, the banks had to remain open to debt rescheduling and softened standards in difficult times because they stood to benefit from the political and economic conditions of that municipality and because their revenues were in part derived from the interest payments they would attain from their debtors. As long as larger-scale economic conditions remained stable and cities did not default, this system of credit was mutually beneficial to cities and commercial lending institutions alike. During the 1970s, however, this system began to disintegrate. The New York City budgetary debacle, during which the city had been given a virtually open line of short-term credit from local banks (Tabb 1982), and the federal government's subsequent refusal to intervene alarmed commercial providers of municipal credit everywhere. Banks were immediately less willing to cover budgetary shortfalls alone. Short- and long-term municipal finance through commercial banks became almost nonexistent. Rising interest rates compounded this obstacle to credit for cities, as bank money simply became more expensive.

This series of events could not have come at a worse economic time for American cities. The "urban crisis" was afoot everywhere,[10] especially in the industrial northeast and midwest. With short-term commercial credit (and federal expenditures) on the ebb, cities increasingly turned to individuals and institutional creditors for both long-term infrastructure and short-term note financing. This process, deemed "disintermediation," effectively removed commercial institutions from municipal debt markets and created an information vacuum for bond investors (Sinclair 1994a, b). To obtain information about the credit applicant (in this case, cities), investors had little choice but to rely upon the judgments of Moody's, Standard and Poor's, or some other rating agency.

During the relatively stable period of municipal debt in the United

9. Swanson and Vogel argue that two-thirds of all municipal debt (including small long-term bonds) was handled either by local investors or banks as recently as the mid-1980s (1986, p. 69).
10. The fiscal crisis spawned a series of important books and articles during the late 1970s and 1980s, including but not limited to Tabb (1982), McDonald and Ward (1984), and Gottdiener (1986).

States following World War II (see Monkkonen 1995), rating agencies were able to satisfy investor demands for information on cities and corporations through relatively cursory evaluations compiled in investment booklets. Investors tolerated this depth of research because municipal debt was a very low-risk investment. But as the 1970s fiscal crisis spawned a series of high-profile defaults,[11] investors grew increasingly nervous about the stability of public debt. Investors clamored for more complete information on the issuing city, and the rating agencies responded by becoming more intrusive and comprehensive than they had been in the past. More detailed financial information was required to issue bonds, and rating agencies began charging issuers to take on the expense of its research.

But while increasingly thorough bond research was designed to benefit investors, it had the effect of creating enormous expectations for rating agency decisions. When the Washington Public Power Supply System (WPPSS) defaulted on a $2.25 billion obligation in 1984, investors sued several of the bond-rating agencies for malpractice (Cantor and Packer 1995). The suit was dropped before a verdict was reached (rating agencies have consistently enjoyed First Amendment protection for their judgments), but it signaled a turn in the position of bond-rating agencies within the municipal market. No longer were rating agencies seen as passive suppliers of information to investors. They were now *expected* to provide infallible advice about issuers. Once little more than market journalists, rating agencies became more influential and intrusive gatekeepers to the municipal bond market in order to maintain their legitimacy. This tendency increased during in the 1980s and early 1990s, as investors grew unnerved by a growing level of municipal default (see figure 2.3). The onerous standards imposed by rating agencies are used by investors who are in a poor position to make informed judgments of their own.[12] Rating agency authority has increased so much in recent years that Moody's and S&P have been able to successfully bill issuers for *unsolicited* credit ratings. Issuing cities and special districts often comply because they fear retaliation in future *solicited* ratings. Noncompliant issuers wishing to challenge Moody's

11. The near-bankruptcy of New York City in 1973, the bond defaults of the New York State Urban Development Corporation (UDC) in 1975, Cleveland in 1978, and the Washington Public Power Supply System (WPPSS) in 1984 were particularly influential in this regard (Lamb and Rappaport 1987).
12. My interview with a top official at Moody's revealed that internal discussions have begun on whether the strict standards of their firm are appropriate, considering a recent study that showed that municipals are almost always safer than corporate issues of the same rating (Litvack 1999). No action has yet been taken, but it has prompted a casual reevaluation of how Moody's rates municipal issues.

TABLE 2.2
Bond ratings in federal regulations in the United States

Year	Regulating agency	Number of ratings required	Policy effect
1931	Federal Reserve and OCC	2	Commercial banks had to appraise speculative securities more modestly.
1936	OCC, FDIC, and Federal Reserve	Not specified	Commercial banks could not purchase speculative securities.
1951	NAIC	N/A	Insurance companies had higher capital requirements if they held speculative securities.
1974	U.S. Congress[a]		Certain pension funds and other institutional investors were prohibited from purchasing speculative-grade bonds.
1975	SEC	N/A	Only the top rating firms were given legal recognition by the SEC.
1975	SEC	2	Bond brokers had higher capital requirements if they held speculative securities.
1982	SEC	1	Investment grade bond issuers were given fewer disclosure requirements.
1989	U.S. Congress[b]	1	S&Ls were prohibited from investing in speculative-grade bonds.
1991	SEC	1	Money market funds had to limit their holdings of speculative securities

Source: Cantor and Packer 1995; and Sinclair 1994a.
Note: OCC = Office of the Comptroller for Currency, FDIC = Federal Deposit Insurance Corporation
[a]Part of the Employee Retirement Income Security Act of 1974.
[b]Part of the Financial Institutions Recovery and Reform Act of 1989.

or S&P have generally not fared well. In one high-profile suit, the Jefferson County School District in Colorado sued Moody's for issuing an unsolicited rating in 1993. The rating cost the taxpayers an estimated $800,000 in extra interest. The Moody's rating was lower than the judgments that they had originally purchased from Fitch and S&P (*Wall Street Journal* 1996b), but the case was thrown out, again on First Amendment grounds. The Justice Department subsequently investigated because of a concern that Moody's was using its power to pressure municipalities unfairly and to squeeze out smaller rating firms like Fitch, which are known to give slightly higher ratings (*Economist* 1996b). Ultimately, no meaningful action resulted, except for a largely unheeded call by the Justice Department to loosen the requirements for becoming an NRSRO (U.S.

Justice Department 1998). The probe did, however, signal a concern that the disintermediation of debt markets was facilitating near-monopoly power for a select number of information providers.

Bond-rating agencies have assumed a central role in the gathering and dissemination of information about municipal bonds—a role that was previously shared with traditional lending institutions. Commercial banks were more willing to bend their standards and renegotiate the terms of debt because they had a huge pecuniary incentive to do so. Rating agency allegiance, by contrast, is to investors who in turn maintain pressure for the firms to keep standards strict and their fiscal research thorough. The connection that cities have with capital markets is determined more than ever by the neoliberal standards enforced by rating agencies.

Local Interactions with Bond-Rating Agencies

With their power enhanced by the aforementioned political and economic shifts, bond-rating agencies now exert more pressure on local governments to become entrepreneurial than ever before. To illustrate how this pressure manifests itself in various contexts, accounts of the recent experience of three cities (New York, Philadelphia, and Detroit) with bond-rating agencies follow (see also table 2.3). The narratives are based on press reports, interviews conducted by the author, and research reports assembled by rating agencies. The cases were chosen not for their ability to represent every urban political reality but rather because of their recent highly publicized interactions (usually conflicts) with one or more of the rating agencies. Their stories are qualitatively useful for understanding how bond-rating agencies affect local autonomy.

New York City

Of the three cities chosen for discussion here, New York has had the most famous relationship with the major bond-rating agencies. The city's financial troubles in the early 1970s became the subject of numerous books and articles on how the city was forced to abandon its experiment with massive redistribution and regulation in favor of a business-friendly, pro-growth form of governance (Tabb 1982; Schefter 1992; Lichten 1986; Fainstein 1992). It is worth revisiting the episode to understand more recent events.

In response to growing unrest in the 1960s, particularly in its minority neighborhoods, City Hall was pressured to increase expenditures for hous-

TABLE 2.3
Historical bond ratings for New York, Philadelphia, and Detroit

	New York City	Philadelphia	Detroit
Rating changes	Aug. 2000 A2	June 2000 Baa1	Oct. 1998 Baa1
	Feb. 1998 A3	May 1998 Baa2	July 1997 Baa2
	Feb. 1991 Baa1	March 1995 Baa	Oct. 1996 Baa
	May 1988 A	April 1993 Ba	July 1992 Ba1
	Dec. 1985 Baa1	Sept. 1990 B	Nov. 1986 Baa
	Nov. 1983 Baa	June 1990 Ba	Aug. 1980 Ba
	Nov. 1981 Ba1	Jan. 1976 Baa	Nov. 1962 Baa
	May 1977 B	Jan. 1975 A	Oct. 1940 A
	Oct. 1975 Caa	Sept. 1968 Baa1	Jan. 1938 Baa
	Oct. 1975 Ba	Jan. 1944 A	
	Dec. 1972 A	Feb. 1939 Baa	
	May 1968 Baa1	Jan. 1938 A	
	July 1965 Baa		
	Jan. 1938 A		

Source: Moody's Investors Service 2000a; 2000b; 1999.

ing, health care, and other social services. Deindustrialization and general population loss was, however, simultaneously dissolving its tax base (see table 2.4). Raising taxes only partially compensated for the hemorrhage of corporations and wealthy people from the city, so the city started issuing short-term notes in the late 1960s and early 1970s to pay for its massive social obligations. In time, the city was forced to issue notes to pay back previous notes. In October 1975 Moody's downgraded the city to specula-tive-grade status (from A to Ba to Caa later in the month) because of this practice, effectively removing it from the debt market. After several pleas for federal relief (one of which resulted in the infamous *Daily News* head-line: "Ford to City: Drop Dead"), the state of New York stepped in to re-structure the city's finances. Unprecedented power was given to two agencies—the Municipal Assistance Corporation and the Emergency Fi-nancial Control Board—to straighten out the city's problems by issuing bonds and slashing social service expenditures. The austerity program in-stituted after the city's debt crisis shook apart the once-solid New Deal coalition in the city. Ed Koch was elected in the resulting power vacuum, and the city's finances were restructured. The city spent less on affordable housing, social services, and hospitals, while an increasing share of the city's public money was devoted to assisting growing sectors of the economy, par-ticularly finance, insurance, and real estate (Fitch 1993).

From a purely fiscal perspective, the move toward entrepreneurialism

TABLE 2.4
Relative population change in New York City, Philadelphia, and Detroit since 1950

	Percentage change over the decade				
	1950s	1960s	1970s	1980s	1990s
United States	18.5	13.4	12.0	9.8	12.5
Cities of:					
New York City	−1.4	1.5	−10.4	3.6	9.4
Philadelphia	−3.3	−2.7	−13.4	−6.1	−4.3
Detroit	−9.7	−9.3	−20.5	−14.6	−7.5
Metropolitan areas:					
New York City	19.3	10.9	−4.2	3.1	8.7
Philadelphia	36.9	12.0	−1.4	−1.9	4.6
Detroit	36.7	13.3	−1.1	−7.9	4.9

Source: U.S. Census
Note: Metropolitan statistical areas change in size over time as outlying regions become functionally integrated into the larger urban economy.

improved the city's situation. In 1983, Moody's upgraded the city's GO bonds to investment-grade and targeted expenditures (mostly tax abatements and incentives for developers) had resulted in modest economic growth. The growth was not, however, without consequence. By the end of the 1980s, New York had become one of the nation's most socially polarized cities (Mollenkopf and Castells 1991; Fainstein et al. 1992), and its abandonment of the industrial sector had encouraged a more volatile economy more attuned to swings in the stock market. When the recession of the early 1990s gutted the real estate market (by then a major component of New York's economic base), the city experienced its second fiscal crisis in fifteen years (Fainstein 1992). The city was downgraded in February 1991 (though not below investment-grade—from A to Baa1), and a second round of budget cuts ensued. Once again, progressive groups in the city were significantly fractured by the crisis, but by this time the notion that cities should behave as corporations had become so commonplace that less political conflict ensued around the further retrenchment of City Hall than in the 1970s. Indeed, the Giuliani administration was consistently rewarded for its efforts to trim City Hall. One element of the city's current mode of operation that Moody's has found encouraging is its ability to combat once-strong public labor unions by cutting back municipal employment. In one fairly recent report on the city, Moody's praised the Giuliani administration's ability to reduce its workforce but expressed concern over how much social service delivery and public sector job creation was still going on at City Hall (2000a, p. 8). The traditional Keynesian relics and labor union sympathies still ensconced in City Hall were framed as threats to the city's future well-being and its current surpluses.

Philadelphia

Like New York, Philadelphia grappled with the difficulty of major industrial employers leaving during the 1960s and 1970s. Also like New York, there was an initial attempt by a predominately Democratic City Hall to deal with the resultant unemployment and economic decline by expanding municipal employment and lobbying for further federal grants. Adding to the already enormous burden for Philadelphia was a $2.5 billion unfunded pension fund debt in the 1980s (Hayllar 1999). City leaders were forced to trim the size of city government in the late 1980s by laying off 2,400 employees (nearly 10 percent of its workforce), selling city-owned property, and borrowing to cover its growing deficits (deCourcy Hinds 1992b). Municipal labor unions became recalcitrant as cutbacks took hold, and the city began exploring the possibility of privatizing city services (Adams 1991). In one particularly bitter episode in 1986, Wilson Goode, the city's mayor, persuaded a judge to order garbage collection employees back to work after a twenty-day strike.

Negotiations over privatizing city services and pay freezes became ineffectual until 1990, when the city was effectively redlined from the bond market after receiving a speculative-grade rating. Past accounting tricks that had kept City Hall afloat, such as issuing debt to service past debt, were made impossible after the downgrade. A bitter fight for City Hall ensued, with a fiscally conservative Democrat, Ed Rendell (now current governor of Pennsylvania and a New Democrat icon) taking office in 1991. Rendell successfully implemented a plan to freeze wages for five years, reduce the municipal workforce by three hundred (many of them mid-level mangers), and take over the management of union-run health plans (deCourcy Hinds 1992a, b). Other departments were restructured, phased out, and summarily eliminated by the new mayor. When, at several points, the city's public labor union attempted to resist the plan, Rendell simply ignored them, and in at least one case, he was vindicated by public disapproval of the unions. After calling a strike in 1993, the city's non-uniformed employees were forced to concede defeat after only sixteen hours because of overwhelming public antagonism (deCourcy Hinds 1993).

All of the bond-rating agencies rewarded the city for its turn toward efficiency. In 1992, Fitch upgraded the city to investment-grade (deCourcy

Hinds 1992a), and the ever-skeptical Moody's upgraded the city to that status in 1995 (Moody's Investors Service 2000b). "The only test for the city," said one Moody's official after the austerity program began, "is to keep up the momentum" (quoted in deCourcy Hinds 1992a, p. B14). Rendell successfully dismantled the local welfare state in Philadelphia with relatively few political consequences by framing the problem within the sufficiently narrow ideological confines of fiscal responsibility. Philadelphia's pro-union democratic coalition was disciplined into acquiescence—that is, agreeing to pay cuts. Resistance waned in the face of a discourse that framed the problem as combination of a bloated City Hall, inordinately powerful labor unions, and an archaic form of governance.

Detroit

In Detroit, city leaders have embraced the virtues of fiscal conservatism since the early 1970s with less reluctance than either Philadelphia or New York. This has not, however, translated into favorable ratings. Detroit has consistently received lower evaluations than either of the other two during the last thirty years. The reason for this probably lies in the degree of economic decline experienced in Detroit during this period, relative to Philadelphia and New York. Detroit experienced a particularly severe version of deindustrialization and suburban capital flight during the 1970s and 1980s. Many in the media blamed Coleman Young, the city's mayor from 1973 to 1993, for exacerbating racial antagonisms and creating an environment unsuitable for business. As *The Economist* (1993) confidently asserted, Coleman Young "is the creature of a discredited school of Democratic politics, over keen on entitlements and given to playing on class and racial antagonisms. Detroit is crying out for a new kind of leadership." Yet despite the smug assessment of the *Economist* (and most of the mainstream press, for that matter), Young was quite popular, and the city actually became more business-friendly than it is often credited for being (see Eisinger 1998, p. 320).[13] During the 1980s, City Hall enthusiastically embraced economic development, gentrification, and the transition to a service economy (Rich 1991). By 1986, Young's City Hall had become business-friendly enough (and successful enough at garnering federal and state help) to achieve an investment-grade rating from Moody's (Baa)—a tremendous feat considering the degree of economic decline affecting Detroit at the time.

13. Its *success* at attracting development was, of course, much more mixed. The point here is that its governing *strategy* conformed quite nicely to the dictates of rating agencies.

The elation of achieving an investment-grade rating was shattered in 1992, when Moody's downgraded the city to Ba1, returning it to speculative status. City leaders were outraged at the downgrading mainly because they had been so aggressive in the previous decade at reigning in the city's finances, improving the perception of corruption, collecting taxes, and pursuing economic development. Moody's noted as much in their evaluation but downgraded the city anyway because of the continued population loss that was jeopardizing its tax base (Noble 1992). Like other governments that are rated, Detroit was in no position to protest the decision. When asked by one newspaper reporter whether the city was going to contest Moody's decision, Detroit's financial director, Bella Marshall, incredulously replied, "Who is going to brawl with the ratings agencies?" (quoted in ibid., p. D1). Basic fiscal prudence was apparently not enough to ensure a favorable opinion from the ratings agencies, and little could be done to resist their judgment.

A protégé of Coleman Young's, Dennis Archer, was elected mayor in 1993 during the fiscal quagmire. He pledged to make Detroit even more business-friendly by continuing to trim City Hall and by encouraging gentrification and economic development throughout the city. Unlike Philadelphia and New York, there has been comparatively little dissent over his vision. City Hall is now a fraction of its previous size, measured both in numbers of workers and expenditures for redistribution. The retrenchment has been successful at garnering rating agency support, at least for now. After 1996, the city was rewarded with three rating upgrades (it is currently Baa) despite continued erosion in the industrial sector (Moody's Investors Service 1999).

Rating Agencies and Local Autonomy

Though it is now common to identify the movement to neoliberal urban governance, it is less common to identify the institutional mechanisms that have facilitated this shift. Rather than being an organic shift in local politics, neoliberal governance has been driven, to a large extent, by non-local forces. Bond-rating agencies, among other institutions, actively encourage this transition by regulating the local connection to capital markets. Financial disintermediation and federal devolution have removed important buffers between the local state and finance capital, while shifts in ideology and investment regulations have strengthened supports for neoliberal local governance. The midcentury Keynesian managerial local state has given way to a mode of governance that is more nakedly exposed to the machinations of the market, and rating agencies have played an important (though not exclusive) role in this transition.

Bond-rating officials regularly meet with city officials in the United States (and, increasingly, abroad) to map out future allocation plans. Of the three cities explored here, however, only New York's virtually wholesale shift in governance since the 1970s has been convincing enough to garner the consistent support of the bond-rating community. The standards are onerous and can impinge upon the ability of an urban populace to choose its own economic and political fate. In each city, jobs and services for labor were cut at the same time that tax abatements for corporations were increased. All were disciplined into becoming more entrepreneurial cities in a relatively short amount of time, and the public pronouncements justifying the change were never effectively challenged. Given the reach of the bond market and the rating agencies, there is little reason to think that these trends are limited to the cities explored in this chapter.[14] Indeed, such shifts are occurring on an increasingly global level. The idea that municipal governments should behave as economically efficient, business-friendly, anti-deficit entities is now an axiom rather than a debated policy shift among city managers.

14. This is not to imply that the experience of these three cities is perfectly representative of all others but rather that wider politico-economic shifts have created a similar context for other cities in the United States and elsewhere.

Chapter 3

The Glocalization of Governance

The summary removal of redistributive state power is the normative ideal for neoliberals, but as Hayek was quick to point out over 40 years ago, *decentralized* state power is the next best thing:

> While it has always been characteristic of those favoring an increase in governmental powers to support maximum concentration of these powers, those mainly concerned with individual liberty have generally advocated decentralization. There are strong reasons why action by local authorities generally offers the next-best solution where private initiative cannot be relied upon to provide certain services and where some sort of collective action is therefore needed; for it has many of the advantages of private enterprise and fewer of the dangers of coercive actions of government. (1960, p. 263)

The theme of decentralized political power has been dominant in American politics since the founding of the country, but the past thirty years have seen an enhancement of this drive to "hollow out" the nation-state, particularly as a way to undermine the Keynesian welfare state. The reduction of federal subsidies for basic welfare provision in the United States is so well-documented that it is hardly worth repeating. Localities are now left with the responsibility of either making up for this shortfall or abandoning the welfare state themselves. Swyngedouw (1997) and others have noted, however, that this well-publicized localization of responsibility (and ostensible regulatory power) is actually accompanied by an equally dramatic *global- ization* of state power to large international institutions and agents. This process of upscaling and downscaling governance away from the nation-state is called "glocalization."

The last chapter addressed the ways that global institutions in this power vacuum are assuming new powers, while this chapter looks at how local institutions are coping with the ostensible devolution of power in the contemporary context. The empirical focus of the chapter is on public housing provision in the United States, but the intent is for the example to serve as a vehicle for understanding much broader changes in the capacity of local authorities to facilitate collective consumption or, more broadly, social reproduction.

The Case of U.S. Public Housing

It is appropriate to ask why the U.S. public housing system would be a useful vehicle through which to understand the wider process of neoliberalism. After all, public housing in the United States is a comparatively minor portion of the overall housing stock, and it was never as important to American Keynesianism as subsidies for homeownership were—and continue to be.[1] Furthermore, it has never held the material or political posture of other aspects of the American welfare state, especially the social security system. In many ways, it has always been a marginalized subsector of the American welfare state. It is, however, precisely this marginality that makes U.S. public housing a useful vehicle through which to observe the process of neoliberalism. First, because it has never enjoyed a broad constituency, public housing has been historically more malleable in the face of ideological shifts than other parts of the welfare state in the United States. The impact of various ideological movements—including but not limited to neoliberalism—tends to be more exaggerated, and thus more readily observable, in this sector than on others with more political support. Second, U.S. public housing is institutionally multiscalar by design. It was constructed and maintained as a system wherein general edicts by the federal government (mainly its housing arm, the U.S. Department of Housing and Ur-

1. Of the 112.3 million total housing units in the United States, merely 1.2 million can be considered "public," in the sense that they were built by or subsidized by a more or less constant stream of federal funding. By comparison, nearly 25 percent of the housing market in the United Kingdom is comprised of public (or "council") housing, while in the Netherlands, the figure is approximately 44 percent (See Doling 1997).

ban Development, or HUD) could be filtered down to local public housing authorities (PHAs), which then had significant autonomy. The institutional architecture of the system is thus ideal for learning about the ways that generalized ideologies (such as neoliberalism) manifest themselves as an actually existing (and locally contingent) set of policies, practices, and experiences.

Public housing provision in the United States is very different than it was thirty years ago. Because of recent policy changes that attempt to distance public housing from its Keynesian roots, the system is not as centrally financed, constructed, or managed as it was during the immediate postwar period. In particular, PHAs—the local regulatory agencies that manage the stock—have been given greater latitude to perform such tasks without direct federal supervision (see J. Smith 2000). Housing researchers and other scholars have understandably linked changes of this sort to the wider turn toward "privatization" (van Vliet 1990; Forrest and Murie 1988; Lundqvist 1988; Swann 1988; Adams 1987), "government failure" (Wallis and Dollery 1999; Chang 1997; Meier 1993; see also Cisneros 1995b; U.S. HUD 1995), "devolution" (Keyes et al. 1996; Adams 1990; see also Staeheli, Kodras, and Flint 1997), "deregulation" (Florida and Feldman 1988; Florida 1986), or some combination of the above. While each explanation partially encompasses the processes involved, they all fall somewhat short of addressing the wider spatial restructuring that is behind such shifts. The intent of this chapter is to explore recent shifts in U.S. public housing policy as an expression of the rescaling of regulation.

Swyngedouw has called such restructuring "glocalization" because it involves neither a localization nor a globalization of regulation per se but rather a simultaneous downward (to local institutions) and upward (to global institutions) diffusion of regulatory power (1997; see also Courchene 1995; Robertson 1995); meanwhile, the erstwhile arbiter (the Keynesian activist state) is rolled back to accommodate a more neoliberal set of practices (Peck and Tickell 2002). On its face, then, *both* global governance institutions (the IMF, WTO, bond rating agencies) *and* local institutions (cities, towns, regulatory districts, public housing authorities) are less "constrained" by Keynesian nation-state politics than they were in the mid–twentieth century.[2] Much recent work has thus focused on the increased importance of subnational governance on the one hand (MacKinnon 2001;

2. The general notion of "institutions" is being employed in this chapter. The idea, borrowing from Regulation Theory, refers to a multiscalar system of relations that filter, articulate, and reproduce the experience of capitalism. "Institutions" are thus both formal organizations, such as public housing authorities, and more abstract relationships such as a prevailing wage rate.

Goodwin and Painter 1996) and the rising importance of global regulatory regimes and institutions on the other (Hackworth 2002; Harmes 1998; Sassen 1996; Sinclair 1994a). But this begs the question of why, given this ostensibly greater latitude for governing autonomy, there has not been a flowering of *local* regulatory approaches that substantively differ from either Keynesian or purely market-oriented governance of years past. To the contrary, as Peck (2001b) points out, the policy imagination in the current regulatory context has narrowed considerably as neoliberalism has risen to hegemonic status (Peck and Tickell 2002; Brenner and Theodore 2002; Jessop 2002). The "opening" of power has been a lopsided affair because it has taken place within a context that heavily favors the aforementioned global institutions at the expense of cities, towns, PHAs, and so on. Moreover, the power propelled "downward" to localities often amounts to little more than an increased responsibility for social reproduction and economic risk, while that propelled "upward" enables greater capital mobility. Many localities are left with little practical choice in this context other than to pursue an "entrepreneurial" path of their own (Hackworth 2000; Hall and Hubbard 1996; Leitner 1990; Harvey 1989b).

This is not to suggest that local institutions are now somehow irrelevant recipients of neoliberalism from higher levels of government. To the contrary, institutional differences are now *more* important sources of regulatory variation than before, despite the nearly worldwide ideological gravitation toward neoliberalism. With the decline of Keynesian economic redistribution and social compensation, local institutions increasingly serve as filters for wider economic processes. Though the boundaries for acceptable policy action have narrowed, localities have been thrust into the position of determining exactly how to address, contest, or embrace larger shifts in the global economy. Thus, while the nation-state has not "given" unqualified power to local institutions, they are nonetheless more important articulators of the global economy than they were under Keynesianism because of the nation-state's restructuring under neoliberalism. One consequence in the United States, the United Kingdom, and other countries that have pursued neoliberal paths is an acceleration of uneven development within and across localities. Local variation in the quality, quantity, and maintenance of public housing, for example, has increased significantly in recent years, less because of differences in federal funding or landscape features conducive to investment than because of the institutional kaleidoscope unleashed by the rescaling of regulation.

This chapter argues that while glocalization is the most comprehensive way to describe and understand the restructuring of public housing in the

United States, we should be cautious not to assume that the upward and downward transfers of power are identical or unqualified. Local institutions—PHAs included—are now arguably more central regulators than before, but their "power" is incredibly qualified and constrained. The first section of this chapter sets the context for this argument by providing an institutional history of public housing in the United States. It shows, above all, that recent changes in provisioning are not easily subsumed under "privatization," "devolution," or "deregulation" explanations alone, because the system has been diffuse and heavily influenced by real estate capital from the start. The second section empirically examines some of the factors influencing local differences in recent provisioning outcomes. The third section compares three very different housing authorities to explain how institutional differences have been unleashed amidst the current rescaling of regulation, leading to the recent emergence of highly unequal production levels and standards for public housing. Drawing on the evidence presented, the chapter concludes by arguing that glocalization has facilitated a set of conditions in which public housing provisioning—now more exposed to relatively global notions of profit—is more prone to inter-local unevenness than ever before.

A Short History of Public Housing in the United States

It is useful to recall the history of the public housing system in the United States as a first step toward understanding recent shifts. The period between 1937 and 1973 saw both the birth and the apex of Keynesian public housing (KPH) in the United States. Though never reaching the level of provision of Western Europe and always sensitive to the needs of real estate capital (see table 3.1), the period can be deemed "Keynesian" to the extent that it was justified on the grounds of redistribution, boosting effective demand, and increasing investment in the built environment. The first major piece of public housing legislation in the United States was the 1937 Housing Act. Successful lobbying by the U.S. Chamber of Commerce and the U.S. Savings and Loan Association kept the act from being a central part of President Franklin D. Roosevelt's New Deal agenda (Marcuse 1998). Roosevelt was persuaded that public housing was "too socialist" a solution to the existing scarcity of homes, and kept it out of the Administration's legislative agenda until the mid-1930s (Bratt 1986). After a bitter, ideological debate in Congress, the act was finally passed in 1937, but not

TABLE 3.1
Major federal public housing legislation accommodating the private sector

Year	Public housing program	Benefit to private interests
1937	Wagner Steagall Housing Act	For construction of public housing to take place, the Act required the elimination of an equal number of substandard units in the nearby community and set income eligibility requirements very low so as not to compete with the private sector.
1949	Federal Housing Act	Public housing built under the Act was prohibited from competing with private market housing through: (a) rent ceilings that were set at 20% lower than the lowest nearby private housing; (b) stigmatizing, austere, physical design; and (c) low operating budgets for PHAs.
1974	Section 8	Part of the 1974 Housing and Community Development Act, the Section 8 "Existing Housing" program provided housing vouchers for tenants to redeem with participating private sector landlords, while the "New Construction/Substantial Rehabilitation" program provided incentives for private sector and nonprofit real estate developers to construct low-income housing.
1990	HOPE VI	Part of the 1990 Cranston-Gonzalez National Affordable Housing Act, the HOPE VI program provides funding for housing authorities to: (a) demolish "severely distressed" units; (b) sell units to tenants; and (c) create partnerships with private sector developers and housing managers to reduce operating expenses.
1998	QHWRA	The Quality Housing and Work Responsibility Act (QHWRA) created legislation to enable housing authorities to turn over management of public units to private managers, among other things.

Source: Vale 2000; Marcuse 1998; Harloe 1995; Bratt 1986.

without significant concessions to the private sector.[3] Among the most significant were requirements that public housing schemes include "equivalent demolition" of housing in the surrounding community (and compensation to the owner) so that no new units were added to the overall stock (Marcuse 1998; Bratt 1986). Furthermore, nearly a third of the units authorized under the act were reserved for military housing, and the remainder of "proper" public housing units were reserved for the working poor, rather than the destitute (Harloe 1995). The 1937 act also established a decentralized system of delivery composed of the PHAs, which were established to receive direct subsidy from the federal government and continue to be responsible for the day-to-day management of housing in cities across the United States. The diffuse nature of public housing governance in the United States would become one of its hallmarks.

Despite its clear shaping by prevailing liberalisms in the United States, public housing nonetheless remained firmly "socialist" in the minds of key congressional leaders even during the Depression (Marcuse 1998). At the same time, many recognized that America's severe shortage of housing would inhibit its ability to build and enlarge military facilities—a key congressional priority as the prospect of war loomed in the late 1930s. The Lanham Act of 1940 was a response to this priority, enabling the construction of thousands of new housing units close to military bases and factories across the United States. But even the special circumstances of this act would not inhibit the private sector from railing against what they saw as unfair competition. In response to the housing lobby, Congress mandated that all Lanham Act housing be transferred to the private sector or demolished outright upon the war's completion (ibid.). This was, of course, very unpopular in many parts of the country, such as Dallas, Texas, where thousands of units had been built to house defense industry workers (see Texas Low Income Housing Information Service 2002) and where, like in many other parts of the United States, affordable housing was in short supply following the war.

Despite severe postwar housing shortages, the first major piece of housing legislation did not come until 1949. By this point, however, the private house construction lobby had achieved even more power than it enjoyed during the 1930s, and it had become even more influential on the legislative process (Checkoway 1980). In addition to being overwhelmingly oriented toward private suburban house construction—which likely wors-

---

3. Even when it did become law, its central purpose was not to provide housing for the poor but rather to relieve unemployment (Marcuse 1998).

ened the inner city conditions necessitating public housing—the 1949 Housing Act public housing measures were severely compromised by private interests (Bratt 1986). Among other things, public housing rents were required to be 20 percent lower than the lowest comparable housing units in the neighborhood (Bratt 1986), eviction authorization was legalized for families exceeding rigid income limits, design limitations were created to make public housing stand out from the average stock (Bristol 1991; Bratt 1986, 1990), and operating budgets for PHAs were set at unsustainably low levels (Bratt 1986). One result of this legislation was a dramatic shift in the tenantry of public housing, from the "temporarily submerged middle class" in the 1930s (Marcuse 1998) to only the most extreme poor by the early 1950s. It not only limited public housing access to all but the "least profitable" (Harloe 1995), but it also substantially undermined the prospect of income diversity in individual housing complexes—a key theme in today's public housing policy discourse. From this point onward, public housing became an increasingly segregated environment for its tenants.

The 1949 Housing Act was the only major legislation affecting public housing until the late 1960s, but there were several demonstration programs and limited changes to existing legislation that continued to be shaped by private interests. In 1959, for example, Congress enacted Section 202 housing, which provided low-interest loans to nonprofit developers to build low-income elderly housing (Bratt 1990). In 1965, Congress unveiled the Section 23 Program, which enabled PHAs to engage in long-term leases with private landlords and to provide continued income subsidies for tenants living in their units, usually based on the difference between a set percentage of their income and the prevailing "market rent" (Bratt 1986). This policy served as an important precedent for the Section 8 voucher program instituted later. Also unveiled in 1965 was the "turnkey" program, which provided subsidies to compensate private developers for building new housing that would eventually be turned over to the PHA at a predetermined price (ibid.). In short, though the years between the 1949 Housing Act and the 1968 Housing and Urban Development Act (HUDA) were nearly devoid of major public housing legislation, smaller "experiments" did occur, and they were affected by the same private sector pressures that had affected the major legislation.

The 1968 HUDA instituted a number of important changes to public housing policy. Two of the most important were Section 235 and 236 housing subsidies. Section 235 provided interest rate subsidies that lowered the lending rate to as low as 1 percent in order to encourage public housing tenants to purchase housing of their own (Bratt 1990). This served as an important precedent for the public housing homeownership policies of the 1980s and marked a turning point wherein public housing tenants were seen as a potential market (rather than a threat to the market) if adequately subsidized by the federal government. Section 236 of the act provided rent subsidies for multi-family housing developers (Feldman and Florida 1990; Bratt 1986), which led to a dramatic surge in unit construction. The total number of housing starts subsidized by the federal government increased from 12 to 25 percent between 1969 and 1970 (Lilley 1980), leading to pro- duction levels between 1968 and 1973 that nearly equaled the total output between 1949 and 1968 (Feldman and Florida 1990; Bratt 1986).

Despite the institutional limitations and relatively small size of KPH, President Nixon and others decided that the program was too expensive and declared a moratorium on all new public housing in 1973, effectively extinguishing the 1968 Housing Act. This basic rollback/destruction of KPH continued through the 1980s and 1990s, as HUD's budget was slashed more aggressively than any other high-level domestic branch of the gov- ernment (Bratt and Keating 1993). This continued through the 1990s when the most active source of public housing funding came in the form of grants to facilitate the demolition and privatization of the stock.

But the neoliberalization of public housing in the United States has in- volved much more than the withdrawal of funding and oversight. The roll- back/destruction of KPH has been accompanied by the roll-*out*/creation of various neoliberal measures that promote "self-sufficiency," entrepre- neurialism, and private governance. In arguably the most extensive mea- sure of this sort, the federal government began foregrounding Section 8 vouchers as the preferred mode of public housing in the early 1970s. Sec- tion 8 vouchers are payments made by the federal government to individ- ual landlords to cover whatever gap exists between the mandated 30 percent of a tenant's income and the prevailing fair market rent (as deter- mined by HUD). Though several demonstration programs in the early 1960s experimented with such demand-side measures, it was not until the 1974 Housing Act that the Section 8 program was officially authorized and expanded as a significant policy device. In the past thirty years, the program has evolved from being a fairly marginal outlay by HUD to being one of its largest.[4] The federal government further institutionalized the belief that the market is a normatively superior way to allocate public housing by ini- tiating the Low Income Housing Tax Credit (LIHTC) Program in 1986.

4. It should also be noted that the Bush Administration recently announced that it was target- ing the Section 8 program for cuts (if not removal). It is possible, in other words, that this roll- out policy could itself fall victim to roll-back destruction.

The LIHTC Program involves the allocation of tax credits to qualifying low-income housing builders. The builders of such units sell the credits to corporations or individuals with high tax liability to create a revenue stream of their own. Central to the expansion of both programs is the belief that the market will be able to allocate goods more efficiently and effectively than the federal government.

Another mechanism used to roll out a neoliberal public housing order has been the encouragement of homeownership as a way to generate "self-sufficiency" among the existing public housing tenantry (U.S. HUD 2003). The first major effort to provide federal homeownership subsidies for low-income families, the Section 235 program, was initiated in the 1968 Housing Act, but it soon faltered because of management problems and the expense of upgrading the stock to sellable shape (Bratt 1990). This was followed by a series of smaller demonstration programs during the 1980s, including the Public Housing Demonstration Program in 1985 and the Nehemiah Program in 1987, but both folded for similar reasons (Silver 1990). The idea of promoting homeownership among public housing tenants resurfaced again in the 1990s as a component of the HOPE VI program, but the same aversion to substantive and widespread federal expenditures for physical improvement remained a constraint.

A further set of roll-out programs sought to link housing to individual work ethic. The idea was to wean the existing tenant base from the federal government by improving their work ethic and entrepreneurialism (U.S. HUD 2003). One of the earliest programs of this sort was the Reagan administration's "Project Self-Sufficiency," which provided assistance for ten thousand single mothers within the public housing system to become economically independent (Vale 2000). The George H. W. Bush administration continued these efforts with "Operation Bootstrap," which included another three thousand families in a similar program in 1989 (ibid.). The programs encouraged job training and included light incentives for working. The Clinton administration's Work and Responsibility Act in 1994 expanded these efforts by providing more incentives for employers to employ welfare recipients, but it was thwarted by the more restrictive Republican-led Personal Responsibility Act. After several years of debate, an agreement was finally reached with the Quality Housing and Work Responsibility Act (QHWRA) of 1998. Among other things, the QHWRA mandated community service requirements and stricter screening for tenants, opened access to public housing for higher-income families, and allowed PHAs to evict tenants for a wider range of reasons (ibid.). It also allowed the newly installed private managers of public housing to enforce such rules. The roll-out neoliberalization of public housing was thus well underway by the early 1990s.

The HOPE VI program, initiated by a federal commission on "severely distressed" public housing and the Cranston-Gonzalez Affordable Housing Act of 1990, folded many of the initiatives discussed earlier (both rollback and roll-out efforts) into a more or less coherent public housing program. The HOPE VI program is an embodiment of both rollback/destruction and roll-out/creation neoliberalism. On the one hand, its mandate is to demolish the country's most "severely distressed" public housing units (U.S. HUD 2003). Beginning in 1995, individual PHAs were awarded grants competitively for this purpose. Initially, the program enjoyed fairly broad political support, as most viewed public housing as a failed model. The early stipulation that all housing units felled as a result of a HOPE VI grant be replaced was sufficient, also, to engender the support of many residents. However, in 1995 this requirement changed and PHAs were no longer required to replace all units. This fundamentally changed the coverage of the program, in particular by emphasizing the fundamentally rollback nature of the initiative. Tenant support soon evaporated as it became increasingly clear that the benefits of HOPE VI would be limited to those lucky enough to land a new housing unit.[5] Most post-1995 HOPE VI plans did not, in fact, replace anywhere close to 100 percent of the felled units. According to HUD data, only slightly more than half of the units to be built with HOPE VI dollars will be even nominally "public"[6] (that is, affordable to the existing tenantry), and only 50.7 percent of these units will actually be available to the residents whose homes were originally demolished.[7] That translates into an actual reduction for the poorest residents in public housing of at least 51,172 units. Using HUD's conservative estimate[8] of household size in HOPE VI communities (2.9), this suggests that as of 2001, at least 148,399 tenants have been or will be removed from the physical public housing stock in the next several years. Some of these families will be given Section 8 vouchers to redeem with private landlords, but with

<hr>

5. Prior to 1995, all HOPE VI plans had to promise at least full-unit retention. Many were unable to deliver on this promise. After the HUD requirement for full-unit retention was removed in 1995, PHAs began submitting plans that did not even intend to replace all (or, in some cases, *any*) of the existing housing units (see Keating 2000).

6. The rest of the units will be either market-rate or more lightly subsidized than current public housing.

7. The remaining units are reserved for tenants in other locations within the PHA system or for those on housing waiting lists.

8. It is "conservative" because it does not take into account doubling up, which can be quite common in public housing.

so many families flooding such markets, many families will have to leave the metropolitan area or face a housing situation even more precarious than the one from which they were removed. Supply has already failed to keep up with demand in places like Chicago and Washington, D.C., where thousands of residents have been displaced.

HOPE VI thus represents much more than a basic divestment of the housing stock. It also represents a more transparent roll-out of neoliberal policy in practice. It has been linked—via the 1998 Quality Housing and Work Reform Act—to the "work responsibility" acts discussed earlier, and the program's promotional material is rife with the language of economic "self-sufficiency" (see ibid.). Increasingly, tenants must behave in "acceptable" ways to continue to receive their housing benefits. PHAs have been given new powers to evict for behavioral or even economic reasons. In HUD's new "One Strike and You Are Out" program, for example, PHAs are able to evict tenants for criminal activity committed by any member of a household on or off the public housing complex grounds.[9] It is part of a more transparently interventionist set of neoliberal state practices.

In general, while U.S. public housing has never been a comprehensive or even completely "public" system of provision, recent efforts to restructure[10] have demonstrably worsened conditions for current tenants. This restructuring has sought broadly to neoliberalize the public housing system by emphasizing "individual responsibility" (the "One Strike and You Are Out" program), the market as social provider (Section 8 housing), and the overall reduction of government oversight (demolition of existing stock, inclusion of private management). The net effect of such changes has been a reduction of housing opportunities paralleled by the expansion of penality for residents.

9. In a recent case brought before the U.S. Supreme Court, the right of PHAs to evict tenants for criminal activity over which they have no direct control was unanimously upheld (see Stout 2002; National Housing Law Project 2000). In the case, three tenants were evicted for criminal behavior committed by someone other than themselves: Pearlie Rucker, 63, was evicted when her mentally disabled daughter—at the time living with Ms. Rucker—was arrested for cocaine possession three blocks away from her apartment building. Willie Lee, 71, and his partner Barbara Hill, 63, were evicted after their grandsons were caught smoking marijuana in the parking lot of the family's housing complex. Herman Walker, 75, was evicted after his in-home caregiver (for medical reasons Mr. Walker is incapable of living alone) was arrested for possession of cocaine in Mr. Walker's apartment on three separate occasions.

10. It should also be noted that various officials (mainly rural Republicans in Newt Gingrich's mid-1990s congressional majority) have recently sought something more ambitious that a mere restructuring of the program. In 1995, there was serious discussion to dismantle HUD completely, along with the housing that it funds and manages. Though ultimately unsuccessful, the "reinvention" of HUD that did occur resulted in a highly compromised (from its Keynesian origins) institution (see U.S. HUD 1995).

Local Differences in Public Housing Provision

In addition to the obvious policy restructuring created by the program, HOPE VI exacerbates an acutely uneven geography. The program has increased authority for local housing authorities while at the same time exposing such institutions to a broader set of more global institutions and forces—the real estate market most abstractly, bond-rating agencies and banks more concretely. There has not been, however, one boilerplate response to this broader shift. In large part, existing geo-institutional differences in PHAs (and in their localities) have shaped the local response to the restructuring of public housing—particularly their ability to retain (or expand) the existing housing stock. Some have wholeheartedly embraced the program as a way to thin out or even eliminate their stock, while others have resisted somewhat, aiming to retain as much housing as possible.

Proponents of HOPE VI have argued that such unevenness the simple result of the award size or, at worst, is the "natural" result of some projects being in very disinvested neighborhoods. Since the program depends heavily upon private funding, so the argument goes, some projects will simply be seen as more profitable than others, so the rebuilt complexes will vary considerably. But this explanation situates the program and its consequences as natural outcomes of local economic geographies rather than the political decisions that they actually are. Moreover, this explanation simply does not square with empirical reality. I evaluated the statistical influence of various HOPE VI awards, neighborhood effects (income, race, and so on of the surrounding area), and private funding, and found that these factors—alone or combined—account for less than 10 percent of the variety of public housing units built after the plan was implemented (see Hackworth 2003 for the full version of this study). Put simply, the surface demography or local economic geography of given neighborhoods is not the reason for such uneven responses to HOPE VI. Deeply ingrained geo-institutional differences that manifest themselves through housing authorities are far more to blame for the differences in quantity and quality of public housing after HOPE VI. Given the highly diffuse regulatory history of public housing in the United States, it is hardly surprising to find such local institutional differences. But it is increasingly evident that existing differences in provisioning approaches have become even more acute in the context of a glocalization that removes the nation-state as an active arbiter and provider of public housing. Those regions that most successfully inhibited the federal government from building public housing in the first place are now able to eviscerate their stock without challenge from the authorities. It would, however, be a mistake to conclude that the inverse of this rule exists to the same extent—relatively pro-public housing areas like New York City are no more able to improve or expand their stock. In such cases, "success" is defined simply as the political power to fend off the clamor from local business leaders and conservative ideologues encouraging the authority to pursue a HOPE VI grant. That is, while it is unquestionably true that the federal government now plays a less active role in the provision of public housing under glocalization, it is not at all true that this has somehow empowered politically progressive localities to create more (or better) social housing. Glocalization, it appears, is a one-way street when it comes to welfare provision. To make this point more clear, it is worth exploring three cities and their very different experiences with the HOPE VI program.

Case Studies of Participating PHAs

Seattle, New York, and Chicago took very different approaches to dealing with a similar set of circumstances—"severely distressed" housing in their local stock. New York chose to retain as much of its public housing as possible, largely ignoring pressure to downsize or diversify its stock. Chicago, by contrast, chose (and continues to choose) to reduce significantly the size of its physical stock by removing as much public housing as possible. Seattle pursued a model of desegregation using HOPE VI dollars to create relatively income-diverse environments. The following section attempts to find out why these cities reacted so differently. The case studies are based on discussions with HOPE VI coordinators and other officials at each PHA,[11] a review of literature printed and posted by the PHA, and an examination of tenant input and activism during the HOPE VI application process.

Seattle

Seattle's population of 563,374 makes it much smaller than either Chicago or New York City, but its embrace of the HOPE VI program implies that it has faced a similar deterioration of its inner city housing stock. The Seat-

---

11. The discussions were open-ended but guided to focus on changes in governance capacity and the PHA's response to these changes. The case studies were also informed by less detailed discussions with fifty other HOPE VI coordinators in other U.S. cities.

tle Housing Authority (SHA) manages 6,305 physical housing units and oversees another 6,955 Section 8 vouchers (U.S. HUD 2002). As of the end of fiscal year 2001, there were 8,268 families on its waiting list. The SHA has been shaped by the city's social democratic political ethos since the mid–twentieth century, and the level of conflict over the siting of public housing has been generally lower there than in other large metropolitan areas in the United States. This history of relative tolerance and adherence to such politics have shaped its approach to the HOPE VI program. The SHA was awarded four HOPE VI grants during the late 1990s—Holly Park, Roxbury House and Village, Rainier Vista Garden Community, and High Point Garden—for a total of $135,137,383 (see table 3.2). The SHA was one of the most assertive in the country at pursuing HOPE VI dollars, but not without local regulation. The Seattle City Council, for example, mandated that every unit felled as part of a HOPE VI plan be replaced and set aside for very low-income tenants. This mandate—the result of pressure from the Seattle Displacement Coalition, a local activist group—assured that, unlike many other cities participating in the program, very low-income tenants would be assured of a unit elsewhere in the PHA's system, but it did not translate into a large percentage of such tenants moving into redeveloped communities. Of the 2,177 units demolished (or scheduled for demolition) since 1995, only 1,211 will be replaced and made available to very low-income tenants on the original development site. The on-site mixture of Seattle's HOPE VI communities is among the highest in the nation, a distinction that came at the cost of some transfer of existing tenants to other sites in the city.

In the High Point Garden Complex, for example, the SHA was able to plan a fairly income-diverse community. As part of the plan, the group reached an agreement with tenants wherein all units would be demolished and replaced with 350 public rentals, 446 other low-income rental and homeowner units, and 804 market rate units. It was able to get the tenants to agree to such a large reduction in public rental units largely because of the citywide one-for-one replacement rule. The SHA sought, and was able to attract, developer interest in the market rate portion of the development, largely because of the city's tight housing market in the late 1990s. The complex, situated in the Puget Sound neighborhood, has attractive views and other amenities for all residents, so it was an easier sell than in other cities. The existing income diversity of the neighborhood also was an important magnet for investors. The median income in the neighborhood (at the time of the development) was approximately 40.1 percent of metropolitan area levels in 1990, much lower than most neighborhoods in down-

TABLE 3.2
Comparison of HOPE VI projects in Seattle, New York, and Chicago, 1993–2000

	Year of HOPE IV award	Award amount	Demolitions	Public rentals	Public homeowner units	Low-income (LI) rentals	LI homeowner units	Market rate (MR) rentals	MR homeowner units
SEATTLE									
Holly Park	1995	$48,116,503.00	871	400	0	334	100	66	300
Roxbury House and Village	1998	$17,020,880.00	60	211	0	30	0	0	0
Rainier Vista Garden Community	1999	$35,000,000.00	496	250	0	0	200	0	300
High Point Garden	2000	$35,000,000.00	750	350	0	366	80	149	655
Total		$135,137,383.00	2,177	1,211	0	730	380	215	1,255
Average		$33,784,345.75	544.25	302.75	0	182.5	95	53.75	313.75
NEW YORK CITY									
Arverne-Edgemere Houses	1995	$67,700,952.00	0	1,789	24	0	0	0	0
Prospect Plaza	1998	$21,405,213.00	102	308	60	0	0	0	0
Total		$89,106,165.00	102	2,097	84	0	0	0	0
Average		$44,553,082.50	51	1048.5	42	0	0	0	0
CHICAGO									
Cabrini-Green	1994	$50,000,000.00	1,324	493	0	0	0	0	0
Henry Horner Homes	1996	$18,435,300.00	746	150	0	0	0	0	0
Robert Taylor Homes	1996	$25,000,000.00	762	251	0	0	0	0	0
ABLA (Brooks Extension)	1996	$24,483,250.00	954	452	0	0	0	0	0
ABLA Homes	1998	$35,000,000.00	1,882	1,052	0	328	1,218	202	0
Madden-Wells-Darrow	2000	$35,000,000.00	2,547	423	0	194	100	316	100
Total		$187,918,550.00	8,215	2,821	0	522	1,318	518	100
Average		$31,319,758.33	1369.17	470.17	0.00	87.00	219.67	86.33	16.67

Source: OPHI 2001; U.S. Census 1990.

town Seattle but much higher than the neighborhoods surrounding most other HOPE VI developments nationwide.

In the High Point Complex and Seattle's other HOPE VI communities, the approach was to create income and ethnic diversity, and to a certain extent they have been successful. By the same token, though, the adherence to the goal of desegregation blinded some to the displacement of very poor tenants needed to make this possible. Tenant dissent was present in Seattle, but the level of resentment did not reach the level seen in many other large cities, in part because activists were initially successful in pressuring the city council to create its own restrictions to the HOPE VI application and development process. While most local officials in other cities chose to avoid formally regulating the HOPE VI application and development process, Seattle's one-for-one unit replacement stipulation served to placate tenants concerned about losing actual housing units. Perhaps because of this, tenants were more receptive to the SHA's proposals than is the case with other public housing communities nationwide. In short, the city's ethos of social democracy, its relatively low level of existing segregation, and the high amenity value of the SHA's properties all shaped its approach to public housing provision under HOPE VI. However, its "success" at achieving these goals has come at the cost of a large transfer of tenants to housing units that are no better than their original situation.

New York City

Managing a stock of 160,430 units and overseeing another 83,303 Section 8 vouchers, the New York City Public Housing Authority (NYCPHA) is the largest in the United States (U.S. HUD 2002). Its history as the most prolific local provider of public housing throughout the twentieth century (Plunz 1990), and its tenants' history as the most organized group of its sort in the country had an important impact on the city's approach to the HOPE VI framework. By and large, it refused to use the program as a way to thin or diversify its housing stock. Many of its physical housing units are in the city's most disinvested neighborhoods, and much of its housing technically qualifies as "severely distressed," but the NYCPHA applied for and won only two HOPE VI grants (see table 3.2). Much of this has to do with housing activism in the mid-1990s that successfully educated tenants about the negative consequences of the program in other cities. Partly in response to this pressure, the NYCPHA chose to pursue HOPE VI dollars only when true tenant support was present and when it was feasible to replace all demolished units.

A closer look at the Arverne-Edgemere complex illuminates the city's approach. The Authority received a HOPE VI grant for $67.7 million in 1995 but took great pains to ensure that the money would not lead to a displacement. The project called for the demolition and replacement of over 1,800 housing units contained in the complex.[12] All of the original units were reserved for existing tenants, twenty of which were set aside for tenant purchase. Though a private consultant was hired to assist with the HOPE VI application, there was no outside private or non-HUD public money used, so there was little private influence on the aims of the development. The tenants were very involved and generally supportive of the development. The surrounding neighborhood had a median income approximately 45 percent of the levels in the New York metropolitan area, which was rather high compared to other New York public housing complexes (and other HOPE VI communities nationwide). This reflected the desire of the NYCPHA to focus first on complexes that are *not* in the most impoverished or isolated neighborhoods. Focusing on very poor neighborhoods often initiates pressure from the federal government to deconcentrate, which in the New York housing market would effectively mean asking a large percentage to leave the city, since few comparatively affordable or available Section 8 units exist.

This approach stood in contrast to most other PHAs nationwide that have either chosen or were pressured to pursue a strategy of physical divestment or income diversification, leading to the displacement of many original tenants from the redeveloped site. New York's institutional and political support of public housing, deeply rooted in the city's history as the leading public housing provider in the country, shaped its approach to the HOPE VI application and development process. Its level of tenant organization and local political support for public housing is unparalleled. Unlike Seattle, the imperative to replace or redevelop the existing stock was not mandated formally by the city council but rather was negotiated at the PHA level in response to pressure by tenants. This pressure has existed in most cities implementing HOPE VI programs, but nowhere has it been as politically successful as in New York. Also unlike Seattle, New York's tight housing market was not interpreted as a way to draw the middle class into a redeveloped complex but rather as a reason for why such a strategy (removing public units to make way for the middle class) was inappropriate. But while the New York developments had the widest tenant support of the

12. Arverne and Edgemere are actually two different developments that were merged as part of the HOPE VI process.

three cities compared here, it was still not sufficient to lead to an *increase* in public rental units. There are very clear limits to "local empowerment" within this context.

Chicago

Though it is the second-largest housing authority in the United States, overseeing 34,699 physical units and 33,852 Section 8 vouchers, the Chicago Housing Authority (CHA) does not have the wider political support enjoyed in New York or Seattle. Chicago's history as a cauldron for land-use disputes associated with the siting of public housing is an important reason for this. Public housing has been and continues to be a deeply divisive issue in Chicago, and its provisioning approach during the past fifteen years reflects this acrimony. The HOPE VI program offered city officials the opportunity to put aside this unparalleled acrimony by simply putting aside public housing. Rather than choose a retention or mixed-income approach, the CHA has used its six grants during the 1990s largely to divest itself of its physical stock (see also Smith 2000; Vale 2000). To be sure, much of this approach was shaped by the federal government takeover of the CHA from 1995 to 2000. But it is equally true that its tenants have been more politically isolated than those in either New York or Seattle and that many of the policies implemented by federal officials (including the takeover itself) were enthusiastically supported by key local leaders.

Over 8,200 units have been or are scheduled to be demolished, but only 2,821 public rentals are planned for replacement as part of the six HOPE VI grants the city received between 1994 and 2000.[13] Unlike the other two case studies, the CHA targeted the most impoverished complexes. As table 3.2 suggests, the average percentage of MSA income (excluding the Cabrini-Green development, which, though extremely poor, is surrounded by wealthy neighborhoods) was very low—between 11 and 18 percent at the time of development. The CHA's HOPE VI plans relied heavily on Section 8 vouchers to accommodate the balance of people whose homes had been demolished. Over 2,000 units have been built or are projected for construction in the coming years, but most of these will not be available to the poorest current residents. Despite militant local activism against the HOPE VI program for the past eight years, no housing authority or city

13. The CHA did apply for and receive two HOPE VI grants after 2001—one for Rockwell Gardens and the other an extension of the existing Robert Taylor Homes project. The actual unit demolition and replacement numbers associated with these grants were not available at the time of this writing, so they are not included in table 2.

council protections exist in this case, and its displacement problem continues to be among the worst nationwide.

As part of Chicago's 2000 Madden-Wells-Darrow grant, for example, 2,547 public rental units were razed and replaced with only 423 comparable units (table 3.2). The expected eventual income mixture is technically high but, as some local activists suggested, also created a fairly substantial displacement of the poorest families. The surrounding neighborhood is one of the poorest in the city, averaging just under 13 percent compared to metropolitan area income levels in 1990. Despite this degree of poverty, there was developer interest as well as interest from outside residents capable of purchasing the planned market rate units. Over $40 million in outside funding was earmarked for the project.

The Madden-Wells-Darrow complex was typical of other HOPE VI activity in Chicago. Its focus was on removing a large portion of the public stock as a means to deconcentrate the poor living in or near the inner city. The very mixed reaction among tenants was also quite typical of the Chicago experience, as some tenants benefited enormously by being able to live in physically redeveloped environments, while most others were forced to navigate the historically unsympathetic Chicago housing market for opportunities with their Section 8 vouchers. The loss of control over various aspects of the HOPE VI process during the federal takeover period was one source of tenant frustration. Though the takeover was in part a response to tenant complaints that the CHA was deaf to their needs, the federal government used the opportunity more as a showcase of divestment than as a true remedy to restore some semblance of tenant democracy. The insensitivity toward their concerns displayed by local housing officials for decades was simply transferred, argued many tenants, to a more powerful agent, the federal government.

These three cases make it clear that there are vast differences in local public housing provisioning systems, differences based in part on existing institutional variations. Such variations are colored by the history of tenant activism, the opposition or support of the real estate community, and existing attitudes toward welfare redistribution, among other factors. Though these factors have been present throughout U.S. public housing history, their salience in the current rescaling of regulation has sharpened. This is not to suggest, however, that PHAs or the localities within which they sit now have more power. As each of the cases demonstrates, actual deviation from a pro-development, anti-public path is politically arduous.

Like many other aspects of the welfare state, public housing has been minimized, privatized, and devolved during the past thirty years. The restructuring of public housing provision is part of a much broader rescaling of regulation, wherein certain regulatory functions that once existed at the national level are being simultaneously propelled upward to larger institutions and economies and downward to various manifestations of the local. As this case shows, however, many localities have not been "empowered" by this realignment. Local PHAs have technically been "given" power, but they must now adhere more to the relatively global notions of profit that are policed by banks, rating agencies, and investors. Like many other local institutions, PHAs are disciplined relatively quickly within this context. "Local control" for PHAs and the tenants they serve often consists of a troubling choice between pursuing, on the one hand, a model that might ultimately undermine the public stock even more through gentrification or, on the other, fighting to retain an already problematic and compromised housing system. By contrast, local real estate developers have been given another set of opportunities, as regulations and other factors discouraging their presence are no longer as acute as they once were.

As much recent work has shown, the rescaling of regulation deals fundamentally with the way capitalism is organized, so it generally moves toward a liberalized set of spatial relationships. Though always compromised by private interests and thus never truly separate from market relations, public housing in the United States has been fundamentally neoliberalized in the past several decades. Gone are the days of the federal government providing direct subsidies to house only the most acutely poor; here, apparently, are the days of a complicated local variability in the quantity, quality, and access to "public" housing.

Chapter 4

The Public-Private Partnership

One of the foundations of neoliberal governance at the local level is public-private cooperation. These alliances can vary considerably in form, but city governments are increasingly expected to serve as market facilitators, rather than salves for market failures. Cities have moved from a managerialist role under Keynesianism to an entrepreneurial one under neoliberalism (Harvey 1989b). No longer are cities as able to establish regulatory barriers to capital; on the contrary, they are expected to lower such barriers. An entire body of academic literature—regime theory—has arisen to address public-private partnerships and such entrepreneurial behavior, but knowledge of how such alliances function within multiscalar capitalism is underdeveloped. In particular, regime theory and much of the mainstream literature on public-private alliances tend to be highly localist in its orientation. That is, it says very little about how local regimes are connected to broader policy shifts, such as the current fervor for federal devolution in the United States. Regime theory also says very little about the market influence and behavior of public-private coalitions, choosing instead to conceptualize the local state and local capital as more or less autonomous entities that just happen to be coalescing around a particular set of development concerns. This chapter attempts to address both gaps by linking the concept of urban regimes to wider policy changes and by considering the local effects of coalitions that have no obvious barriers between public and private. The goal is to examining regime theory critically through the use of a case study of such cooperation in New Brunswick, New Jersey, during the past thirty years.

Regime Theory and the Local State

Urban regimes are collectives of public and private interests that join forces to initiate development or retard disinvestment in a particular city. Their public participants include city hall, development authorities, housing authorities, and the like, while their private participants can range from wealthy individuals to influential local corporations. Regime theory is helpful in understanding neoliberal urban governance insofar as it emphasizes the increasingly murky boundaries between private and public institutions in the land development process, but there are serious deficiencies in its approach, as a brief history of the literature shows.

Stone's study of urban development in Atlanta, Georgia, is often cited as the nominal beginning of regime theory (1989), but important antecedents were undertaken several years earlier by Norman and Susan Fainstein (1983, 1985) in their work on the changing role of the local state in New York City. Regime theory is best understood intellectually as a rapprochement of competing local state theories and empirically as a set of ideas about the future of local government amidst widespread urban decline following the 1970s. During the 1950s and 1960s, one of the more salient debates in urban studies addressed the general question of who governs at the local level. Generally, there were two strands of thought on this subject: pluralism and elitism. Pluralists argued that power at the local level was not the domain of any one group or constituency but rather was formed through political coalitions. Postwar metropolitan fragmentation in the United States, which divided power into smaller geographical units, fueled this sentiment. Power was "up for grabs" according to pluralists, and the mechanism of the general election was the chief (though not the only) mechanism for achieving this power. Dahl's *Who Governs* is a classic articulation and defense of pluralist local political theory (1961). In this book, Dahl chronicles the formation of a mayor-centered electoral coalition in New Haven, Connecticut, that was eventually responsible for redeveloping the downtown area of the city. The importance of economic restructuring, the financial power of coalition participants, and the links to wider processes are generally missing in this and other pluralist narratives.

The work of Dahl and the pluralists more generally was criticized by practitioners of elite theory[1] as being blind to an existing economic power structure that places enormous power in the hands of elite businesspeople. To elite theorists, local power is not open to all who are organized enough to reach for it but rather is an obvious by-product of economic power. Miliband's instrumentalist model of the local state was in line with elite conceptions when it posited a veritable conspiracy between local business elites and local political elites (1969; see also Clark and Dear 1981). The argument runs that elites from both worlds (business and politics) exchange roles freely—business elites become political elites, and vice versa. Miliband and some other elite theorists thus suggested that a real understanding of local politics is actually more economic than that proposed by Dahl and the pluralists. In the elite model, we need only understand the individual career behavior of a locality's most economically powerful people.[2]

Regime theory developed initially as an attempt to reconcile the strength of both pluralist and elitist notions of local power. The regime literature during the 1980s was composed primarily of case study research, but more recently some practitioners have developed general theoretical statements so that we can begin to speak more clearly about the idea of regimes (Horan 1991; Stone 1993; Stoker 1995; Lauria 1997b). Regime theory emphasizes the following: (a) the importance of coalition building, a central tenet of pluralist theory; (b) the ability to provide leadership in a complex and changing environment; and (c) the importance of economic and institutional power. In essence, as Stone explains, "regime analysis concedes to pluralism the unlikelihood that any group can exercise comprehensive social control but also holds that the absence of monolithic control is so universal as to be uninteresting" (1993, p. 8). In contrast to elite theory, though, "regime theory recognizes that any [one] group is unlikely to be able to exercise comprehensive social control in a complex world" (Stoker 1995, p. 59). That is, regime theory recognizes that political actors are beholden at least in part to the economy and more specifically to economic actors but at the same time attempts to steer clear of the economic determinism of elite theory by arguing that power is more complicated than simple access to resources. Power, according to regime theory, is de-

1. Some, such as Lauria (1997b), have deemed this school of thought "structuralism" rather than elite theory.
2. This view was disputed on the left by Poulantzas, who argued that while economically powerful people often become politically powerful, the relationship is more structural than interpersonal or cronyistic per se (1969). That is, it is the position of economic power within liberal capitalism that confers political power, not the particular connection of individuals currently residing in those positions.

pendent also upon electoral power, the nature of coalitions in a locality, and technical knowledge (ibid., p. 60).

While most general statements on regime theory tend to explain it in relation to pluralism and elitism, Brown (1999) has argued that regime theory's emphasis on the nexus between the public and private is reminiscent of the commercial republic, which is a product of classical liberal thought. Brown's placement of regime theory into the liberal tradition relates it more closely with the pluralist model, which emphasizes individual choice and diffuse electoral democracy. Though some have refuted this conception of regime theory (see in particular Feldman 1997), at a minimum it is true that its tendency to focus on the uniqueness of individual coalitions in particular places blinds us to the ways in which such coalitions are connected to broader restructuring processes. Stone's work provides a good (but by no means the only) example of this tendency (1989). In his study of coalition building in Atlanta, Stone presents a relatively liberal notion of local politics. He argues that a regime was formed whose core was a coalition between the sizeable black middle class and downtown business elites, particularly those associated with Coca-Cola. His emphasis on this coalition was an important contribution for understanding the group psychology of a power alliance in a city undergoing restructuring. Yet because of this emphasis on the power created by this coalition, Stone struggles to represent adequately the nonlocal sources of economic and political power that were driving the regime in question (see Lauria 1997b). "Consequently," as Lauria points out, "the abstraction of theoretical insights [in this case and others] becomes confined to behavioral microeconomic, and possibly pluralistic, explanations of the social production of cooperation and political coalition building" (ibid., p. 5). To this extent, then, Brown is not alone in his concern that regime theory devolves into a liberal pluralist and often highly local understanding of public-private cooperation.

But orthodox regime theory is not the only source of insight on public-private cooperation. Some scholars have taken a wider view of regimes and have thus been able to think more clearly about their connections to broader activity. Norman and Susan Fainstein's attempts to understand the state in urban development (1983, 1985) and more recently Lauria's project to weave regulation theory into regime theory (1997a) are two important examples of this approach. Lauria's project culminated in an edited collection of mostly neo-Marxian pieces that debated the relative merits of weaving the hitherto very local regime theory with the nation-state–scaled regulation theory. Regulation theory posits that forms of governance are created at the national level to ensure economic stability and peace between capital and labor. The idea with the marriage was to move beyond the relatively simplistic assumptions of individual choice that had characterized the urban regime literature. While raising important issues, however, Lauria was only partially successful at using regulation theory as a way to "structuralize" and "de-localize" regime theory (1997c). Though both literatures developed out of a similar set of conditions, their empirical foci are so radically different that such a rapprochement is very difficult to achieve. Perhaps the most important insight that emerged from this exercise was that certain important antecedents to the literature—particularly the work of Norman and Susan Fainstein—may provide a better model for how to do this than previously thought. The time has come, Lauria suggests (1997b, p. 5) to "revert back to a Fainsteinesque approach that focuses on the connections to external economic relations."

Though they did not themselves use the language of "regimes," Fainstein and Fainstein developed an important historical (and multiscalar) typology of postwar urban development coalitions that provides an early framework for how to understand local variability, and demonstrated how such alliances are constrained by the imperatives of the capitalist urban system in the United States (1983, 1985). They argued that federal urban policies were particularly important at shaping the local coalitions during the twentieth century, and that three observable periods of regime formation could be identified: (1) the Directive Period, 1950–64; (2) the Concessionary Period, 1965–74; and (3) the Conserving Period, 1975–84. By basing their typology on the experience of five very different cities,[3] they were able to develop the typology without falling into the trap of a "one size fits all" economic determinism. Their comparison highlights how local politics matter, because they use larger political and economic change as the starting point rather than as a tangential side-note buried in their conclusions. Their typology is a useful framework for understanding the activities of contemporary public-private alliances,[4] so it will be explained here.

Local coalitions formed during the Directive Period were typically intent upon sustaining postwar growth and restoring the vitality of downtown areas, which in many cities had fallen into physical disrepair. Federal urban policies encouraged slum clearance as a means to achieve these goals, and local participation was minimal, as vast areas of major urban cores were eviscerated in this political context. In New York City, for example, promi-

---

3. New Haven, Detroit, New Orleans, Denver, and San Francisco, and later New York City.
4. They were certainly not arguing—nor am I—that these phases descended upon cities at *exactly* the same time, with exactly the same consequences. The phases highlight, and are only meant to highlight, a generalized structural context for regime formation.

nent officials like Robert Moses and powerful institutions like the Port Authority of New York and New Jersey demolished neighborhoods mainly to make way for freeways and bridges (Warf 1988; Caro 1975). Over time, local protest, primarily emanating from minority neighborhoods—frequent targets of slum clearance—became effective at stopping such activity. Federal urban policy was forced to change in the 1960s along with local coalitions as the social costs of this form of slum clearance became clear.

The Concessionary Period emerged from the ashes of the Directive Period. It is largely defined by the mildly redistributive programs that developed under President Johnson's "Great Society" and "War on Poverty" initiatives. The 1964 Civil Rights Act and rising minority (particularly African-American) power in cities essentially forced the shift. During the Concessionary Period, coalitions at the local level focused on community development more than on community replacement, housing more than freeways. These coalitions were facilitated by a spate of regional programs and institutions established to revive inner city areas with new housing. For example, the New York State's Urban Development Corporation (UDC) was formed in 1968 to provide public and affordable housing for the urban minority poor in the state. It was given enormous power to override local zoning restrictions and opposition and to issue bonds in order to site such facilities. The UDC was, however, among the first regional government agencies to realize that without a parallel change in the federal redistribution of income, their goals were unprofitable. They were effectively bankrupt by 1975, forced to shift their focus to more profitable real estate activities. The experience of the UDC is emblematic of the larger historical regime typology that the Fainsteins developed.

Largely because of such financial hardship, regime formation, they argue, moved into a third phase in 1975: the Conserving Period. During the conserving period, cities were forced to respond to the harsh fiscal realities of the mid-1970s by focusing more attention on property tax generation than on social service provision. Agencies like the UDC shifted to highly profitable commercial redevelopments, while at the federal level New Deal and Great Society safety net reforms were slowly unraveled. "Entrepreneurial coalitions"—also known as public-private alliances—formed in this era as a response to economic restructuring (Fainstein and Fainstein 1985; Harvey 1989b; Leitner 1990). These alliances were varied in purpose and extent but generally involved the deployment of local statecraft in ways that differed from the Keynesian era. As Susan Fainstein would later remark, "Cities, like private corporations, are increasingly in the business of making deals. But the kinds of deals public officials can make are limited to what conforms to business strategies" (1995, p. 38).

According to Harvey, four development foci emerged among entrepreneurial coalitions after the 1970s (1989b). First, cities attempted to enhance their ability to compete within the increasingly global division of labor by defraying costs of technology and labor force training for capital. Universities and research centers became the predominant vehicles for pursuing this strategy. Second, cities attempted to enhance their position within the spatial division of consumption, particularly in areas of upscale retail and tourism. With manufacturing income on the ebb, many cities opted for consumption-oriented, tourist-friendly inner cities. Third, cities attempted to attain "command functions" within the global economy (Sassen 1991). That is, they attempted to lure corporations and interests with global reach to their municipality by offering tax breaks and other incentives—the idea being, of course, to "ground" some of the profits being experienced by global finance capital. Finally, as Harvey points out, there was some continuance of the erstwhile goal of competing for federal redistribution of one sort or another (1989b). Competition for defense industry contracts and military bases during the Reagan buildup of the 1980s was a particularly acute example of this strategy in action.

Urban Regimes in a Devolved Context

The structural conditions prodding local governments to behave in a more entrepreneurial way sharpened in 1994 with the Republican Contract with America—a highly devolutionary tract partially built on the ideas of classical liberalism (Staeheli et al. 1997; Eisinger 1998).[5] The ostensible goal of devolving federal power was to give states and localities more political autonomy (Staeheli et al. 1997), but most local governments were relatively powerless on their own at realizing the "autonomy" that sat before them. Capital was relatively well-situated to acquire the devolved power (Kodras 1997), but it could not work alone either, and it often depended upon the local state to defray some of its self-imposed costs. Zoning enforcement,

5. It is important to note that this document and the politics that led to it were motivated by concerns that included, but were not limited to neoliberalism. In particular, there is a strong social conservatism that pervades this document and the American Right in general. This social conservatism, though frequently allying with neoliberal politics, is nonetheless a different strand of political thought, with a different genealogy.

neighborhood policing, and utility costs are all typically beyond the capacity of individual fractions of capital to absorb, so the local state is often deployed to cover them. In essence, then, it is neither the local state nor capital which stood *ipso facto* to gain from federal devolution; rather, an organized relationship between the two entities would be necessary. Urban regimes thus became increasingly important institutional mechanisms for acquiring power released from the federal state.

As mentioned earlier, contemporary regime theory evolved from case studies that correctly assumed that the local state is embedded in a larger economic context (for example, see Stone 1989; Jones and Bachelor 1993) but devoted enormous attention to *extra-economic* concerns like race and culture to demonstrate why local coalitions matter (Fainstein 1995; Stoker 1995; Brown 1999). Because of this extra-economic bias, we still know little about how regimes behave as capitalist agents at the local level and, perhaps more important, about how they relate to the larger political economy (Jessop et al. 1999; MacLeod and Goodwin 1999). Such issues are assumed rather than explained in this literature (Lauria 1997b), so it is important to return to a more basic political economy literature for answers. We know, for example, that capitalism is wrought with internal contradictions that collide to form an unevenly developed socioeconomic landscape (Harvey 1985; N. Smith 1990; 1996). Uneven development is derived in particular from the tension between capital's need to equalize the conditions of production (to expand), on the one hand, and its conflicting need to differentiate those conditions (to exclude), on the other (Plotkin 1987; N. Smith 1990). As a dialectic, exclusion and expansion are at once in opposition to one another and at the same time necessitate each other's continued presence. "In capitalism," as Sidney Plotkin observes, "the logic is inescapable: expansion is the condition of exclusion just as exclusion is the condition of expansion" (1987, p. 10). We know, furthermore, that the state intervenes at several scales to manage the spatial effects of this contradiction. Land-use zoning, for example, is an explicit attempt by the state to protect real estate capital's need to differentiate economic space. As Eisinger has pointed out, the recent devolution in federal power has required local states to ally with capital (in the form of regimes) even more directly than before (1998). However, because the *raison d'être* of regime theory has thus far been to focus on extra-economic political behavior to understand uneven development, there has been little explicit attempt to understand regimes as capitalist agents within this dialectic. Though a more materialist understanding of urban regimes in the United States has been needed since the mid-1970s, it has become increasingly important since the mid-1990s, as the federal state has restructured.

Regime Formation in New Brunswick, New Jersey

The following case study describes the formation of an urban regime in New Brunswick, New Jersey, within the context of the capitalist expansion-exclusion dialectic to illustrate both the connections to wider-scale politico-economic restructuring and the capacity of public-private coalitions to become more or less autonomous participants in the market. A regime was formed in New Brunswick to redevelop the city's central business district (CBD) after years of disinvestment. One ancillary goal of the regime has been to demolish a nearby public housing complex as a way to protect local property values in the adjacent CBD. An exploration of this case highlights the way in which local regimes become locked into the maelstrom of expansion and exclusion and how, as a result, geographic scale gets produced and dissolved. This process is most easily understood by breaking the history of redevelopment in New Brunswick into three phases.

1975–1981

Like many cities in the northeastern United States, by the mid-1970s New Brunswick had found itself embroiled in a fiscal crisis. Its main employers were fleeing to areas where labor and land were cheaper and where regulations and taxes were more relaxed (Beauregard and Holcomb 1984; Holcomb 1997). The primary circuit of the larger regional economy was in crisis, so a revival of manufacturing seemed an improbable strategy for increasingly desperate city leaders to pursue. A strategy that could tap into the enormous transfer of capital into the built environment that was afoot (Harvey 1978) was more likely to be successful. Yet the regional profitability landscape was grossly uneven by the mid-1970s, so there were significant barriers to real estate investment in New Brunswick. The city had rent control, high taxes, and relatively expensive labor; on top of that, its volatile race politics had been chronicled in the infamous *Kerner Commission Report* several years earlier (1968). Investors were squeamish about planting their capital in New Brunswick during the mid-1970s because of barriers—both perceived and material—in the regionally differentiated profit landscape.

Just as things apparently could not get worse for city officials, the city's largest private sector employer, Johnson and Johnson, began serious deliberation on whether they should join the exodus from New Brunswick and move their headquarters closer to their manufacturing facilities in Texas. In a vote that was eventually decided by the chairman of the corporation, Johnson and Johnson decided to stay in New Brunswick, but only on the condition that the city devote itself more seriously to removing the aforementioned obstacles to real estate reinvestment in the downtown area. Some of the obstacle removal would necessarily involve the local state, while other goals were dependent on capital, so a public-private coalition was formed to facilitate the redevelopment. The coalition was named The New Brunswick Development Corporation (DevCo), and, along with a sister organization called New Brunswick Tomorrow (NBT), it was responsible for facilitating the redevelopment of downtown New Brunswick and devising more privatized methods of service provision. A regime was thus born to handle the increasingly complex task of governance in an economically devastated city. It is interesting to note that, although its primary focus was on a very specific geographic area—the central business district of New Brunswick—few leaders of the regime actually lived in New Brunswick, much less near the downtown. This membership structure remained intact largely because neither of the two key public-private organizations had democratically elected boards (Beauregard and Holcomb 1984).

With the institutional apparatus for redevelopment in place, Johnson and Johnson affirmed its commitment to the city by constructing corporate headquarters complex in 1978 costing $70 million (see figure 4.1). This investment served as an important material foundation to the more ethereal business-friendly atmosphere that was sought by the public-private coalition. The new headquarters building directly encouraged the construction of the Hyatt Regency Hotel and indirectly encouraged the Trenton-assisted beautification of George Street and the construction of Ferren Mall and the Plaza II Building. These initial projects improved investor confidence—an important condition for tapping into the wider property boom that would arrive in the 1980s.

1982–1989

During the second phase of New Brunswick's redevelopment, the real estate capital planted in phase one expanded southward within the CBD. As figure 4.1 depicts, real estate capital had become implanted in the northern portion of the CBD and was now migrating southward. The growth

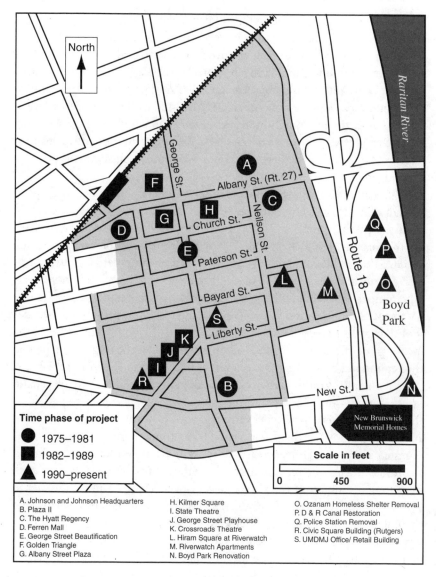

Time phase of project

● 1975–1981
■ 1982–1989
▲ 1990–present

A. Johnson and Johnson Headquarters
B. Plaza II
C. The Hyatt Regency
D. Ferren Mall
E. George Street Beautification
F. Golden Triangle
G. Albany Street Plaza

H. Kilmer Square
I. State Theatre
J. George Street Playhouse
K. Crossroads Theatre
L. Hiram Square at Riverwatch
M. Riverwatch Apartments
N. Boyd Park Renovation

O. Ozanam Homeless Shelter Removal
P. D & R Canal Restoration
Q. Police Station Removal
R. Civic Square Building (Rutgers)
S. UMDMJ Office/ Retail Building

Figure 4.1 Development in New Brunswick, NJ, 1975–present

occurred because of the regime's, and particularly DevCo's, continued efforts at removing barriers to reinvestment vis-à-vis surrounding cities. This continued to be the primary governance motive throughout the second period, and it was met with continued success as reinvestment poured into the area. Yet precisely because an expansion was occurring within its jurisdiction, the local regime became confronted with the need to exclude. That is, after the implantation of real estate capital and some growth during the late 1970s, it became necessary to differentiate the central business district as a means of facilitating growth within it—to exclude in order to expand.

The year 1982 marks the onset of the second phase for precisely this reason. In that year, the city's mayor, John Lynch—a key figure in the extant regime—publicly announced for the first time the city's intent to demolish the nearby New Brunswick Memorial Homes Complex (Rubin 1990; NBHA 1996). The complex sat at the fringe of the putative central business district and was seen as an obstacle to urban redevelopment in the area. The removal of the complex was therefore proposed, but because the Department of Housing and Urban Development (HUD) prohibited local demolition plans that could not guarantee one-to-one unit replacement, the local regime could not afford to follow through. Despite its growing power, the regime did not possess the resources necessary to overcome the regulatory constraints on its activities. For a demolition plan to take place, 246 housing units would have had to be built elsewhere in New Brunswick, so the mayor and his supporters eventually withdrew the proposal. With obstacles to removing the Memorial Homes seemingly insurmountable, regime participants concentrated on other more veiled forms of exclusion to protect and expand real estate capital in the central business district, such as the establishment of the City Market Special Improvement District in 1987. The district served to protect local real estate capital by assuring that the CBD was more attractive, better-served, and safer than the rest of the city. The emphasis on protecting CBD real estate investment at the expense of nearby residents generated a more public (and racialized) form of social conflict in the city. One local activist angrily summarized the tension that was developing between city residents and regime participants; while castigating Mayor John Lynch at a meeting during the 1980s, activist David Harris stated, "There is a substantial minority presence downtown. After each of your projects there is none at all. That disturbs me" (quoted in Todd 1989, p. A1). Exclusion as a means of expansion was plainly unacceptable to nearby residents, but because their electoral power was being progressively eroded by the material power of real estate capital in the regime, New

Brunswick residents became even more marginal in city politics than they had been at the beginning of the decade.

1990–Present

If exclusive measures that facilitated expansion characterized the second phase of New Brunswick's redevelopment, the capital expansion that produced exclusion is the identifying theme of the third phase. The dialectical sea change took place in 1990 with the formal announcement of an expansion beyond the current CBD. Lynch, still mayor of the city and key participant of the regime, proudly announced that the central business district was going to leapfrog Route 18 and expand into the waterfront park. The Riverwatch Luxury Housing Complex, built on several sites, was going to form the cornerstone of the expansion (Parisi and Holcomb 1995; Patterson 1997). Several months later, Lynch unveiled the requisite exclusionary piece of the expansionary puzzle: a formal funded plan to demolish the Memorial Homes Complex (Wallace 1990). The complex was adjacent to the only bridge linking the existing central business district to the waterfront and was seen as an obstacle to expansion. Lynch summarized the regime's exclusionary sentiment in his characteristically unvarnished way. "It is clear," he noted, "that from a marketing standpoint, you would not be able to market the waterfront with the presence of the Memorial Homes" (quoted in Rubin 1990, p. A1).

The demolition proposal included public and private money to rebuild and scatter the existing Memorial Homes units throughout the city (Fazzi 1990). The fact that local capital was even willing to help finance such an expensive plan is a telling gauge of how threatening the Memorial Homes were to the CBD expansion. Yet while construction on the Riverwatch portion of the plan began almost immediately after the 1990 announcement, the private financing for the demolition plan began to evaporate as the early 1990s recession took hold. The first phase of Riverwatch eventually opened in 1993, the nadir of the recession for regional housing markets, so support for this portion of the plan eventually began to evaporate too. For Riverwatch to expand, the recession would have to abate, and the local regime would once again have to find a way to underwrite the replacement of the units in the Memorial Homes, because HUD still required one-for-one unit replacement.

Several years after the completion of Riverwatch's first phase, the recession finally subsided. The southward progression of real estate investment within the central business district resumed, and the waterfront tracts were redeveloped for a possible expansion (see figure 4.1). Yet the expensive project of replacing the 246 units in the Memorial Homes still remained an onerous obstacle for the local regime. Just as it was beginning to appear that Riverwatch's expansion was going to necessitate the enormously expensive project of moving several hundred very poor families, the devolution of the federal state gave the local regime the requisite power to expand without the extant requirement. As part of HUD's "reinvention"—itself part of the larger federal devolution—the one-to-one unit requirement for local demolition plans was removed. Furthermore, the HOPE VI program had begun encouraging demolition nationwide by providing funding for such plans. With this regulatory hurdle absent and a possible funding source in place, the New Brunswick Housing Authority, in regular consultation with local regime leaders (Clarke 1997a), submitted a HOPE VI proposal to HUD in 1996. In line with the new, less stringent regulations, this plan only sought to replace 102 of the 246 existing units with newly built houses (NBHA 1996). HUD eventually rejected the proposal, so the New Brunswick Housing Authority submitted a similar plan the following year, which drew upon local capital for demolition costs (Clarke 1997b). HUD approved this iteration of the plan but offered only housing vouchers (no new units) as a means of replacement. Because the New Brunswick affordable housing market is saturated by Rutgers University students, this virtually guaranteed that most Memorial Homes residents would be forced to relocate elsewhere. In effect, the local regime had acquired the lever of exclusion to complement its power to expand and, in so doing, effectively eliminated a perceived threat to local real estate growth. The complex was demolished on August 18, 2001, and development has begun on the Boyd Park area of the city. As Mayor Cahill blithely pointed out in 2002, the gentrification of inner New Brunswick during the previous ten years had been nothing short of astonishing: "In 1991, if one were to have said that New Brunswick, over the course of the next ten or so years, would see the development of over 1,000 upscale and luxury housing units, the demolition of Memorial Homes, . . . and the realization of over 1.1 billion dollars of investment within our revitalization efforts, most would have thought that individual was dreaming" (Cahill 2002).

The Expansion-Exclusion Dialectic

The real estate capital that was expanding within New Brunswick's CBD during the 1980s began to expand beyond its boundaries during the 1990s.

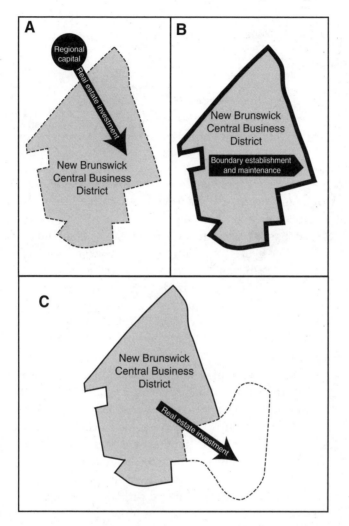

Figure 4.2 Three phrases of real estate development in downtown New Brunswick, 1975–present

The local regime aggressively facilitated this expansion by attempting to finance the removal of the nearby Memorial Homes complex. Yet only with federal devolution was the regime given the effective power to realize this particular goal. Expansion was deemed possible only through exclusion, yet the effective power to exclude prior to 1995 was still embedded in the federal state. After this power was devolved, the regime was empowered to manipulate more directly the expansion-exclusion dialectic in and around the central business district.

TABLE 4.1
Redevelopment phase by predominant spatial strategy

Redevelopment phase	Spatial goals of the regime		
	Primary	Secondary	Tertiary
1975–1981	Capital enticement		
1982–1989	Capital enticement	CBD exclusion	CBD expansion
1990-present	CBD expansion	CBD exclusion	Capital enticement

The New Brunswick case demonstrates capital's need to exclude in order to expand (and vice versa) and its ability to do so through the mechanism of an urban regime. The initial motivation of the regime was to dissolve the barriers to real estate investment that had built up over time—to entice capital (see figure 4.2). With the initial goal of constructing a scale of profitability successfully met, the regime's spatial strategy diversified and shifted (see table 4.1). A more localized—and thus more controllable—expansion-exclusion dialectic took hold as the regime and its participants acquired more power. The regime's survival became virtually dependent on facilitating the expansion of this scale—a goal that could be accomplished only through the exclusion of perceived threats in the landscape.

The regime's acquisition of power over time and its subsequent immersion into the contradictions of the urban land market were accelerated by events occurring at higher political scales, especially the devolution of the federal state in 1994–95. It is thus reasonable to conclude that the New Brunswick case is not anomalous and that urban regimes elsewhere are increasingly better understood according to the calculus of capitalism than according to the extra-economic behavior of their participants. If carefully done, this understanding can be achieved without returning to the economistic cul-de-sac of state theory's past, but it does involve a reversal of the classic emphasis in regime theory. Rather than assume that regimes operate in a murky economic context while describing their unique political attributes, it has become increasingly important to assume that such local details exist while devoting more attention to the regime's role as an agent of capitalism.

PART 2

THE ACCELERATION OF UNEVEN DEVELOPMENT

It may seem curious, and perhaps abrupt, to switch from a discussion of neoliberal urban governance to a consideration of real estate investment during the past thirty years. But as Fainstein among others has argued, real estate has become an increasingly common and quasi-autonomous vehicle for economic development in cities throughout the advanced capitalist world (2001). This has happened in the face of a globalized political economy that makes the basic manufacturing so prevalent during the mid–twentieth century all but impossible to sustain in wealthy core cities. American cities have turned to the development of producer services, "soft" industries, and—most relevant to this section—real estate as a way to improve the fortunes of local economies. Real estate has become quasi-autonomous because cities and capital have become increasingly reliant on it as a sector independent of the rest of the regional economy. Real estate investment of this sort is arguably the leading edge of neoliberal urbanization at the local scale.

But while the importance of real estate as a quasi-autonomous growth sector has increased in recent years, the general connection between real estate investment and the state is much older and worth consideration before delving into the empirics of recent changes in cities. Harvey's famous theorization of the "spatial fix" to the Great Depression provides the richest model of the mutual dependence of the state and real estate capital (1989a; 1985). In this model, Harvey suggests that the massive postwar suburbanization in the United States was part of an overall strategy to create and maintain a long-term cycle of growth. It was supported by allied commercial interests like the automobile and consumer durables industries and by the state in the form of massive subsidies for homeownership, freeways, and military bases that redistributed wealth across the country. This arrangement was "spatial" not least because it entailed a massive physical expansion of cities, and it was a "fix" because it revived real growth in the national economy. But as Lake (1995) more recently argued, the mid–twentieth century spatial fix that Harvey so elegantly describes likely had petered out by the early 1990s. True, cities were still growing outward after the early 1990s, but they were also displaying characteristics that were not common in the mid–twentieth century variant, such as massive investment in the urban core, greater volatility replacing generalized growth, and an overall acceleration of uneven development between and within cities. If the Keynesian managerialist city was characterized by outward growth, inner city decline, regulated development, and public investments in infrastructure, the neoliberal city is increasingly characterized by a curious combination of inner city and exurban private investment, disinvestment in the inner suburbs, the relaxation of land use controls, and the reduction of public investment that is not likely to lead to an immediate profit. If public housing and middle-class suburban housing were icons of the Keynesian managerialist city, then gentrified neighborhoods and downtown commercial mega-projects are the icons of the neoliberal city. City governments have facilitated this not only through the relaxation of erstwhile regulations like zoning but also with the selective deployment of statecraft to spur real estate development in certain sections of the city.

This section considers changes in production and management and in the spatiality of these changes. Chapter 5 examines changes to the ten largest metropolitan areas in the United States, while chapter 6 focuses on its largest individual city (New York). Chapter 7 considers changes at the neighborhood scale in New York City, while Chapter 8 looks at individual commercial real estate projects in Phoenix, Arizona. The overall intent of the section is fourfold. First, I argue (along with many others) that real estate investment and the local state are extremely intertwined and that, more recently, the former has become the primary economic vehicle of neoliberalism at the local scale. Second, I suggest that the spatial fix to the Great Depression has been replaced by an emerging spatial fix—whose characteristics are only now becoming clear—to the economic travails of the 1970s. Third, I argue that the emerging fix is characterized primarily by the acceleration of uneven development between and within cities. Finally, I argue that the emerging pattern of development in cities is the spatial corollary to wider social polarization so often discussed in the global political economy literature.

Chapter 5

The Neoliberal Spatial Fix

Cities have long been considered very physical expressions of social relations, movements, and ideologies (Fainstein 2001; Harvey 1985), so it stands to reason that physical changes can provide some insight into broader political change—neoliberalism being one example—that converge to produce and reproduce everyday urban life. Unfortunately, the connection between urban form and neoliberalism is ignored by most scholars of neoliberalism. For a consideration of this connection, we must turn to a more explicitly geographical scholarship. The work of Harvey (1989a; 1985) and N. Smith (1996; 1990) provides a particularly useful schema for understanding the connection between political restructuring and physical landscape change. Their narratives focus particular attention on the political fallout from economic turmoil in the United States during the 1970s, when the OPEC oil embargo sent the American economy into recession. This relatively isolated political event was paralleled by more secular forces—not least the growing productivity of German and Japanese automobile manufacturers—that adversely affected American dominance in that industry and introduced a phase of economic reorganization that hit the nation's large cities with particularly force (Harvey 1989a). The decline in productivity and rise in prices quickly diffused into many other parts of the nation's economy. Not since the Great Depression of the 1930s was economic stagnation so acute and widespread.[1] But the "spatial fix" to the

1. It is true that there were deeper short-term recessions in the United States between the Great

Great Depression of the 1930s—which involved an interrelated and government-supported mixture of massive suburbanization, growth in the automobile industry, and expansion within key consumer durables markets (washing machines, televisions)—was suddenly less effective at dealing with the complex problems of the 1970s (Walker 1977; Harvey 1982).

A very different spatial fix would have to form to meet the demands of and deal with the unique problems posed by the mid-1970s crisis (Warf 1999; Gilmore 1998; Lake 1995). Federal outlays to cities were slashed, and city governments became more entrepreneurial in their orientation (Harvey 1989a; Leitner 1990). Industrial decline accelerated as cities reoriented themselves around finance, insurance, and real estate (Fainstein 2001; Fitch 1993). Urban form was stretched, torn, and reshaped to accommodate the larger-scale economic restructuring as well. Many cities actively encouraged real estate investment close to their struggling central business districts in order to offset declining production by increasing consumption. Investment in commercial real estate (offices, shopping malls), and affluent central city housing increased (slowly in places, more rapidly in others) as cities offered unprecedented incentives for such activities to locate close to downtown (Fainstein 2001; Harvey 1989b). Unlike the spatial fix to the Great Depression, which was unambiguously centrifugal, the mid-1970s fix involved a complex mixture of centralization and decentralization in real estate investment. The effect of this paradox has only recently become discernable.

At least three major urban forms have emerged within this context. First, the process of inner city gentrification has received enormous attention as a process fundamental to contemporary urbanization (see, among others, N. Smith 1996; Ley 1996). Discursively marginalized as little more than "islands of renewal in seas of decay" as recently as the mid-1980s (Berry 1985; see also Bourne 1993a), gentrification became widespread in many cities after the early 1990s recession (Wyly and Hammel 1999). Hundreds of thousands of once-accessible inner housing units continue to remain off limits to the urban poor in places like New York, San Francisco, and Boston and, increasingly, in places like Cleveland, Miami, and Pittsburgh as well. Second, inner suburban devalorization has begun to emerge in a variety of locations, challenging the notion that its presence is entirely local (see Smith, Caris, and Wyly 2001; Soja 2000; Harvey 1996). Some of this is related to the aforementioned gentrification of the inner city, which has

---

Depression and the 1970s, but the mid-1970s saw an unprecedented combination of inflation and declining productivity (also known as "stagflation").

pushed a belt of disinvestment to the very different physical environment of the postwar suburbs, but much of it is also the simple result of generalized devalorization in the housing stock. This has created a very different contour to urban poverty, challenging existing modes of service delivery and community development designed to deal with a more concentrated form of poverty. A third process backgrounded by the emphasis on complexity is the continued physical expansion of metropolitan areas. Sudjic's prediction of the "100 mile city" is already a reality in several locations in the United States and elsewhere (1993). Thousands of hectares of land per day are being turned over to urban residential use for largely the same reasons, again challenging the notion that such processes are completely local in orientation.

Despite the relatively widespread emergence of these forms, however, much of the urban form literature still emphasizes an overwhelming complexity (Lewis 1983) or even "randomness" (Dear and Flusty 1998) of urban patterns or the notion that the urban periphery is the locale of most change, much as it was during the Keynesian managerialist period (Lang 2003; Dear and Flusty 1998). The latter has prompted some to go so far as to suggest that the erstwhile economic importance of the urban core has expired (Castells 1989; 1996). When viewed in a more comparative light over a longer period of time, however, both mainstream notions—chaotic urban form and periphery dominated conurbations—begin to break down. Changes in the ten largest United States conurbations between 1970 and 2000 clearly contradict these contemporary assumptions about urban form. They lose explanatory power once one looks beyond Los Angeles—the locus of most such studies. This can be seen in two ways. First, although suburban expansion continues apace, it is just one feature of the neoliberal city—two others being the revalorization of the inner core and the devalorization of the inner suburbs.[2] Second, the neoliberal spatial fix is not an atomized, individual site process (although local variation is important); rather, it is happening in a number of places and so must be thought of as something other than a purely local phenomenon.

2. The language of "valorization," "revalorization," and "devalorization" is used in this chapter to denote the broad process of investment and disinvestment in real estate. Neighborhoods "valorize," for example, when investment causes land prices to rise and "devalorize" when disinvestment leads to a decline. For a more comprehensive discussion of these processes, see Harvey (1982) and Smith (1990).

Landscape Change in Large Conurbations

To assess issues of landscape complexity across a diverse array of metropolitan areas, I consider the locational changes of valorizing and devalorizing zones in each conurbation, using rent, house value, and income data.[3] Overall, the shape of the rent gradients over time has remained remarkably constant when generalized at this level. Differences in the location of high and low rent belts seem to have "smoothed out" over time, with smaller differences between intervals in 2000 than in 1970. The partial exceptions were New York and Boston, which saw fairly dramatic rent level increases in the center of their metropolitan areas. This parallels moderate increases in the center of other metropolitan areas. By and large, however, the rent gradients portray a remarkable level of stasis: most metropolitan areas had very similar shapes in 1970 and 2000 when generalized at this scale. Relative differences in the standard deviation for rents between 1970 and 2000 for each zone were also recorded to identify changes in variance across the city surface. Changes in standard deviation were generally low but composed mostly of increases over time; variability is relatively ubiquitous. There were several exceptions, however, most notably (1) Los Angeles, which experienced major decreases in standard deviation in its inner core; and (2) Houston, which experienced major decreases in its outermost zone. Both cases imply that the overall increases in variability are relatively isolated and that, in particular, the Los Angeles inner zone and the Houston outer zone are becoming less heterogeneous than they were in 1970.

3. The first step of this process involves the creation of visual cross-sections for each metropolitan area. The cross-sections were created by averaging the individual census tract values within ten-kilometer zones emanating from the historical core of the CMSA. Rather than describe changes in each 10-km zone, this chapter focuses on changes in four locations: (1) the "inner city" (also referred to as the "inner core")—the main historic core to the CMSA; (2) the "inner suburbs"—suburban housing built between 1945 and 1970; (3) the "newer suburbs"— fringe housing built after 1970; and (4) the "outermost fringe"—a heterogeneous zone of primary industry communities and wealthy exurban recreational retreats. For example, average contract rent for the census tracts in each 10-km belt emanating from the CMSA center were recorded as a cross-section that could be visually analyzed. This process was repeated for house values and incomes for each census year in question (1970, 1980, 1990, 2000) to examine changes in high and low value zones over time. The figures used to derive a value for each zone were then evaluated for their level of standard deviation. This allowed for a consideration not only of those zones that possessed the greatest degree of internal variation, but also of which zones have become more (or less) variable over the past thirty years. Areas of increasing standard deviation imply zones of the city that are becoming more heterogeneous, while those with low values indicate a more statistically homogeneous zone. To preserve space, the cross section figures are not presented here but rather will be summarized. A more complete and specific depiction of this work can be found in Hackworth (2005).

A number of patterns also emerged from the house value gradients. First, there are very sharp increases in relative house values in the inner core for all but three cases (Philadelphia, Los Angeles, and Detroit). In most cases, the inner core was the location of the lowest relative house values in 1970 but among the highest by 2000. In those cases where the inner city is experiencing such growth (all but Philadelphia, Los Angeles, and Detroit), comparatively sharp decreases in relative house value have occurred in the inner suburbs. Though house values in the inner suburbs rarely decreased in actual terms between 1970 and 2000, their relative value (vis-à-vis the CMSA average) generally declined. The inner suburbs formed a noticeable and enduring "trough" on the gradients through 2000. Newer suburban areas, by contrast, began high in 1970 and remained high throughout the time period in question. Setting aside the aforementioned increases in the inner city and several anomalous increments, the newer suburbs were the location of the highest relative house values in each CMSA from 1970 to 2000. The outermost fringe areas, by contrast, did not fare as well. With the exception of Los Angeles, whose outermost areas include wealthy communities such as Palm Springs, the outer zone was the location of low relative house values for the metropolitan areas in this sample. This is at least partly the result of a very liberal definition of metropolitan area used by the U.S. Census. The areas in question are often rural, primarily industry-centered (or warehousing-centered) locales that have generally not prospered economically in the past thirty years—that is, they are not new suburbs.

On the whole then, change was minimal in most zones except for the inner core, which experienced large increases in certain cases. The inner core is, however, also the zone of greatest increases in house value standard deviation, suggesting that the aforementioned increases are not monolithic but rather segmented and uneven. Such increases were most pronounced in those places experiencing high rises in aggregate inner city house values, but they were also seen in Detroit and Philadelphia, suggesting that increased volatility is more a characteristic of inner city real estate markets than generalized increases. In most other zones of each urban area, standard deviation increases were minimal but generally positive, suggesting a higher aggregate degree of heterogeneity in the landscape.

Income was also converted into a transect to analyze in this way, and several interesting patterns emerged. For half of the sample (Boston, Detroit, Los Angeles, Philadelphia, Washington, D.C.–Baltimore), the 1970 gradients reveal a picture of relatively low incomes in the inner city that slope upward as one moves toward the newer suburbs, only to fall again on the fringes of the city. By 2000, this picture had changed somewhat; for all cases except Los Angeles and Detroit, the inner core experienced relative growth between 1970 and 2000. This pattern was particularly marked in Chicago, Dallas–Fort Worth, Houston, New York, and San Francisco–Oakland. The New York area also experienced notable increases in the inner sub-urbs, though this pattern was ambiguous in other cities. Notable exurban valorization occurred in New York, Los Angeles, and Philadelphia, though the latter two should be interpreted cautiously because they are largely the result of census agglomeration (adding Palm Springs and Atlantic City, re-spectively, during the past thirty years to their CMSA).[4] Notable outer fringe decline was evident in Boston and San Francisco–Oakland, but, again, these stood in contrast to slower changes elsewhere. In all but one case (outer fringe of Houston), landscape variability was low but on the rise, implying incipient change. The inner city was the location of the highest increases in volatility—where change was occurring most unevenly and rapidly. As with rent and house value, Detroit and Los Angeles stood out—in this case as metropolitan areas where income variability was not in-creasing in the inner city.

Overall, inner city landscapes have become the locations of relative greatest variability, but the salient point emerging from this analysis is that stasis, not volatility, is more common in city landscapes. Though there was no trend common to all metropolitan areas, there were important similar-ities and, most important, remarkable consistency (in shape and volatility) over time. This suggests that the form of these cities may be complex, but it is not random. Some cities have grown more polycentric, with the rise of edge cities, but no conurbation can be called "chaotic," even when gener-alized at this scale. It is also evident that cities were exceedingly complex in 1970, contradicting the suggestion that such changes are of recent or en-tirely local origin. Finally, it is apparent that the historic center of each met-ropolitan area continues to have a somewhat centripetal landscape function for population density, house values, and rents, though income patterns are more complicated. This gravitational pull is likely related to the larger switch of capital to real estate, tourism, and generalized recreation in the urban core.

This pattern challenges much contemporary urban theory situating the urban core as moribund or increasingly diluted by the outward expansion

4. Both of these outer cities are only very loosely connected to the metropolitan area's central urbanized area. They function, along with several other examples from other CMSAs, more as points of destination for a wider hinterland than as the home of workers commuting into the central city.

of conurbations in the United States. While it is impossible to deny the existence of such outward expansion, the evidence suggests that cities are no more diffuse than they were thirty years ago and, in certain cases, have actually become more centrally oriented in investment—and people. I base this assertion not only the aforementioned figures but also on the creation of eight hundred "scatterplots" (eighty per metropolitan area) measuring the relationship between rent, income, house value, and population density, on the one hand, and distance to the main urban core, on the other (see Hackworth 2005 for a fuller description of this analysis). This shows the degree of diversion from an ideal-type monocentric model during the past thirty years by using several types of statistical "best fit" lines to each resultant distance gradient scatterplot.[5] The r-square values for each line were then recorded into a matrix to assess change in statistical fit over time. This specifies exactly how monocentric the metropolitan areas were in 1970 and how de-centered and variable (or not) their landscapes have become since then. A value of 0 for a particular year would suggest complete statistical randomness (and thus no center, or centers, to the metropolitan area), while a value of 1 would imply that the type of line used explains all variability in the city. Multinodality tends to register high r-square scores when represented by polynomial lines.

Population density was the first variable plotted in this way. Population density, as a variable, yields far higher r-square values than any of the value-oriented variables discussed below. Eight of the ten urban areas registered r-square values of at least .5 during some point in the past thirty years—though with different types of lines—and all were statistically coherent enough by 2000 that at least one type of statistical line could explain 30 percent of the variation (over 50 percent, in many cases). A few temporal patterns also emerged from the basic analysis of population density gradients in the ten metropolitan areas. First, r-square values for population density in each metropolitan area have declined over the past thirty years, suggesting greater variability in the absolute location of high-density areas. Second, polynomial lines, especially higher-order ones, were generally better able to account for variations in 1990 and 2000 than were linear equations, suggesting an increase in polycentric urbanization, but not randomness.[6] The emergence of case groupings (according to the other variables) of at least three metropolitan areas occurred with each of the

5. Linear and exponential, as well as second-, fourth-, and sixth-order polynomial approaches were used here.
6. See Bunting, Filion, and Priston 2000a, b for similar findings in their study of population density gradients for Canadian cities.

variables examined, suggesting that while inter-city differences exist, there are important inter-city commonalities as well.

Rent variables were also used to examine centricity in the landscape. Several patterns emerged from this analysis. First, relatively high fourth- and sixth-order polynomial line fits (over .4 in Chicago, for example) exist as early as 1970. This suggests a form of incipient polycentricity early in the study period. Second, decreases (virtually without exception) in r-square values were unambiguous during the past thirty years. In most cities, the r-square value for every line was very small in 2000—the partial (and curious) exception being Washington D.C.–Baltimore, which yielded sixth-order polynomial values in 2000 (.292) that were nearly identical to those recorded for 1970 (.294, despite the aforementioned change to the size and contents of the CMSA in the 1990s). The geography of rent values in each of the ten CMSAs was complicated in 1970, growing only more complicated during the subsequent three decades.

When converted into distance gradients, the geography of house values appears to be very complicated. R-square values were generally low (below .3) for 2000 in almost every case, but they were high in comparison to rent and income from 1970 through 1990. Though linear and exponential equations explained the variance poorly, a noticeably better degree of fit occurred with polynomial lines in most cities, suggesting that polycentricity (rather than random variability) was driving the shape of cities in very different contexts. The highest value recorded was .566 for Chicago in 1970 using a sixth-order polynomial line, suggesting the presence of a fairly coherent (statistically) polycentric city very early. Though only two values exceeded .4, multiple cases, including Boston (1970–90), Chicago (1970–2000), Detroit (1970–2000), and New York (1970–90), saw values exceed .3 with most polynomial lines. Sharp decreases do, however, occur in most cities during the 1980s and 1990s, indicating a shift in the organization of house values that, among other things, lags a bit behind comparable drops in rents. In general, the distant gradient method yielded better statistical coherence for house values than for rents. However, as with the rent gradients, it is only possible to make statements about the actual shape of these urban areas by generalizing the findings to a more manageable scale.

When income is plotted in relation to the distance from the center of each metropolitan area, interesting parallels and diversions (with the other three variables) emerge. Of the four variables used in this chapter, income r-squares dropped the most emphatically between 1970 and 2000. By 2000, all results for income gradients were below .1 in each case except for Detroit; in most cases the values were below .05. Declines in r-square were most evident during the 1980s, partly because of census agglomeration but also, of course, because of increased variation. Detroit, curiously, is a stark anomaly to this trend, with comparatively high (over .225) and stable polynomial r-square values throughout the thirty-year period. It is also clear that linear regression was less effective at predicting the location of income than it was for rent or house values, but polynomial lines did fare better (>.25) for explaining early (1970 and 1980) variations in Boston, Chicago, Philadelphia, and Washington D.C.–Baltimore, suggesting some ordered polycentricity in these locations prior to 1990.

Temporal changes in the four variables suggest, among other things, that the neoliberal spatial fix is not a "galactic" or "random" expansion of cities, as Lewis or Dear and Flusty would have it, but rather a more organized affair. Though suburban downtowns have emerged as more important magnets in recent years, their growth has been paralleled by growth in urban cores. Furthermore, it is not at all clear (or probable) that the polycentric growth being witnessed now is entirely new. Several conurbations in this sample either have not become discernibly more periphery-focused or have become even more core-focused in the past thirty years.

Emergent Forms in Large Conurbations

When mapped, the conceptual features of the neoliberal spatial fix become even clearer (see figure 5.1). A variety of maps were made to identify the location of valorization and devalorization in urban landscapes. These maps were disaggregated by variable (rent, income, and house value), but because of space considerations, only the maps identifying aggregate changes are presented here (but all, including the disaggregated maps, are described below). Figure 5.1 identifies both areas experiencing relative increases in more than one of the aforementioned variables (rent, house value, income) and those experiencing a relative decreases in more than one of the variables. Mapping the landscape changes permits the identification of some important changes that are occurring *without* specific reference to the center of the city, a suburban center, or any center at all. They provide, in short, an extra dimension to the portrait of the neoliberal spatial fix.

When combined, a picture of pronounced inner city revalorization emerges in over half of the cities being studied: Boston, Chicago, Houston (though sectoral and primarily westward), New York, San Francisco–Oakland and Washington D.C.–Baltimore. These agglomerations of value-change vary in size and are certainly not monolithic, but they are significant

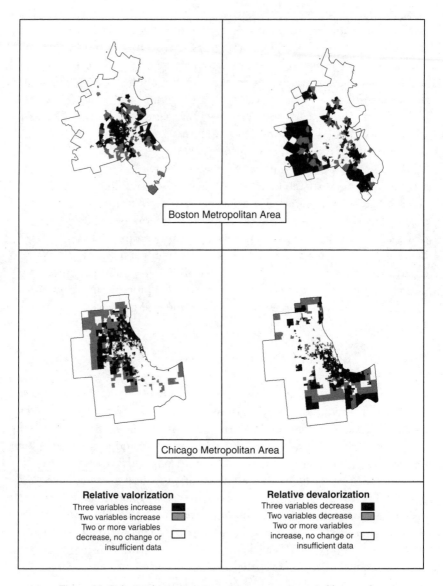

Figure 5.1: Relative changes in contract rent, owner-occupied house value,
and per capita income, 1970–2000

Source: U.S. Census

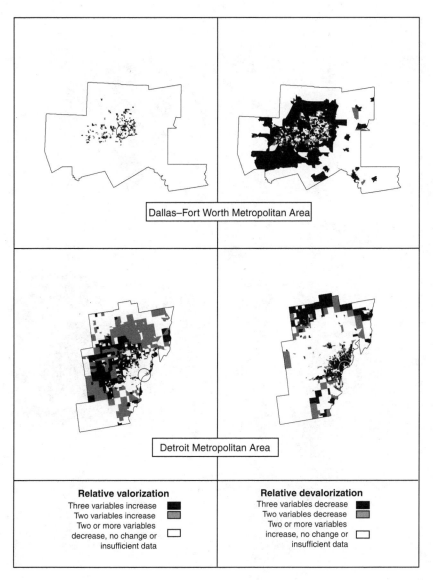

Figure 5.1 (continued)

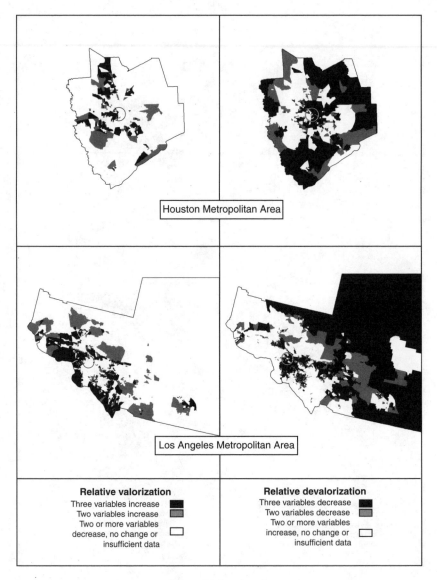

Figure 5.1 (continued)

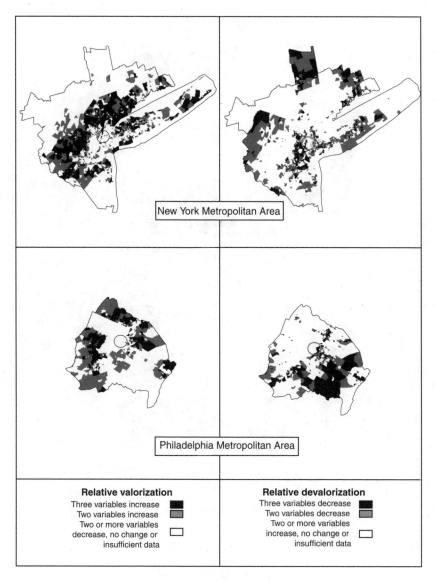

Figure 5.1 (continued)

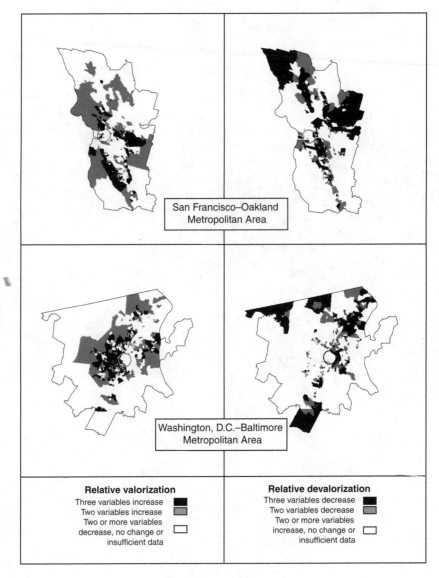

San Francisco–Oakland
Metropolitan Area

Washington, D.C.–Baltimore
Metropolitan Area

Relative valorization
Three variables increase
Two variables increase
Two or more variables
decrease, no change or
insufficient data

Relative devalorization
Three variables decrease
Two variables decrease
Two or more variables
increase, no change or
insufficient data

Figure 5.1 (continued)

enough to note. A prevailing tendency toward inner city devalorization between 1970 and 2000, by contrast, was experienced in Detroit, Los Angeles, and, to a more limited extent, Philadelphia. The inner suburbs experienced a notable devalorization in Chicago, New York, Detroit, and Los Angeles, while a more ambiguous pattern emerged in all other cases. Newer suburbs experienced an almost unqualified valorization (or, in some places, revalorization), except where decline occurred along sectors (Houston in particular) or where the physical geography of the city deeply influenced the location of valuable real estate (usually ocean and mountain views), such as San Francisco–Oakland and Los Angeles. One interesting deviation from this general picture is Chicago, where a large swath of disinvestment extends from the central city southward through the inner and newer suburbs on the south side. Landscape change in the outer fringe of Chicago was notable in its variability.

Further reinforcement of these patterns is revealed by disaggregating the data into separate variables (again, these maps are omitted here to conserve space). Mapping changes in rental prices between 1970 and 2000, for example, reveals some interesting internal patterns and inter-metropolitan groupings. In New York, San Francisco–Oakland, Boston, and, to a certain extent, Washington D.C.–Baltimore, Chicago, and Philadelphia, some variation of the following pattern emerged: (1) inner city revalorization, (2) inner suburb devalorization, (3) newer suburb valorization, and (4) outer zone devalorization. In Los Angeles, Detroit, and Houston, by contrast, the inner city and inner suburbs have disinvested rapidly, while the newer suburbs are experiencing major rent increases that contrast with outer zone decreases. The main difference seems to be stark inner zone rental increases in one category with a the lack of such rent increases in the other. Dallas–Fort Worth defies categorization in either. Generally, the inner zone of Dallas–Fort Worth experienced relative revalorization and the outermost zones devalorization, but the landscape is far too fragmented to make this assertion with confidence. It could be, as Waddell and others have suggested, that the Dallas–Fort Worth area is one of the most truly dispersed metropolises in the United States; it may be not polycentric but rather truly fragmented (Waddell 1994; Hoch and Waddell 1993; Waddell and Shakla 1993. In any case, it stands as an anomaly to the two categories of urban areas that have emerged thus far.

House value changes revealed a similar pattern to that unearthed via rents. Similar, though not identical, groupings of cities emerge from this exercise. The largest group includes New York, San Francisco–Oakland, Boston, and, to a certain extent, Washington D.C.–Baltimore, Chicago, and Philadelphia, and is characterized by: (1) reinvestment in the inner city, (2) disinvestment in the inner suburbs, (3) investment in the new suburbs, and (4) disinvestment in the outer zone. In Los Angeles, Detroit, and Houston, by contrast, the inner city and inner suburbs have experienced decline, with new suburbs thriving and the outermost zones not. Again, Dallas–Fort Worth defies strict categorization with an almost kaleidoscopic pattern of house values.

Generally, the inner zone experienced relative increases and the outermost zones decreases, but most of the landscape is extremely segmented. Though most pronounced in this area, each metropolis was home to important pockets of house value inflation among otherwise declining areas (and vice versa), but relatively coherent visual patterns did emerge. Also important (especially in Houston), some of this growth is occurring along corridors somewhat reminiscent of the sectors that Hoyt (1939) identified over sixty-five years ago. Compared to rent, house value change in the newer suburbs exhibited higher and more consistent increases during the thirty-year period in question. Also, compared to rent, inner city house values tended to be more segmented and varied, as were inner suburban areas (especially in New York), implying that these areas are home to the greatest degree of current housing market volatility.

Mapping income changes revealed findings similar to those found for rent and house value—somewhat surprising, given the lack of apparent pattern in the r-square values described earlier. As with the other two landscape variables, the inner city experienced relative income increase in all cases except Detroit, Los Angeles, and to a partial extent Philadelphia. Patterns in the inner suburbs are ambiguous in Boston, Dallas–Fort Worth, Houston, San Francisco–Oakland, and Washington D.C.–Baltimore, while there are notable decreases in this zone for other cities. Newer suburbs have experienced generalized increases, though there are important deviations from this trend in all cities. The outer fringe of each city reveals a mosaic of increases and decreases (but more of the latter), a pattern especially marked in Boston, Houston, Los Angeles, Philadelphia (on the New Jersey side), San Francisco–Oakland, and Washington D.C.–Baltimore. The maps also reveal several localized patterns worthy of note: (1) there is a notable corridor of general decrease in the Washington D.C.–Baltimore area adjacent to Interstate 95; (2) Houston's pattern of income growth and decline is highly sectoral; and (3) the Dallas–Fort Worth income landscape is highly varied, almost to the point of defying categorization.

Overall, the last three decades have seen continued valorization in outer fringe places like Palm Springs on the eastern edge of the Los Angeles CMSA, but it has also seen the continued decline of outer fringe communities with economies organized around a waning portion of the primary sector or warehousing, such as Pike County, Pennsylvania (on the western edge of the New York CMSA). Though each city has areas that are more varied than others, clear patterns are emerging. Among these patterns is the generalized revalorization of the inner city in several metropolitan areas. Though Los Angeles and Detroit run patently counter to this trend, it is evident that processes of inner city revalorization are occurring, at least in part, above the neighborhood scale. Furthermore, most cities displayed some inner suburban devalorization combined with continued outer suburban growth. Though certainly not identical, the presence of these processes in such disparate landscapes hints at the possibility of a systemic, uneven development that operates at a more general level than any individual locality.

These specific findings support some general observations. First, the metropolitan areas in this sample do exhibit a more polycentric and generally more complicated landscape mosaic than that viewed through the lens of received urban theory. However, there are extremely important caveats to this statement, not least that all of the cases were already very complicated in the early 1970s and that any new complexity "discovered" as having emerged recently is misleading and overstated. Second, intra- and inter-city differences certainly exist; it would be naïve to engage in a project of this sort without expecting them. Just as important, however, are the more or less coherent categories into which most cities fall. Finally, the replication of shapes and patterns in different cities suggests the presence of important emergent forms that can best be understood through comparative rather than idiographic research.

The Neoliberal Spatial Fix

The geography of political restructuring following the Great Depression resulted in what Harvey deemed "the spatial fix" (1982). The spatial fix to the Great Depression was a uniformly centrifugal one, consisting largely of massive suburbanization and economic growth on the peripheries of cities. Industries related to this growth prospered, while economic decline spread in many inner city locations. Government policy supported this "fix," but it was much more than a simple policy event. The spatial fix was an intersection of capital, policy, and individual preference on the urban landscape. By the 1970s, this machine of growth began to expire or at least transform. Much like the Keynesian managerialist period, cities have continued their outward growth, but unlike the earlier period, the pattern is being joined by considerable inner city reinvestment and inner suburban disinvestment. But these parallel processes were relatively minor in extent until recently, so geographers and social scientists rarely connected them to wider economic change. No one dared speak of a "spatial fix" to mid-1970s economic travails, largely because processes like gentrification and inner city real estate development seemed both minor and unconnected to wider economic restructuring. By the 1990s, however, it started to become clear that these processes were not only important but were also connected to a wider reorganization that was occurring in a variety of industries. In particular, the inner city became restructured by niche real estate, service sector employment, tourism, and other replacements for waning heavy manufacturing. Capital had "switched" into finance, insurance, and real estate, and the urban fabric was morphing to accommodate these changes.

This chapter was an initial attempt to map the geography of this switch across a variety of cities. At least three findings emerge from this analysis. First, cities do not grow in the same way, nor were they connected in the same way to mid–twentieth century forms of economic growth, but it is an extra and unjustified step, I argue, to suggest that the urban landscape is now random or chaotic, as some have recently done. Such a conclusion both underestimates the level of landscape variability that existed in the "more coherent" Keynesian managerialist city and downplays the similarity in patterns occurring in contemporary ones. Recent proclamations of unambiguous urban centrifuge also appear to be overstated or at least incomplete. This analysis reveals obvious growth on the periphery of cities in the past thirty years but much less change in population and real estate investment in the inner core than much of the literature on contemporary suburbanization implies. The areas of greatest decline and volatility are generally not the inner city, but rather the inner suburbs.

Finally, at a less abstract scale, three emergent forms appear to dominate the neoliberal spatial fix. Suburbanization continues at a rapid pace, but it is not a simple extension of the Keynesian managerialist patterns. Current outward growth appears to be deeply connected to broader social polarization. The places of most active suburban growth are often places where second homes and leisure activities dominate. By contrast, the suburban housing of the Keynesian managerialist period (inner suburbs) is largely falling victim to disinvestment, as the wealthy flee for either the gentrified neighborhoods of the inner city or the gated ones of the exurbs. The inner core, moreover, appears to be revalorizing in a variety of cities, casting some doubt on the description of gentrification as an isolated neighborhood process. However, in order to make a tighter connection between urban form and the neoliberal turn, it is important to complement this portrait with a consideration of smaller-scale processes—gentrification and inner city redevelopment in particular. The following three chapters attempt to connect the neoliberal turn and urban form changes through exactly this method. Chapter 6 examines inner core change in one city, while chapter 7 examines it in three neighborhoods. Finally, chapter 8 examines it by looking at individual redevelopment projects.

Chapter 6

The Reinvested Urban Core

Perhaps the most striking feature of the investment maps presented in chapter 5 is the dramatic restructuring of the inner city—even in places that are completely dominated by their suburbs. Beneath the abstraction of these maps is a process often referred to as "gentrification," as it involves the restructuring of urban space for a wealthier clientele. On the most basic material level, this involves the revaluation of inner city space—the replacement or displacement of the poor by the more affluent. On a symbolic level it represents much more. Gentrification can be seen as the material and symbolic knife-edge of neoliberal urbanism representing the erosion of the physical and symbolic embodiment of neoliberal urbanism's putative other—the Keynesian activist state. In other words, gentrification is much more than a politically neutral expression of the real estate market; it involves the replacement of physical expressions of Keynesian egalitarianism like public housing with a privately led segmentation of inner city space. This chapter attempts to examine the physical and institutional progression of the process in one city, New York, to shed light on its current significance to the broader project of neoliberal urbanism.

Theorizing Gentrification's Significance

For a variety of reasons, gentrification has been one of the most common and hotly contested concepts within urban studies during the past thirty years. Researchers have debated its causes, its normative value, its spatial significance, and its linkages to wider restructuring, among other attributes (see N. Smith 1996; Ley 1996; Caulfield 1994). One intriguing aspect of this literature is that much of it was written during the 1970s and 1980s, when gentrification, according to Berry, represented little more than "islands of renewal in seas of decay" (1985). More recently, the literature has ebbed in size and importance (Bondi 1999) at the same time that gentrification, paradoxically, has transformed from an idiosyncratic anomaly in select housing markets to an apparently systemic process integral to the near future of advanced capitalist urbanization. No longer confined to large global cities like London, New York, San Francisco, and Toronto, it is now beginning to pop up in places like Columbus, Ohio, Tampa, Florida, and Austin, Texas. Furthermore, what was once a highly neighborhood-based process is now spreading in such a way as to create a largely "reinvested core" in many cities. Wyly and Hammel (1999) have even suggested that Berry's famous maxim should be reversed, as the inner core of many large cities is now dominated by tony neighborhoods, commercial mega-projects, luxury condominiums, and expensive boutique retail shops.

The 1990s were an extremely important time for this transition. Not only did it mark the physical continuation of pocketed reinvestment that began in the 1970s and 1980s, but more importantly it settled a debate about the wider significance of gentrification in general. This debate emerged from the recessional conditions of the late 1980s and early 1990s. The recession was infamous both for its effects on real estate and for its relationship to financial markets. By the time that the New York Stock Exchange crashed in October 1987, the real estate industry was so intertwined with financial markets throughout the world (Ball 1994; Coakley 1994; Logan 1993; Pugh 1991a, b) that the property sector soon plummeted in most of the world's major cities. By the early 1990s, the flood of inner city real estate investment characteristic of the 1980s had reduced to a trickle. Unlike earlier recessions, in which gentrification had displayed a mild pattern of countercyclicity (Ley 1992), it began to show signs of slowing as well. For some, such as Bourne (1993a, b), the early 1990s property glut mirrored nothing less than the curtailment of the conditions that produce gentrification. The recession in property markets coincided, he argued, with a saturation in the supply of easily gentrifiable housing units and a reduction in the number of its potential consumers—young baby boomers, who would hereafter choose to retire in the suburbs. "Gentrification," Bourne concluded, "will be of decreasing importance as we move beyond the recession of the early 1990s" (1993b, p. 183). Other commentators (Lueck

1991; Bagli 1991) joined Bourne in dismissing gentrification as just another example of 1980s excess; the "post-gentrification era" was afoot. In one oft-quoted article, Lueck quipped, "Gentrification may be remembered, along with junk bonds, stretch limousines and television evangelism, as just another grand excess of the 1980s" (1994, p. 1).

Despite the conviction and, in the case of Bourne, thoroughness of their analyses, however, the post-gentrification school was not without its critics. Ley, for example, argued that the early 1990s slowdown was actually a precursor to *accelerated* gentrification—baby boomers, he argued, will choose the inner city as a place of retirement (1996). Also skeptical of the post-gentrification thesis, Badcock found that certain forms of inner city investment had actually *resurged* in Australian cities during the recession because local government had effectively smoothed the switch of glutted commercial real estate capital into residential markets in 1991 (1993, 1995). More recently, Smith and Defilippis took issue with the post-gentrification idea by arguing that the recession was only a temporary interlude to an accelerated post-recession reinvestment of real estate capital in New York (1999).[1]

The subsequent experience of real estate investment in New York and elsewhere during the 1990s (particularly the late 1990s) has generally vindicated this latter viewpoint. Signs of reinvestment abounded—commercial, residential, and institutional—as disinvestment got pushed to the inner suburbs. The novelty of gentrification wore off once it resurged again in U.S. cities after the recession. Signs of disinvestment were increasingly anomalous as the tide of reinvestment saturated inner city real estate markets. It is perhaps for this reason that gentrification lost its panache as a cutting-edge theoretical concept. It was no longer the exception in need of explanation. Increasingly it served as a systemic part of neoliberal urbanization in American cities.

The following chapters explore this process at three different scales. This chapter explores the wider process of inner city reinvestment at the scale of one city (New York) to set the context for an examination of gentrification at the neighborhood (chapter 7) and project-based (chapter 8)

---

1. *Reinvestment* is defined in this chapter as the return of investment to a building or neighborhood whose productive potential has been removed or undermined by disinvestment. *Disinvestment* is the secular process wherein a building or entire neighborhood's capacity to generate its highest potential rent is slowly removed by a decline or cessation of maintenance or other forms of investment designed to counteract the physical deterioration of the structure or structures.

level. The first section of this chapter reviews the pre-recession history of inner core reinvestment in New York City in order to contextualize the second portion of the chapter, which explores whether the early 1990s recession was a meaningful interruption in the broader, apparently secular pattern of investment capital returning to inner core housing markets. The third section maps and explains changes in the core of reinvestment since the recession. The overall intent is to describe the transformation of gentrification from a "localized" anomaly to a process that is increasingly systemic to the future of neoliberal urbanization.

The Pre-Recession Valorization of New York's Urban Core

Though some neighborhoods in New York's inner city, like the Upper East Side of Manhattan, never experienced a notable bout of disinvestment, much of the city did during the middle part of the twentieth century (figure 6.1). The famously deep bouts of disinvestment in northern Manhattan, central Brooklyn, and the south Bronx were paralleled by smaller but still significant bouts in southern Manhattan's sundry neighborhoods. The islands of wealth in the inner city were isolated anomalies within the seas of high-rent residential areas to the city's north and east (see Hoyt 1966). Wealth had been almost completely exiled to the suburbs, while the inner city was left to disinvest. Now just as noted as the midcentury disinvestment, the subsequent return of real estate investment to Manhattan below 96th Street (and even above it—see Schaeffer and Smith 1986) has transformed the borough into one of the most exclusive districts in the world. Early gentrification during the 1950s in Greenwich Village was followed by loft conversions in SoHo (Zukin 1982) and the more recent gentrification of the Lower East Side (N. Smith 1996; Abu-Lughod 1994), to name but several examples. The collective effect is now an old story: a major reinvestment of the city center and the creation of a reinvested core (RC) for New York, namely Manhattan below 96th Street and northwestern Brooklyn. Susan and Norman Fainstein describe the qualitative result of these changes in southern Manhattan, the heart of the RC:

> By the 1980s, the social and functional heterogeneity of southern Manhattan was noticeably reduced. . . . An uncounted number of factories had disappeared or had been converted to other uses, and large expanses of proletarian tenements had been replaced by expensive apartment towers. Chic restaurants occupied abandoned factory

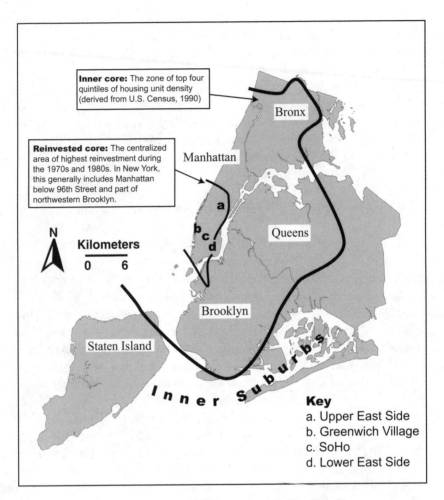

Figure 6.1: Inner core and reinvested core in New York City

showrooms. The fabric of the central business district had changed: many strands of its previous industrial woof had been exchanged for the golden threads of late capitalism. (1989, p. 59)

The acceleration and spatial focus of reinvestment during the 1980s can be measured through various means. Residential building alterations, for example, were highly clustered in the reinvested core during the 1980s, while demolitions were clustered in the extant zones of deep disinvestment—the south Bronx, northern Manhattan, and northeastern Brooklyn (figure 6.2).

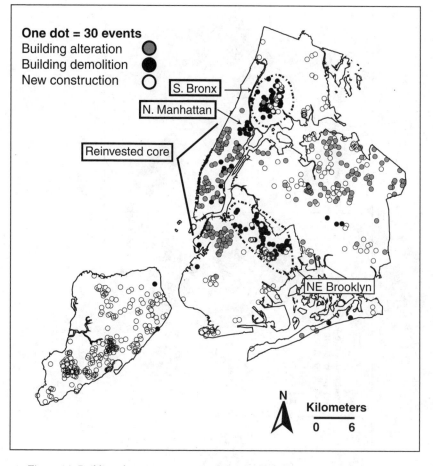

Figure 6.2: Building alterations, new construction, and demolitions in New York City, 1983–1989

Source: NYC Department of Buildings

New construction activity was relegated mostly to the suburban fringe of the city—predominately Staten Island and eastern Queens. The pattern of real estate investment (through building alteration in the inner city and new construction on the fringe of the city) corresponded closely to the areas of the city experiencing higher-than-average rent and income upgrades during the decade (figure 6.3). The highest absolute gains in rent and income were clustered in the RC, with the notable exceptions of the suburban fringe and the Lower East Side, Chelsea, and Hell's Kitchen in Manhattan.

Figure 6.3: Rent and income change in New York City census tracts during the 1980s

Source: U.S. Census

104

The most intense clusters of lower-than-average rent and income change during the decade were isolated in the aforementioned zones of disinvestment in the city.

These maps, however cursory, reveal a reinvestment of inner core housing markets in New York that had congealed by the 1980s to create an identifiable reinvested core. What these maps do not show, of course, are the neighborhood-level processes like gentrification, incumbent upgrading, and commercial redevelopment, not to mention the attendant social problems such as the displacement of the working class from the increasingly affluent central city. Such local processes are an important but different concern that is taken up elsewhere (Smith and Defilippis 1999; Wyly and Hammel 1999). The intent of this chapter is to identify a coherent scale of inner city reinvestment and evaluate its reaction to the recession and its subsequent (current) real estate boom.

Housing Market Investment in Recession and Boom

After nearly a decade of growth during the 1980s, the American economy (and most others closely linked to it) went into a sharp recession in 1990. Though relatively short in duration, the national recession of 1990–91 swiftly translated into heightened unemployment. Much of the multi-sector job growth of the 1980s was dissolved in the span of one year. Recession losses in the United States were paralleled by declines in other industrialized portions of the world, particularly Japan. The decline of property markets only served to exacerbate the downturn further. Yet while the impact of the early 1990s recession was fairly widespread for at least one year, it is also true that certain regions within the United States (and elsewhere) were hit more severely and affected for a longer duration than national figures would suggest. The New York Metropolitan Region and the larger northeastern United States was one such area. The recession there was both longer and more severe than in other areas of the country. As Yaro and Hiss explain in the most recent New York Regional Plan,

> From 1989 to 1992, the [New York Metropolitan] region lost 770,000 jobs—*the largest job loss of any U.S. metropolitan region since World War II*—eliminating virtually all of the region's growth during the 1980s. While national employment grew by 5% from the end of the 1990 to 1991 recession through 1994, jobs in the region grew by only 1%

since the bottom of the recession in 1992. (1996, p. 7; emphasis in original)

Much of the job loss was experienced in the tertiary and quaternary sectors of the economy, which had become hallmarks of the neoliberal spatial fix. Yet while we know that the early 1990s recession was severe in the region and that it hit certain labor markets particularly hard, there is much less certainty about its long-term impact on the reinvested core. Addressing this relationship involves an analysis of both reinvestment and active disinvestment, as they are but different sides of the same larger process.

Disinvestment Citywide

At the urban scale, the recession appears to have had little impact on overt forms of disinvestment. Measures of vacancy and demolition are broad indicators of disinvestment insofar as they indicate a removal of productivity from the built environment (see Beauregard 1993). Tax arrears data, on the other hand, is used in housing studies (e.g. Smith, Duncan, and Reid 1989; Lake 1979) to measure a less obvious form of disinvestment: tax delinquency. Through basic mapping techniques with this data, it is possible to document the impact of economic recession on different parts of the city. The intent of this section is to examine the impact of recession on disinvestment citywide.

Vacancy data provide a starting point for this analysis. The number of vacant residential buildings had been on the ebb since 1981, after several years of increase in the late 1970s (figure 6.4). Though there was a slight increase in the number of vacant buildings in 1988, the gradual decline of the 1980s continued, virtually unchecked, through New York's 1989–92 recession; the number of vacant buildings dropped by 751 between 1989 and 1992. The decline of vacancy continued after the recession with a slight reversal after 1995. Overall, though, it appears that the tendency of declining vacancies was unaffected by either the recession or subsequent economic boom.

Building demolitions were slightly more sensitive to the larger recession, but overall the broader pattern toward reduced disinvestment was uninterrupted (figure 6.5a). After seven years of decline in building demolitions per annum, the number bottomed out in 1990, only to increase by 313 the following year. Apparently, the recession encouraged a brief increase in this form of disinvestment. After 1991, however, the secular trend toward a decline in building demolitions continued. Between 1991 and

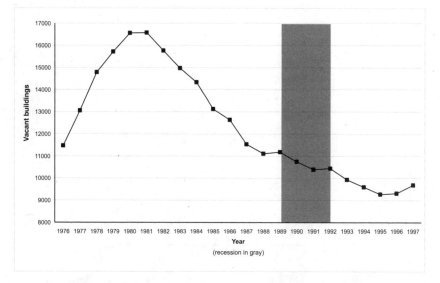

Figure 6.4: Vacant residential buildings in New York City, 1976–1997

Source: Sanborn Building Survey

1997, the number of demolitions per year dropped by 445. The recession facilitated a short-term acceleration in demolitions, but the subsequent economic boom appears to have encouraged a resumption of the decline that began during the 1980s. Though much of the city (including the reinvested core) experienced little or no change in the number of demolitions per annum during the recession, northeastern Brooklyn, northern Manhattan, and portions of the south Bronx did experience notable increases in this type of disinvestment (figure 6.5b). By contrast, much of central Queens experienced a decrease in the number of demolitions during the recession, suggesting that disinvestment there was slowing. Massive immigration throughout the 1990s has kept demand for housing there strong. Southwestern Brooklyn and the entire borough of Staten Island experienced a mixture of increasing and decreasing disinvestment during the recession, implying a destabilized housing market. After the recession, northeastern Brooklyn, northern Manhattan, and the south Bronx experienced a partial reversal of the earlier increase in demolitions—unlike most of the city, which maintained a stable level of demolitions (usually zero per census tract) after the recession (figure 6.5c). Staten Island and southwestern Brooklyn again display features of housing market flux with a polyglot

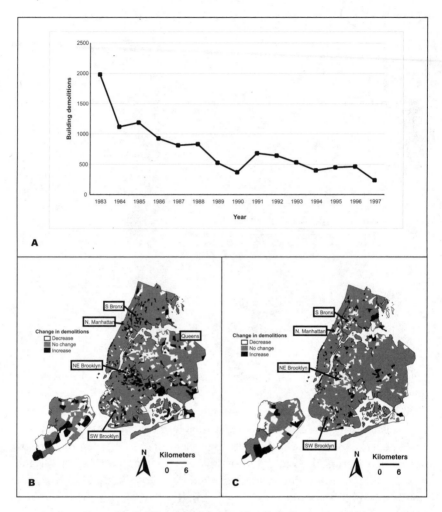

Figure 6.5: Building demolitions in New York City, 1983–1997

Source: NYC Dept. of Buildings, Sanborn Building Survey

Note: (a) Number of demolitions per annum, 1983–1997; (b) Change in number
of demolitions per tract between 1989 and 1992; (c) Change in number of demolitions
per tract between 1993 and 1997

mixture of divergent tracts. The most conspicuous forms of disinvestment (vacancies and demolitions) appear, in sum, to have been only mildly affected by the 1989–92 recession.

Subtle forms of disinvestment like tax delinquency, on the other hand, were more directly affected by the larger economic downturn. Figure 6.6a reveals that the number of buildings in arrears with the city increased by 10,863 during the recession and continued to climb rapidly until 1996, before falling thereafter. Most of the increase during the recession was contained within the mild (three to four quarters in arrears) and moderate (five to twelve quarters in arrears) categories, but the aggregate increase is remarkable since it translated into 7.5 percent of all tax lots in arrears citywide by 1996. Though all categories of arrearage continued to increase after the recession, moderate arrearage was the first to drop, in 1994. Severe arrearage (over twelve quarters), by contrast, began to rise in 1989, and did not fall until 1996. As figure 6.6b shows, the pattern of increased tax delinquency during the recession was nearly ubiquitous across the surface of the city. Closer analysis reveals that inner core tax delinquency tended to be more severe (five or more quarters), while increases along the suburban fringe were typically limited to mild arrearage (three to four quarters). The recession inspired a deeper glut closer to the core relative to the suburbs. Yet after the recession (figure 6.6c), inner core disinvestment was reversed, while disinvestment in suburban areas of the Bronx, Queens, and Brooklyn actually deepened. Though much of Staten Island also experienced an increase in arrearage after the recession, the wide swath of decreases along its western edge confuse the pattern enough to imply a housing market in flux. Nearly all of Manhattan, northwestern Brooklyn, western Queens, and parts of the south Bronx experienced a decline in tax delinquency after the recession, while aggregate increases were the prevailing pattern for the balance of the city. Above all, disinvestment had largely subsided in the inner core by 1997, but much of the low-density suburban fringe of the city was still in decline.

Reinvestment

If the impact on aggregate disinvestment was ambiguous, the effects of recession on measures of reinvestment were unmistakably sharp. Examining the effect of recession on reinvestment—expenditures made to improve the productive capacity of real estate—can be done through a variety of means. Here, new construction, housing alteration, and sales exchange data are

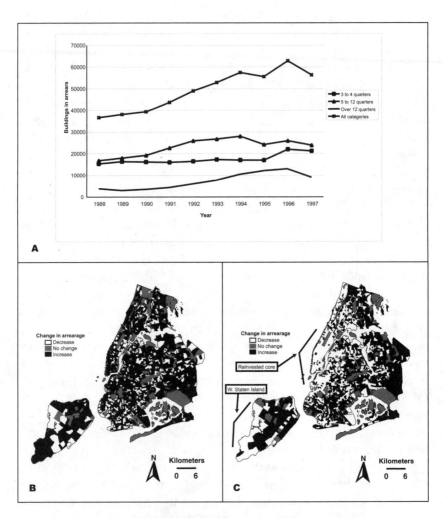

Figure 6.6: Tax-delinquent buildings per annum in New York City, 1989–1997

Source: NYC Dept. of Finance

Note: (a) Buildings in arrears by level of severity, 1989–1997; (b) Change in number of tax-delinquent buildings per tract between 1989 and 1992; (c) Change in number of tax-delinquent buildings per tract between 1993 and 1997.

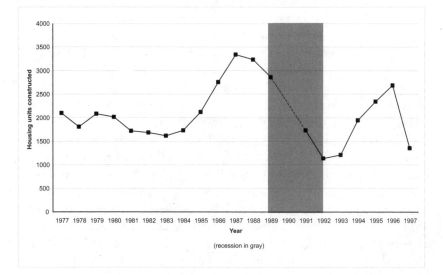

Figure 6.7: New construction in New York City, 1977–1997

Source: NYC Dept. of Buildings, Sanborn Building Survey

mapped to examine aggregate reinvestment.[2] Each of these measures has been used before to examine housing market investment.

The application of this data to New York reveals that the economic downturn retarded positive housing market investment several years before the rest of the economy sank. New construction data—a basic measure of housing market investment—provide the first indication of this pattern (figure 6.7). After rising markedly between 1983 and 1987, the level of new residential construction plummeted thereafter. Between 1987 and 1992, there was a 2203-unit drop in the level of new construction, with most of this occurring during the 1989–92 recession. After 1992, new construction began to increase again but fell sharply after 1996. Though interesting in sectoral terms (overall housing investment), it is likely that the drop was more the result of saturated opportunities for new construction on the suburban fringe (where most of this activity takes place) than any cooling of the post-recession real estate boom in the inner core.

2. Sales exchange is a measure designed to convey the sense of capital flows into and out of various housing markets. It is derived by multiplying the sales volume (for example, the number of sales per community district) by the average sales price (per community district) for a given year.

Data on residential sales activity (sales prices and volumes) provide a more geographically useful tool for examining changes to the reinvested core and citywide. By multiplying aggregate sales volume by average sales price, it is possible to chart the history of real estate exchange since 1984 (figure 6.8a). High levels of exchange generally parallel high levels of housing market investment citywide. Similar to new construction trends, the level of residential exchange began to sputter in 1986 after two very strong years of growth. Sales prices in both multi-family and single-family housing sectors continued to rise until 1989, but sales volume for both sectors dropped considerably in 1986, after the Tax Reform Act restricted certain types of speculative investment. The 1987 New York Stock Exchange crash also left investors uncertain about the future. Other than a short increase in residential property exchange in 1988, the descent in sales activity from 1986 was unambiguously sharp. After peaking at over $11.2 billion in residential property transactions in 1986, the level dropped to $5.8 billion in 1992. Much of the initial drop (1986–88) was caused by falling sales volume (price actually increased until 1988), while the drop in the latter period (1988–92) was caused by a parallel reduction in volume *and* price. After the recession, sales prices and volumes increased almost immediately. The subsequent rise between 1993 and 1998 was smooth, save for 1994–95, when ambiguous signals in the securities industry alarmed investors in New York and elsewhere (O'Cleireacain 1997).

Figure 6.8b reveals the geography of residential real estate sales during the recession in New York. The reinvested core (Manhattan below 96th Street and northwestern Brooklyn) experienced the highest percentage losses in sales during the recession despite having the highest base (sales price) figures in the city. Northern Manhattan, the southern two-thirds of Brooklyn, central Queens, northern Staten Island, and much of the Bronx also experienced major percentage decreases in residential sales during the recession, but because the sales price base level in these areas was relatively lower in 1989, the change is less significant in absolute terms than decreases in the expensive markets of the reinvested core. Five community districts in the south Bronx and northeastern Brooklyn lie in stark contrast to this pattern because they experienced *increases* in the level of investment during the recession. In the former case (the south Bronx), the increase was countercyclical—there were decreases after the recession—while growth in the latter area was sustained after the recession. The suburban areas of eastern Queens, southern Staten Island, and the east Bronx experienced a more mild reduction of sales activity during the recession than the inner core.

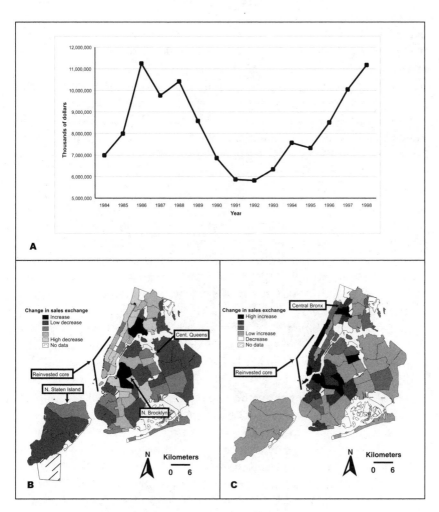

Figure 6.8: Residential sales in New York City, 1984–1998

Source: NYC Dept. of Finance

Note: (a) Residential sales per annum, 1984–1998; (b) Change in residential sales per community district between 1989 and 1992; (c) Change in residential sales per community district between 1993 and 1998

113

After the recession, this pattern was reversed (figure 6.8c)—the highest percentage gains in sales activity were experienced in the inner core, while the suburban fringe experienced a more limited rise. In addition to the reinvested core, portions of central Bronx and the northern half of Brooklyn also experienced a disproportionately high increase in residential sales activity after the recession. A notable spine of growth extends through northeastern Brooklyn. Outer areas of the Bronx, Queens, Brooklyn, and Staten Island, by contrast, experienced only a mild increase in this form of reinvestment, while three districts in the Bronx experienced a reduction.

If the recession and subsequent expansion clearly affected new construction and real estate sales, their impact on building alterations was less obvious. Because they reflect improvements made to existing structures, building alteration data are an index of reinvestment. Figure 6.9a shows that the level of building alterations increased steadily between 1983 and 1986 and then more rapidly until 1988. The fantastic rate of growth during the 1980s boom was surpassed only by the rate of decline thereafter. Between 1988 and 1990, the number of alterations per annum dropped from 2404 to 160. Not unlike real estate sales activity and new construction then, building alteration activity was adversely affected by the 1989–92 recession and continued to slump during the subsequent property boom. After 1991, the yearly level of alterations grew by less than 300 but never exceeded 500. In fact, there was a notable decline after 1993 despite the clear signals of growth in the larger (regional, national, and global) economy. The recession thus appears to have triggered a larger reaction in the rate of building alterations despite spawning a temporary episode of decline for other forms of reinvestment. The reasons for this are complicated but undoubtedly include a reduced proclivity to enforce regulations by the city in the 1990s, which likely means that there are many more *illegal* alterations (that is, unrecorded) than before (see Lobbia 1998). Inflation in subcontracting costs and saturation in the supply of profitably upgradeable housing units (after a swell of such activity during the 1980s) were also to blame for the fall. Overall, building alterations were slowed considerably during the recession, but other factors appear to be at play in suppressing the level since the recession.

As Figure 6.9b reveals, the most notable drop in alterations were clustered in the reinvested core during the recession. Building alterations per annum in this portion of the city were disproportionately high in the late 1980s but were significantly reduced as the recession suppressed expendable income and investor enthusiasm. Staten Island emerges again as a housing market in flux, but most of its census tracts experienced a reduction in the

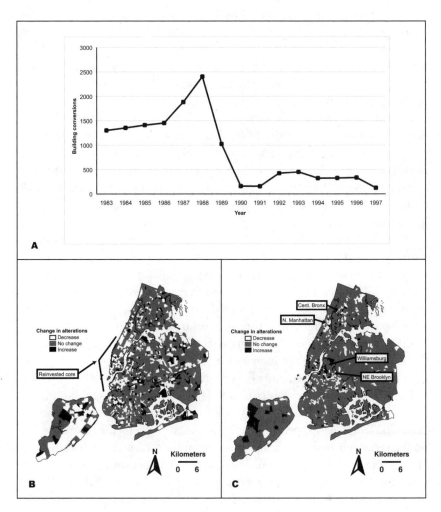

Figure 6.9: Building alterations in New York City, 1983–1997

Source: NYC Dept. of Buildings, Sanborn Building Survey

Note: (a) Number of alterations per annum, 1983–1997; (b) Change in number
of alterations per tract between 1989 and 1992; (c) Change in number
of alterations per tract between 1993 and 1997

number of alterations. Much of the city experienced an odd mixture of increasing and declining alterations during the recession, but the most common tendency was to remain static. This pattern was likely the result of ambiguous signals in the economy, which made investors more cautious.

After the recession (Figure 6.9c), by contrast, the level of rehabilitation remained relatively constant throughout much of the city. Northeast Brooklyn, particularly the neighborhood of Williamsburg, experienced a notable increase in the number of alterations, but as one travels southeast from this point, the predominant pattern actually indicates reduced investment. In northern Manhattan, the prevailing pattern since the recession has been that of declining alteration activity, likely as a result of inflated renovation costs. In central Bronx, the housing market is more volatile, with a divergent mixture of increasing and declining census tracts.

Overall, the effect of the 1989–92 recession and subsequent boom are spatially varied but indicate a general tendency toward a more rapid response (to recession and economic recovery) within inner core housing markets. Though there was a fairly ubiquitous increase in certain forms of disinvestment during the recession, reductions in positive investment were palpably sharper in the inner core than on the suburban fringe of the city. Reduced levels of sales and building alteration activity were more severe in the reinvested core, while increases in demolitions were most notable in the swath of land immediately beyond this portion of the city (northeastern Brooklyn, northern Manhattan, and the south Bronx). The suburbs, by contrast, experienced a comparatively mild recession, except for parts of Staten Island, which appear to have been destabilized by the downturn. After the recession, disinvestment subsided only in the inner core, while outer areas either remained the same or experienced a deepening decline. Reinvestment, on the other hand, generally increased, but the sharpest growth (in residential sales and alterations) was within the reinvested core—the same portion of the city that was pummeled by the 1989–92 recession. While the fringe experienced a milder recession, it was nonetheless slower to recover afterward. By 1997, large areas along the suburban fringe were still experiencing disinvestment, while the inner core (especially the RC) had already rebounded several years earlier.

Post-Recession Expansion

Since the end of the 1989–92 recession, reinvested core property markets have recovered and become even more exclusive than before. As a consequence, it has become virtually impossible to find affordable housing in lower Manhattan and northeastern Brooklyn. But the resurgence of property markets in the extant reinvested core is only half of the story. *New* growth in property markets in northwestern and central Brooklyn indicates that the reinvested core is expanding outward. This expansion of new investment has delivered gentrification to places as remote (in social and geographical terms) as Bedford-Stuyvesant—a neighborhood that once was deemed ungentrifiable but is nonetheless now considered one of the "hottest" by the local real estate press (see Hall 2000). The expansion of reinvestment is most clearly illustrated when changes in the *relative* focus of real estate investment are mapped.

To measure relative change, I devised an index to determine the degree of investment change between the 1980s boom and 1990s boom (that is, pre- and post-recession) for each census tract. Demolition data (a measure of disinvestment) and alteration data (a measure of reinvestment) are used in the index because of their efficacy at conveying broad patterns of investment change in previous studies (see especially Beauregard 1993). The index is created by dividing the level of activity (either alterations or demolitions) per census tract during the 1990s property boom ("post-recession") by the level of activity citywide during the same period. That figure is then subtracted by an identical computation of activity per tract for the 1980s boom ("pre-recession"). When mapped, the computation reveals changes in the share of total reinvestment (equation 1a) and disinvestment (equation 1b) between the two time periods. The equations are represented below. Figures derived from these equations are applied to each census

Measure of reinvestment: (1A)

$$\Delta TI_{CT} = \frac{1990sBoom\ TA_{CT}}{1990sBoom\ TA_{NYC}} - \frac{1980sBoom\ TA_{CT}}{1980sBoom\ TA_{NYC}}$$

Where:
TA_{CT} = Total alterations per census tract
TA_{NYC} = Total alterations in New York City

Measure of disinvestment: (1B)

$$\Delta TDI_{CT} = \frac{1990sBoom\ TD_{CT}}{1990sBoom\ TD_{NYC}} - \frac{1980sBoom\ TD_{CT}}{1980sBoom\ TD_{NYC}}$$

Where:
TD_{CT} = Total demolitions per census tract
TD_{NYC} = Total demolitions in New York City

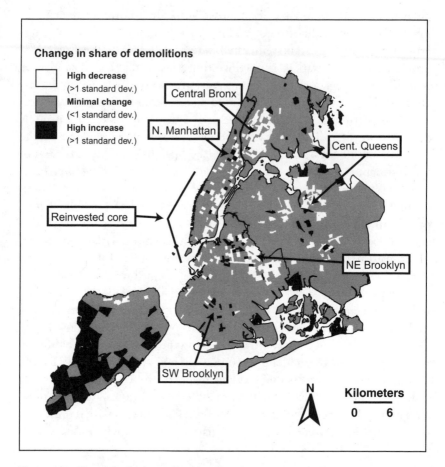

Figure 6.10: Change in the share of building demolitions per tract, 1983–1988 vs. 1993–1997

Source: NYC Dept. of Buildings, Sanborn Building Survey

tract and mapped. The actual figures are then grouped according to the degree of quantitative change measured. "High decreases" and "high increases" refer to census tracts that received a figure greater than one standard deviation from the mean for all census tracts. "Little or no change" refers to census tracts that received figures of zero (the mean), or figures closer than one standard deviation from the mean.

Figure 6.10 maps the results of this computation for total demolitions (using 1b)—a measure of disinvestment. Several patterns become immediately obvious. First, the reinvested core experienced a general decrease in disinvestment vis-à-vis the 1980s. In addition to mild reductions, the RC contained several clusters of high relative decreases in disinvestment. This shows that while *new* investment was slowing in this portion of the city, as we shall see, disinvestment there was also on the ebb (sharply in places). Central Bronx and northeastern Brooklyn were also experiencing relatively high decreases in disinvestment, but for a different reason. The cluster of high decreases likely signaled a turning point toward reinvestment, as the pockets of disinvestment were being shoved further from the central city. One further suggestion that the zone of deepest disinvestment in the city was diffusing outward is displayed on Staten Island and southwestern Brooklyn, which both experienced high relative increases in demolitions. Secular disinvestment is a relatively new event for both of these inner suburban locations. Central and western Queens also experienced the negative results of this movement as indicated by the scattered pattern of rising *and* falling disinvestment—a sign of housing market volatility.

Patterns of new investment also indicate a post-recession RC expansion. Figure 6.11 maps changes in the relative share of alteration activity between the two booms. The reinvested core appears to have experienced a relative reduction in its share of building alterations after the recession, because so much of that type of investment (building rehabilitation) took place there during the 1980s. The new foci of this activity were mostly beyond the reinvested core: northeastern Brooklyn, northern Manhattan, central Bronx, and northern Staten Island in particular. The key difference between these areas and the housing markets on the suburban fringe is that the former were also zones of reduced disinvestment (see figure 6.10) while the latter (suburban fringe) only experienced the *introduction* and acceleration of disinvestment during the 1990s. This pattern should not come as much of a surprise in light of urban theoretical and empirical work in the last twenty-five years showing a demonstrable (if apparently paradoxical) tendency toward continued sprawl (geographical decentralization of investment) and inner city reinvestment (geographical recentralization of investment). Inner suburbs like central Queens and central Staten Island are the increasing foci of disinvestment (see also Harvey 1996, p. 405; and Smith, Caris, and Wyly 2000 for a more detailed discussion) as the reinvested core expands outward, pushing urban decay into the inner suburbs (figure 6.12). Though it is too early to tell whether the RC's expansion will congeal into a level of affluence similar to that in the extant reinvested core, we can be certain that a disproportionate amount of the city's housing market investment is currently occurring there, and as such the ongoing reinvestment of the central city has not only continued but actually expanded.

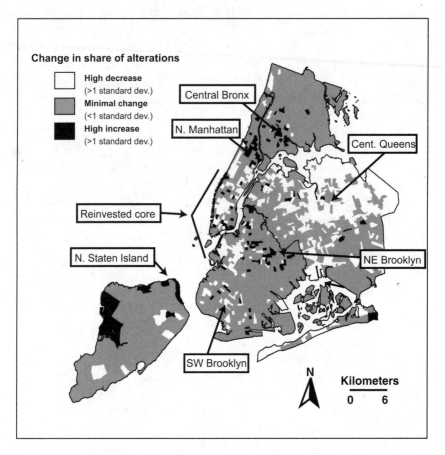

Change in share of alterations

☐ High decrease
   (>1 standard dev.)
▨ Minimal change
   (<1 standard dev.)
■ High increase
   (>1 standard dev.)

Central Bronx

N. Manhattan

Cent. Queens

Reinvested core

N. Staten Island

NE Brooklyn

SW Brooklyn

N

Kilometers
0   6

Figure 6.11: Change in share of building alterations per tract, 1983–1988 vs. 1993–1997

Source: NYC Dept. of Buildings, Sanborn Building Survey

Though much of the literature fetishizes gentrification as separate from wider processes occurring at the regional, national, and global scales, the key argument of this chapter is that gentrification is part of a broader restructuring of space. Moreover, it is not only connected to the broader process of neoliberal urbanism but can be seen as its knife-edge. Gentrification is much more than the physical renovation of residential and commercial spaces. It marks the replacement of the publicly regulated Keynesian inner city—replete with physical and institutional remnants of a system designed to ameliorate the inequality of capitalism—with privately regulated

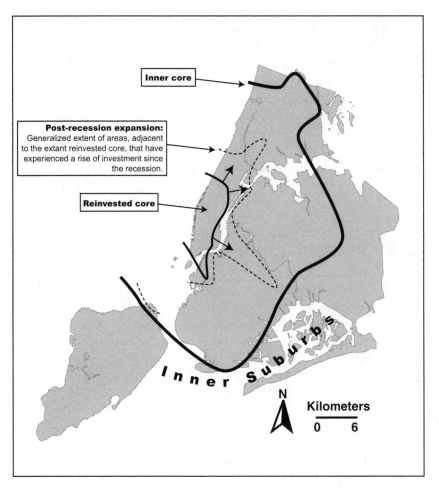

Figure 6.12: Schematic summary of post-recession reinvested core expansion

neoliberalized spaces of exclusion. Gentrification is also much more than the small, idiosyncratic neighborhood process that it is often framed to be. No longer limited to "islands of renewal in seas of decay," redeveloped pockets have melded into a larger zone of exclusion that now forms the reinvested core. Though the conditions for gentrification have been present in New York and elsewhere for at least four decades, the congealment of the reinvested core has really taken place since the last major global real estate recession.

Since the early 1990s recession, there has also been a notable expansion of the reinvested core into previously disinvested parts of northeastern and central Brooklyn. Though gentrification theory has already predicted that such locations are ripe for the process, its post-recession occurrence in neighborhoods like Bedford-Stuyvesant has surprised even the most experienced analysts of New York real estate patterns. But the significance of gentrification extends far beyond its physical expansion. The nature of gentrification here partly reflects the wider integration of property and finance capital (see Coakley 1994). It is being initiated not by risk-taking owner-occupiers who want to rehabilitate the neighborhood's brownstones for personal use (the predominant mode of gentrification during the 1970s and 1980s) but rather by more globally linked corporate brokerage firms like the Corcoran Group (Hall 2000). Despite the presence of such corporations, however, the financial risks to such geographically remote gentrification schemes are still formidable, perhaps more so than during the 1980s, when more investment took place in or near "tamed" neighborhoods. In response to developer concerns, urban policy has become more assertive at removing such obstacles during the 1990s (Wyly and Hammel 1999, 2000). This is particularly interesting in New York, where local resistance was strong enough during the 1980s to slow pro-gentrification governmental forces (Hackworth and Smith 2001) but has been all but erased from the urban political scene more recently (see Wilson and Grammenos 2000). Hotbeds of 1980s resistance like the Lower East Side are now less likely to resist (see Jacobs 1998), and newly gentrifying ones like Bed-Stuy do not appear to be spawning a contemporary replication of earlier militancy. The picture created here is not, of course, perfectly replicated in every city, but the identification of such patterns in New York—which has experienced as much gentrification as any city in the world—has in the past foreshadowed events that were to follow in other cities. At a minimum, it is clear from this and other recent research that gentrification is changing, both quantitatively and qualitatively, and that it can usefully be seen as part of a much broader neoliberalization of the inner city. The next chapter attempts to elaborate on this point by focusing on the nature of this process in three specific neighborhoods.

Chapter 7

Neoliberal Gentrification

Though gentrification clearly has the potential to materialize at the super-neighborhood level, much of the interest in gentrification is linked to the understanding that it is a highly localized process that articulates broader politico-economic forces like globalization (N. Smith 2002), uneven development (N. Smith 1982), and culture change (Ley 1996). That is, gentrification can serve as a revealing window into much broader processes like neoliberalism. But exactly how processes like neoliberalism articulate themselves locally is anything but straightforward. The location, history, and demographics of a particular neighborhood are all important factors in how neoliberalism gets localized through gentrification. Conversely, changes to the way that neoliberalism is articulated and policed globally affect the way that gentrification plays out. The relationship is broadly dialectical in this way.

Unfortunately, however, the literature on gentrification is not much more specific on this relationship. We have to turn to fragments in the literature to see how the neoliberal city affects gentrification and how gentrification affects the neoliberal city in turn. Much of this literature points to a series of changes to gentrification that are related to recent broader-scale events, especially the early 1990s real estate recession. Lees, for example, argues that gentrification is now fundamentally different than it was in the 1970s and 1980s, but neglects to detail how (2000). Smith and Defilippis (1999) are a bit more specific when they argue that contemporary gentrification is driven more by profit-seeking land development firms than the individual owner-occupiers that drove earlier waves of the process, but their portrait is still incomplete. Wyly and Hammel (1999) emphasize yet another change, arguing that important changes in urban policy are now fueling gentrification. Others (see for example Bondi 1999; Ley 1996) hint that the process is different than it was before but provide even less of a summary of what those changes might be. There is, in other words, no composite summary of contemporary gentrification, despite several statements and research articles showing that the process has indeed changed. This is unfortunate, because gentrification has long been theorized as a window into larger processes of economic and social restructuring. Understanding its most recent manifestation could thus reveal important clues about the nature of neoliberalism at the local scale.

The primary intent of this chapter is to explore how gentrification has been changed by the broader-scale processes described in this book. Such an understanding not only helps to underline the importance of gentrification for neoliberal urbanism, but, more importantly, it also demonstrates the important connections between relatively global ideological shifts (like the one toward neoliberalism) and neighborhood-based processes. After building this framework, this chapter also explores the local articulation of recent gentrification in three New York City neighborhoods: Long Island City (LIC), DUMBO ("Down Under the Manhattan Bridge Overpass"), and Clinton (see figure 7.1).

Each neighborhood has been identified by the New York real estate press (Dunlap 1998; Lobbia 1998; Cohen 1996) as a recently intensified locale for gentrification, but all were more or less spared the process during the 1970s and 1980s. An exploration of recent gentrification in these three neighborhoods offers important clues as to the local articulation of general changes observed by researchers in several contexts and locations. Though New York is hardly a typical American city, its experience of gentrification and related changes has generally preceded the same process in other U.S. cities by a decade or more. Understanding the recent gentrification history of New York City neighborhoods could thus reveal much about the immediate future of the process elsewhere.

Gentrification, Before and After the Early 1990s Recession

The composite of gentrification prior to the early 1990s is well developed (see Hackworth and Smith 2001). Depending on the city, gentrification started to occur sometime between 1950 and 1980, when small-scale

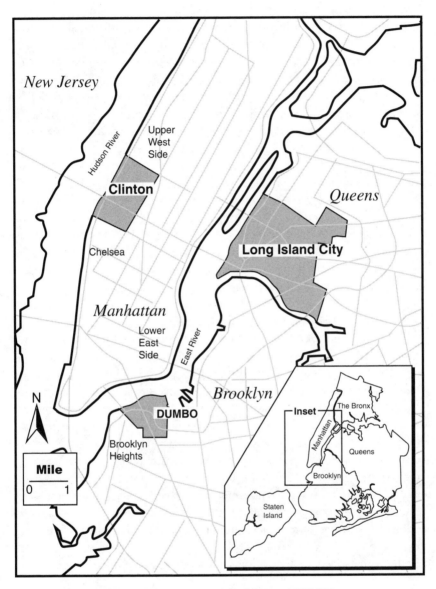

Figure 7.1: Clinton, Long Island City, and DUMBO

owner-occupiers entered disinvested neighborhoods to rehabilitate individual homes for personal consumption. If enough individual investors came to the neighborhood, the process sometimes became more corporate, with development firms entering the "tamed"[1] market to sell condominiums, brownstones, and townhouses to less adventurous buyers (Ley 1996; Berry 1985; Laska and Spain 1980). In some situations, the process led to the direct displacement of vibrant working-class communities (Atkinson 2000; N. Smith 1996; Marcuse 1986). Resistance movements coalesced around the threat of displacement and grew quite violent in highly polarized cities like New York (N. Smith 1996; Abu-Lughod 1994). This general picture was repeated in large world cities during the 1960s and 1970s, but by the 1980s, gentrification was a process affecting a wider range of cities down the urban hierarchy. Increasingly, places like Edinburgh, Boston, and Budapest were subject to gentrification as well. Despite its intercity diffusion, though, the process remained qualitatively similar to its earlier manifestation in larger cities—small investors at first, followed by developers, displacement, and resistance.

More recent literature suggests that recession of the early 1990s facilitated a restructuring of the gentrification process itself. Though some of the cited changes appear to be a continuation or exaggeration of earlier patterns, some aspects are more novel. Though no researcher has given the early 1990s recession primary *causal* significance in these changes, a consensus is developing that, for whatever reasons, gentrification now operates differently than it did before the recession and that these changes can be linked to the neoliberal turn. Four changes have been particularly salient. First, the process is more often initiated by corporate developers because of restructuring in the real estate industry. Second, local and federal government intervention in the process has become more open and assertive. Third, opposition movements to urban redevelopment and gentrification appear more marginal than in earlier decades. Finally, gentrification has diffused into more remote neighborhoods, intensifying the pressure on ungentrified tracts of land closer to the urban core and altering the land economics that produced earlier waves of the process.

Corporatized Gentrification

Recent economic restructuring appears to have altered the real estate industry in such a way as to encourage the presence of large corporate gentrifiers more than small-scale owner-occupiers (Smith and Defilippis 1999). Though the involvement of corporate real estate capital in gentrification is well documented in neighborhoods that have already been "tamed" (see Ley 1996; Zukin 1982), until recently the involvement of corporate actors at the early stages of the process in "untamed" neighborhoods occurred less frequently. Much of the impetus for corporatized inner city real estate investment lies in 1970s economic change, but more recent political and economic restructuring intensified those pressures and made gentrification (one of several forms of investment) more corporate.

Property and financial markets experienced substantial integration during the 1980s (Ball 1994; Coakley 1994; Logan 1993; Pugh 1991a, b) as a result of deregulation in finance, the expansion of credit (Squires 1992; Harvey 1982), and a general reorientation of core manufacturing economies toward real estate (Fainstein 2001; Fitch 1993). But the intrinsic instability of this "switch" to the secondary circuit (see Harvey 1978) morphed into a crisis when several core economies went into recession in the early 1990s. Sale prices plummeted and homeowners in Britain and the United States were immediately saddled with negative equity. Highly leveraged land developers and the lending community were also in a precarious position. High profile (and overextended) developers like Donald Trump, Olympia and York, and William Zeckendorf were hit very hard by the recession (Fainstein 2001), as were several banks that had overinvested in real estate. Most attempted to liquidate their holdings as quickly as possible but were quickly thwarted by the deepening recession. Some avoided bankruptcy, but most lost an enormous amount of money during the downturn.

Yet rather than withering away, inner city real estate capital simply reorganized, mostly, though not entirely, through consolidation (see Linneman 1997). Already-large inner city developers, real estate investment trusts, and mortgage brokers merged with smaller firms to create a more consolidated industry (Campbell, Ghosh, and Sirmans 1998; Linneman 1997; Logan 1993; see also Chandrashekaran and Young 1999). The global reach of development firms increased in concert with this consolidation, and the real estate trade became less local (Logan 1993), becoming even more integrated with finance capital. But just as development firms were growing in power, the availability of profitable opportunities for the small-scale classic gentrifier was shrinking. By the 1980s, many of the most easily gentrified neighborhoods had already appreciated in value to the point where the smallest investors could no longer enter the market without sizeable down payments or assistance from local government. The remaining neighborhoods would require a larger infusion of capital and organization in order to turn a profit. It would take more than individual renovations to overcome the remaining obstacles to house value appreciation in many of the remaining neighborhoods. By the mid-1990s, corporate real estate capital was in a much better position than individual investors to overcome these obstacles.

One result of these changes is that highly capitalized neighborhoods, such as Brooklyn Heights in New York, are now experiencing "financification" (Lees 2000), wherein workers and capital from the finance industry pour into already-gentrified neighborhoods, accentuating previous levels of exclusivity. Another result is that development corporations appear more commonly at early stages of gentrification as "pioneers" because the remaining markets are more challenging. In New York's Bedford-Stuyvesant, for example, corporate brokers like the Corcoran Group are facilitating the onset of gentrification (Hall 2000) in a way that would have been unlikely fifteen years earlier. Studies on other cities are necessary to determine the extent of these changes, but that they are being prodded by large-scale economic shifts indicates that they are not limited to New York. The pioneer metaphor describing gentrifiers is now not only problematic for its cultural connotations (see N. Smith 1992b) but also increasingly because the "hearty individual" is less a part of the gentrification process than before. Corporate participation is no longer simply the "maturation" of gentrification in individual neighborhoods. Firms are increasingly the first to invest and redevelop property for more affluent users.

State Intervention and Gentrification

Within the limited number of cities that experienced gentrification in the 1950s and 1960s, the state—usually, though not exclusively, through the device of local government—played a crucial role in the process. In Philadelphia, for example, local government helped with land assembly, zoning changes, incentives for banks, and informal marketing attempts to bring patrician families into the burgeoning Society Hill district during the late 1950s (N. Smith 1979a). In New York, the city government attempted to make marginal industrial space in SoHo attractive by dropping its support for manufacturing tenants, relaxing fire codes, and providing targeted incentives for artists to reside there (Zukin 1982). In other instances, the role of municipal government was less neighborhood-specific but no less influential. As Hamnett (1973) showed in London, for example, central government improvement grants were often crucial in catalyzing the process there in the 1960s. The advantage of such intervention for capital was fairly obvious: it served to offset some of the risks associated with inner city reinvestment. But because Keynesian welfare governance was still so prevalent in western states until the mid-1970s and because gentrification was displacing certain residents from their homes, the state's role as an agent of social reproduction grew more tenuous (Hackworth and Smith 2001). Openly encouraging a process that would displace a given group for the sake of another would have to be offset by more progressive parallel regulation and ideology if the welfare state balance was to be maintained. The Special Clinton District in New York City stands as an example of this trend. Though City Hall was generally pro-gentrification during the 1960s and 1970s, it responded to protest in Clinton by providing a special district within which gentrification was made all but impossible. This measure was created at precisely the same time as efforts were made elsewhere in the city to *encourage* gentrification, including (but not limited to) efforts in SoHo several blocks to the south. This apparent paradox was replicated by other local governments dealing with gentrification at the time. The ostensibly ambivalent nature of state involvement in gentrification during the 1960s reflected the state's arbitrating orientation.

Since the early 1970s, however, this orientation has withered, along with the economic conditions that supported it (N. Smith 1999; Warf 1999; Gilmore 1998; Harvey 1989a). Many of the political obstacles to providing open support for gentrification were lifted after the 1970s, as neighborhood activism became more fragmented, unions withered, and redistribution declined. A brief period of federally inspired, locally implemented laissez-faire urban governance ensued, wherein public policy provided incentives for success, such as enterprise zones, without *directly* intervening in the process as much as before (Gaffakin and Warf 1993). For example, tax breaks to developers became rampant—but often with the proviso that the builders obtain significant commitments from private lenders beforehand. The expansion of credit and the deregulation of finance capital made this a relatively small burden for most, but it is an important one to mention in the context of more recent state involvement, which tends to come without this proviso. Since the early 1990s recession, state support has become more direct again, but this time outside of the Keynesian context. So while recent intervention is qualitatively distinct from state involvement in the 1960s and 1970s, it has nonetheless recently become more direct after a period of relatively indirect involvement during the 1980s (Hackworth and Smith 2001). This support exists on two relevant levels: national urban policy and municipal entrepreneurialism.

Wyly and Hammel (1999, 2000) have recently argued that the 1990s property boom in American cities was being facilitated in part by targeted federal expenditures that served to expand extant pockets of gentrification. Public housing is one of the few obstacles left to gentrification spreading within some inner city neighborhoods, but since the implementation of the Department of Housing and Urban Development's (HUD) HOPE VI program, these obstacles quite literally are falling (see chapters 3, 4, and 9). Wyly and Hammel (1999) found that many of these grants tend to be awarded to complexes that sit amidst otherwise gentrified neighborhoods. HOPE VI appears to be part of a much broader restructuring of the American state that began in the 1970s but accelerated in the mid-1990s with the rapid and strategic devolution of certain redistributive and regulatory functions at the national level (Hackworth 2000; Staeheli, Kodras, and Flint 1997). In the case of HOPE VI, the mid-1990s state devolution was crucial to its impact. This recent bout of state restructuring expanded the capacity of local development authorities to demolish public housing without full replacement—an important and expensive requirement during the 1980s and early 1990s (ABT Associates 1996). With this and other Keynesianesque forms of regulation removed, national urban policy has become a more effective instrument at facilitating gentrification. Other research reminds us that these events were more than simply mid-1990s American exceptionalism. Some have argued, for example, that not only is the neoliberalization of national urban policy occurring elsewhere but that the shift is also an ongoing response to economic crisis in the 1970s (N. Smith 1999; Gilmore 1998; Gaffakin and Warf 1993)—likely much deeper than a capricious swing of American or British electoral politics.

Heightened state involvement has occurred through the device of local government. Because of the decline in general outlays to municipalities, there is an even greater reliance on tax revenue than before. The pressures that facilitated entrepreneurial governance (Hall and Hubbard 1996, 1999; Leitner 1990; Harvey 1989) are now even more common than they were before, but the political and theoretical reasons for why these concepts were once controversial are suddenly less obvious. It is simply accepted as axiomatic that city governments should become more direct players in real estate (see, for example, Varady and Raffel 1995). In short, the late 1990s represent the culmination of several decades of neoliberal ascendance. There are now fewer political consequences for consorting directly with real estate capital to facilitate growth. The days of Keynesian urban policy seem to have expired—or at least gone into hibernation—and city governments have adapted to the new conditions. Compounding the larger political shift is the expansion of gentrification to more remote neighborhoods where the needs for state involvement—that is, to offset barriers to profit—are greater than before. At times, those barriers are simply a function of geographical distance from the central city, but very often they involve a complex mixture of zoning barriers, existing measures designed to assist the poor, and infrastructure expenses.

Resistance to Gentrification

During the 1970s and 1980s, the threat and reality of displacement from gentrification often motivated working-class groups to fight the process when it entered their neighborhoods. Though usually unsuccessful at stopping the process outright, such groups often did procure limited agreements from banks, developers, and the state to make the process less deleterious to the existing community (Wilson and Grammenos 2000; Robinson 1995; Squires 1992). By the end of the 1980s, though, neighborhood-based opposition began to lose the support of the erstwhile Keynesian activist state (Lake 1995, 1997) and sometimes became more militant as a result (N. Smith 1996). In the last decade, however, anti-gentrification (and anti-redevelopment) groups have become less militant and more marginal within the urban political sphere (Wilson and Grammenos 2000). Overall, anti-gentrification activism has been pushed in two different directions. For groups whose politics and purpose are too expensive for the state to absorb, on the one hand, confrontation with City Hall is the increasingly common outcome of protest. For anti-gentrification groups in New York's Lower East Side, this was already becoming the case by the end of the 1980s (N. Smith 1996; Abu-Lughod 1994). Their calls for the city to stop encouraging gentrification were met with violent police action and a series of laws restricting further protests in and around Tompkins Square Park. Participation in such protest withered in part because of continued attempts by pro-gentrification city leaders to keep this form of activism out of the public sphere. In San Francisco's Tenderloin District, the reaction by City Hall was less violent but no less confrontational as the pro-growth underpinnings of the city's major regime sought to pursue gentrification (Robinson 1995). Though activists in San Francisco were more successful than those in New York at obtaining concessions from the local government, they nonetheless had to endure an increasingly oppositional City Hall in the process. Anti-gentrification groups elsewhere have often splintered under similar pressures.

For less militant groups, on the other hand, with less threatening politics, the recent political context has been friendlier. Many groups that agitated for help in financing affordable housing during the 1980s, for example, morphed into community development corporations (CDCs). CDCs have become an important feature of the post-Keynesian city and have functioned as partial replacements for the removal of certain social functions that were once organized by the state (Kodras 1997; Harvey 1996, 425), especially affordable housing provision. The politics of CDCs are palpably different than the politics of militant anti-gentrification groups, not least because most CDCs are dependent on the state for some (if not all) of their revenue. Even CDCs with more militant roots are limited by this position. Open criticism of pro-development urban policy is made very difficult because of their ties to the state. As the Pratt Area CDC in Brooklyn found out in the late 1990s, for example, toeing the line between critic of City Hall and recipient of funding that flows through local government can be untenable (*City Limits* 1999). The Pratt Area CDC's funding was summarily rescinded in the late 1990s after its leaders openly criticized Mayor Giuliani's affordable housing policy. Being reliant on state funding is a precarious position for any critical community group. So while the fraction of anti-gentrification activism that morphed into community service provision has had a better reception by the post-Keynesian state, it is more vulnerable to fiscal disciplining and less likely to retain a critical bent.

Compounding the tricky political position of community-based opposition are the aggregate spatial effects of continued reinvestment in the inner city. As gentrification continues and the working class is less able, as a whole, to afford rents in neighborhoods close to the central business district (CBD), prospects of an oppositional collective consciousness are reduced. The density of working-class populations in places like the Lower East Side and Clinton fostered relatively cohesive anti-gentrification struggles in the 1970s and 1980s. Propinquity made communication easier and enabled participants to see firsthand what was happening to their neighborhood. But as the poor continue to move into inner-ring suburbs, the benefits of density are removed. Though activist groups certainly still exist in gentrifying inner city neighborhoods, the stance of such groups has on the whole softened, particularly because they are increasingly composed of gentrification's beneficiaries. This has happened in places where militant anti-gentrification struggles occurred only a few years prior, like the Lower East Side. A ten-year retrospective on the Tompkins Square struggles in the *New York Times* (Jacobs 1998) found that many of the previous anti-gentrification leaders have either been priced out of the neighborhood or gotten jobs lucrative enough to stay there and softened their stance—

"grown up," to use the language of one ex-protestor. Once-militant activism there has been diluted by the expansion of gentrification. This expansion appears to be facilitating a similar pattern elsewhere.

The Diffusion of Gentrification

This collection of qualitative changes to gentrification has facilitated an outward diffusion of the process in many cities that experienced it before and facilitated its debut in many cities left relatively untouched in earlier periods. The implications of this expansion—both within and between cities—loom large for inner city land economics (see figure 7.2).

Though gentrification was quite common throughout the 1970s, as of the mid-1980s most still considered the process spatially insignificant. Berry was particularly skeptical, deeming the process little more than "islands of renewal in seas of decay" (1985). But with the recent expansion of gentrification, it appears that the process is inching toward spatial significance in some cities (see chapters 5 and 6). Wyly and Hammel (1999) have boldly argued that it is already time to reverse Berry's oft-quoted maxim because several American inner cities are now beginning to resemble "islands of decay in seas of renewal."

While contemporary gentrification continues to affect many of the central urban neighborhoods that started to gentrify several decades earlier—a process that Lees (2000) calls "regentrification"—the most profound change has been its outward diffusion into areas once thought ungentrifiable (in New York, to Bedford-Stuyvesant, Harlem, even the south Bronx). Here, housing markets are in flux as the reinvested core shoves the once monolithic belt of disinvestment (the land value valley) outward from the urban core (figure 7.2). The most notable zones of disinvestment are being shifted into the inner-ring suburbs as a result (see Smith, Caris, and Wyly 2001; Soja 2000; Caris 1996; Harvey 1996).

Paralleling this outward diffusion is an in-fill of ungentrified spaces closer to the core (for example, public housing, rent-controlled apartments, the remaining SROs). In New York, these spaces are often the last vestige of the working class within otherwise gentrified neighborhoods. Though many were under some development pressure during the 1980s, the political and material support for removing them had not yet coalesced, and they remained in place. But continued investment in adjacent neighborhoods has made these spaces more vulnerable. The rent gap (see N. Smith 1979b) for these parcels is yawning more sharply than before since

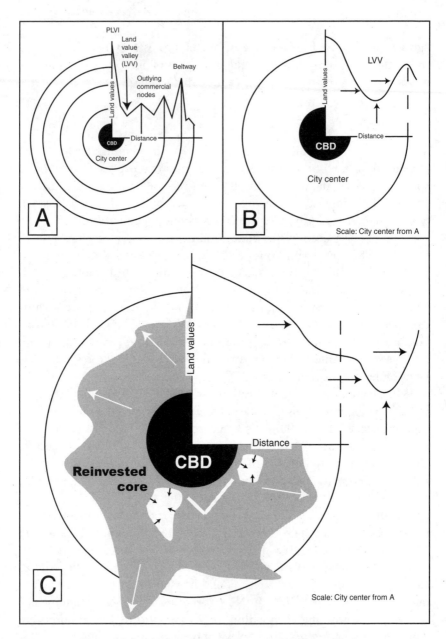

Figure 7.2: Land value surface and the expansion of gentrification

Source: Hartshorn 1992; Hoyt 1993; Smith 1996

Note: (a) Urban land surface; (b) Scale of gentrification and land value after it occurs;
(c) Land value after several decades of gentrification

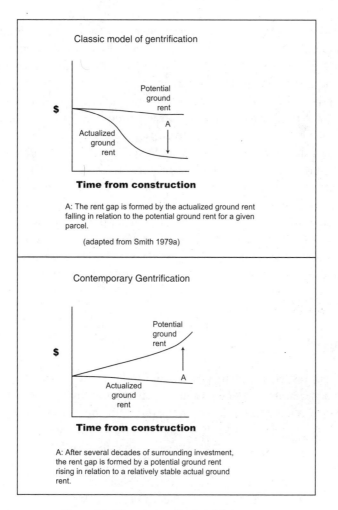

Figure 7.3: Changing mechanics of the rent gap

the recession. While a widening rent gap was the necessary precursor for the gentrification that occurred during the 1970s and 1980s, the mechanics of the gap have changed in some cities since the recession (see figure 7.3). During the earlier waves of reinvestment, actualized ground rent (at the parcel level) tended to fall in relation to a relatively inelastic potential ground rent level before gentrification took place (Clark 1995; N. Smith 1979b). When the appropriate political and economic forces combined, gentrification closed the gap as investors rehabilitated the property to actualize its higher potential rent. Since the recession, however, the actualized ground rent has remained relatively stable (or even increased) while the potential ground rent has risen sharply (for a similar argument, see Hammel 1999), because the surrounding core of reinvestment has lifted the economic potential of all centrally located parcels. The pressure that speculators—developers, banks, and landlords—have placed on city hall to bring about the development of socially useful but as yet ungentrified spaces has been notable since the recession. Yet more so than in the past, the parcels slated for redevelopment already attract rents high enough to stave off earlier waves of gentrification—that is, the actualized ground rent is now relatively inelastic. Thus, even public housing and rent-controlled apartments, both of which bring in some revenue, are now being gentrified more frequently than before because the opportunity cost of their relative underdevelopment has grown so significantly in the last fifteen years due to inner city reinvestment. The reinvested core of earlier waves has tightened the pressure already exerted on affordable housing close to the core.

Neighborhood Case Studies

While some aspects of gentrification may indeed be changing everywhere, there are certainly local geographies that are modifying and filtering in ways that problematize a general description of the process. The remainder of this chapter will explore neoliberal gentrification in three New York City neighborhoods to illustrate how the aforementioned general changes are manifesting themselves within different localities. The neighborhoods were not chosen to reflect the complete spectrum of gentrification as it stands today but rather because they each began to experience a significant bout of the process only recently. Exploring neighborhoods that are only now beginning to experience the process can reveal more clearly than neighborhoods with a longer history of such activity how the salient characteristics of contemporary gentrification are playing themselves out in the landscape. To assess changes, we identified major landholders and recent changes in ownership and then conducted interviews with gentrifiers new and old, city planners, developers, and community district officials from each neighborhood. Planning documents, news clippings, and agency web sites supplemented the interviews. The brief descriptions below are the result of this research.

Clinton

Clinton is located just west of Manhattan's exclusive Midtown office district and adjacent to two heavily gentrified neighborhoods, Chelsea to the south and the Upper West Side to the north. Though some gentrification took place in Clinton during the 1970s and 1980s, neighborhood activism stymied its expansion and kept the impact of displacement in check. Tables 7.1 and 7.2 express this pattern nicely. While increasing in relative terms, housing and income indicators remained below citywide averages in both 1980 and 1990 but above it in 2000. Wealthier professionals who could benefit from the neighborhood's location typically chose to buy or rent rehabilitated apartments in nearby neighborhoods rather than in Clinton because the prospect of sustained growth was more convincing elsewhere (in Chelsea and the Upper West Side in particular). The Special Clinton District (SCD)—a zoning designation established to fight gentrification in the early 1970s—made development expensive and suppressed property value appreciation throughout the 1980s. In many cases, larger investors opted to warehouse their property while court challenges to the SCD's legality were being decided rather than to develop immediately (see HKNA 2000; Sclar 1993; Dunlap 1988). After several of the strictest SCD regulations were relaxed in 1990, gentrification expanded very quickly in the neighborhood, led by the only group that could afford to invest there in the 1980s on a widespread basis: corporate development firms.

Clinton was the subject of several real estate articles marveling at the pace of 1990s investment (Lobbia 1998; Deutsch 1996; Cawley 1995; Finotti 1995). The yearly percentage of buildings in tax arrears has declined sharply since 1991 (see figure 7.4), and sales prices for tenement buildings (figure 7.5) and small walk-ups (figure 7.6) have outpaced the white-hot Manhattan real estate market overall. As gentrification unfolds, however, it is virtually devoid of smaller investors because larger actors, who speculated that the SCD would be weakened in the late 1980s, have already absorbed much of the easily gentrifiable property. In this context, then, the recent tendency toward corporate real estate investment has not manifested as a transition from small investor to large but more as an alleviation of fiscal burdens to corporate capital already in place.

Clinton also represents an interesting manifestation of state intervention in gentrification. Local government *assisted* with the project of resisting gentrification for two decades (through the SCD) by requiring detailed documentation that tenant harassment had not taken place in a property slated for development and by limiting demolitions and alterations. Mili-

TABLE 7.1
Aggregate socioeconomic change in New York City, 1960–2000

	1960	1970	60–70 ch.	1980	70–80 ch.	1990	80–90 ch.	2000	90–00 ch.
Population	7,781,984	7,891,251	1.40%	7,070,424	−10.40%	7,322,670	3.57%	8,008,278	9.36%
Number of professionals	368,418	502,068	36.28%	492,319	−1.94%	656,304	33.31%	764,856	16.54%
Percent of professionals	4.73%	6.36%	34.39%	6.96%	9.44%	7.58%	8.90%	9.55%	25.95%
Median income	$6,091.00	$9,682.00	58.96%	$16,818.00	73.70%	$31,534.37	87.50%	$41,056.01	30.19%
Housing units	2,758,116	2,917,428	5.78%	2,941,850	0.84%	2,992,212	1.71%	3,200,912	6.97%
Med. home value	$17,000.00	$30,420.00	78.94%	$60,500.00	98.88%	$200,317.84	231.10%	$257,462.80	28.53%
Median rent	$65.00	$102.60	57.85%	$256.10	149.61%	$543.50	112.22%	$754.40	38.80%

Source: U.S. Census

138

TABLE 7.2
Aggregate socioeconomic change in Clinton, 1960–2000

	1960	1970	60–70 ch.	1980	70–80 ch.	1990	80–90 ch.	2000	90–00 ch.
Population	47,761	38,735	−18.90%	40,740	5.18%	42,515	4.36%	46,088	8.40%
Number of professionals	2,547	3,534	38.75%	5,883	66.47%	8,108	37.82%	10,029	23.69%
Percent of professionals	5.33%	9.10%	70.63%	13.08%	43.73%	17.02%	30.12%	21.76%	27.87%
Median income	$4,996.38	$7,340.90	46.92%	$13,893.40	89.26%	$26,263.60	89.04%	$44,171.50	68.19%
Housing units	22,854	21,551	−5.70%	24,266	12.60%	27,389	12.87%	28,139	2.74%
Med. home value	n.d.	n.d.	n.d.	$65,433.33	n.d.	$237,500.00	262.96%	$556,250.50	134.21%
Median rent	$42.45	$68.50	61.35%	$211.30	208.47%	$477.30	125.89%	$865.30	81.29%

Source: U.S. Census

139

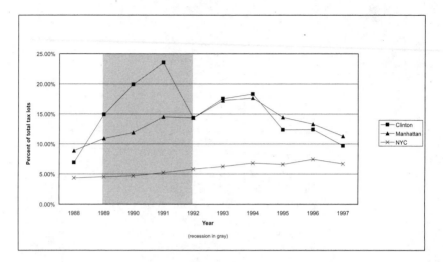

Figure 7.4: Yearly percentage of buildings in arrears in Clinton, Manhattan, and New York City, 1988–1997

Source: NYC Dept. of Finance

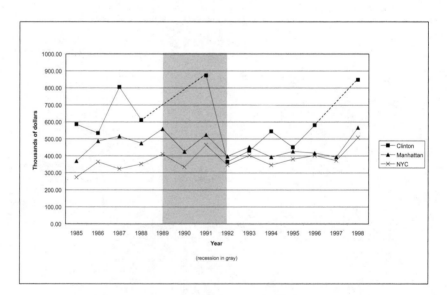

Figure 7.5: Average tenement building sales prices in Clinton, Manhattan, and New York City, 1985–1998

Source: NYC Dept. of Finance

140

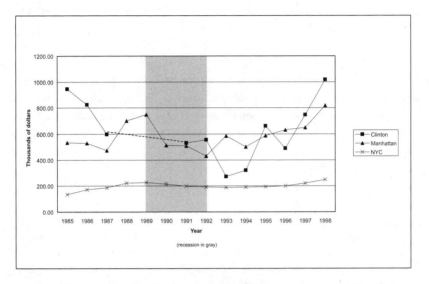

Figure 7.6: Average small walk-up sales prices in Clinton, Manhattan, and New York
City, 1985–1998

Source: NYC Dept. of Finance

tant anti-gentrification activism led to the formation of the SCD in the
early 1970s. Despite the political pressure to succumb to outside reinvestment during the 1980s, resistance to gentrification remained relatively successful. Paralleling this resistance were the efforts of community-based
groups like Housing Conservation Coordinators and the Clinton Housing
Development Corporation, which attempted to build affordable housing
in the neighborhood (HKNA 2000). Much of the funding for these two
groups, however, comes from public sources, as did the enforcement mechanisms for the SCD. As the state became more entrepreneurial during the
1980s and 1990s, the oppositional potential of the groups began to erode.
The praxis of recently established activist groups in the neighborhood,
such as the Hell's Kitchen Neighborhood Alliance, filled this void with a
palpably softer stance on gentrification and redevelopment largely because
many of its members are, unlike their predecessors, the beneficiaries of the
process. The remaining activists in the neighborhood now complain that
their work assists the middle-class newcomers more than the working-class
residents (see also Hackworth and Smith 2001; Gwertzmann 1997). The
most notable shift in state involvement since the recession—dissolution of

the SCD—is thus actually a departure from earlier regulation rather than a proactive immersion into the process.

Long Island City

In Long Island City small pockets of "classic" gentrification took place in the 1970s and early 1980s, but because it is a mixed-use neighborhood, banks remained reluctant to lend there, and the pockets remained isolated. Table 7.3 reflects this general pattern. Much like Clinton, Long Island City experienced relative gains in income and rent during the 1970s and 1980s but had lower absolute figures in both areas in 1970 and 1980. With the 1982 announcement of the Queens West Project—a multi-stage mixed-use plan to redevelop the neighborhood—prospects for widespread gentrification appeared to be changing. The neighborhood was deluged almost immediately with corporate real estate actors, including the Mitsubishi Bank and William Zeckendorf's MO Associates (Passell 1996; Moss 1990), hoping to cash in on the ensuing development. But progress on Queens West could not begin without significant assistance from the public sector. The neighborhood's zoning would have to become more uniformly residential, and the Queens West developers would need mortgage insurance before the requisite financing would fall into place. Both obstacles eventually fell in the early 1990s (during the recession, actually), thanks in large part to assistance by various ex-public officials who were hired by the development team (Moss 1990). Their advocacy was crucial in moving the Queens West Project forward; construction on the first Queens West building is already complete, with eighteen more residential and office structures slated for construction over the next several years (Port Authority 2000). The revival of Queens West has also spawned a revival of the surrounding neighborhood. Figure 7.7 depicts the apparent curtailment of neighborhood-wide disinvestment, as measured through tax arrears data. Figure 7.8 conversely demonstrates that this has been paralleled by an infusion of real estate investment. Recent changes in federal housing policy have been very important at facilitating the Queens West Project and Long Island City gentrification. During the 1980s (when the development process for Queens West began), the federal government was not as likely to guarantee mortgages for luxury housing. In 1996, though, the Federal Housing Administration (FHA) agreed to provide mortgage insurance for the Queens West Project (Passell 1996). Without the insurance, it is doubtful that a private lender would have financed the project despite the significant assistance from quasi-public institutions like the Port Authority and

TABLE 7.3
Aggregate socioeconomic change in Long Island City, 1960–2000

	1960	1970	60–70 ch.	1980	70–80 ch.	1990	80–90 ch.	2000	90–00 ch.
Population	29,552	33,223	12.42%	29,534	−11.10%	29,664	0.44%	31,398	5.85%
Number of professionals	711	971	36.57%	835	−14.01%	1,871	124.07%	2,550	36.29%
Percent of professionals	2.41%	2.92%	21.48%	2.83%	−3.26%	6.31%	123.09%	8.12%	28.76%
Median income	$5,879.44	$8,941.23	52.08%	$13,563.86	51.70%	$25,284.64	86.41%	$37,853.36	49.71%
Housing units	9,928	11,939	20.26%	12,475	4.49%	11,854	−4.98%	12,473	5.22%
Med. home value	$14,350.00	$18,472.73	28.73%	$35,363.64	91.44%	$153,740.00	334.74%	$212,070.00	37.94%
Median rent	$53.90	$77.71	44.18%	$205.29	164.16%	$491.73	139.53%	$734.57	49.38%

Source: U.S. Census

143

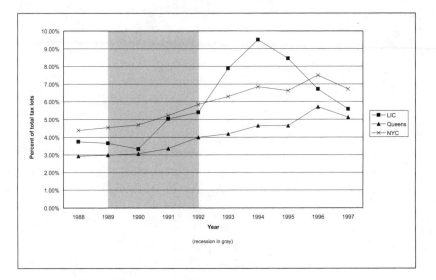

Figure 7.7: Yearly percentage of buildings in arrears in Long Island City, Queens, and New York City, 1988–1997

Source: NYC Dept. of Finance

the State Urban Development Corporation and the $16 million in tax abatements from City Hall (Moss 1990; Fainstein and Fainstein 1987). The FHA's involvement signaled a shift to more open relations between the federal government and real estate capital and served as a reminder that the Keynesian aversion to unbalanced supply-side incentives is no longer a significant obstacle to gentrification. Community opposition to gentrification in Long Island City has focused on quality-of-life issues such as the visual impact of Queens West and the noise made by the project's builders (see HPCC 1996). Though the danger of displacement is mentioned in the group's promotional material, their main thrust is not on the problems associated with gentrification but rather on the *type* of development embodied by Queens West. Complaints revolve around the lack of involvement in the plan, City Hall's willful deafness to community concerns, and the lack of connection on the part of the new residents to the existing community.

DUMBO

Though a small trickle of artists started to gentrify DUMBO in the 1980s (Richardson 1995), contemporary gentrification in the neighborhood is

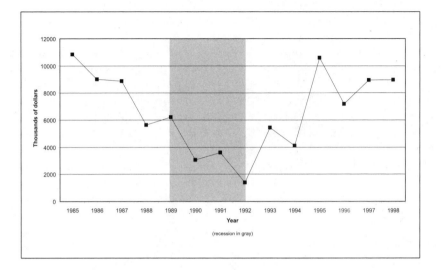

Figure 7.8: Residential sales exchange in Long Island City, 1985–1998

Source: NYC Dept. of Finance

Note: Sales exchange is measured by multiplying the sales volume
per year by the average sales price per year.

being orchestrated almost exclusively by one firm: David Walentas's Two
Trees Development Corporation. In the early 1980s, Two Trees purchased
almost all of DUMBO's turn-of-the-century industrial loft buildings and
began to refurbish them. At that time, DUMBO was a small neighborhood
of moderate income and rent levels (see table 7.4). Relatively affluent artists
and craftspeople began moving into the lofts of DUMBO in the mid-
1980s, but their demographic effect was muted by the very poor eastern
part of the neighborhood, which is dominated by the Farragut Public Housing Complex.

Upon his arrival, Walentas evicted many of the artists that resided in his
buildings and moved aggressively to improve the area's amenity value
(Dunlap 1998; Garbarine 1998). Their plan to redevelop the adjacent waterfront was paralleled by efforts to bring art galleries (as opposed to resident artists) to the neighborhood. As was the case in LIC, though, various
bureaucratic and financing obstacles impeded the Two Trees plan from becoming a reality, and the minor rehabilitations were stopped. During the
mid-1990s, Walentas encountered a more politically receptive City Hall,

TABLE 7.4
Aggregate socioeconomic change in DUMBO, 1960–2000

	1960	1970	60–70 ch.	1980	70–80 ch.	1990	80–90 ch.	2000	90–00 ch.
Population	7,437	5,759	−22.56%	5,303	−7.92%	5,628	6.13%	5,659	0.55%
Number of professionals	70	89	27.14%	54	−39.33%	123	127.78%	476.00	286.99%
Percent of professionals	0.94%	1.55%	64.19%	1.02%	−34.11%	2.19%	114.62%	8.41%	284.87%
Median income	4,121.50	6,899.50	67.40%	13,063.50	89.34%	30,327.00	132.15%	42,170.00	39.05%
Housing units	1,797	1,474	−17.97%	1,624	10.18%	1,701	4.74%	2,123	24.81%
Med. home value	n.d.	n.d.	n.d.	$29,400.00	n.d.	$193,750.00	559.01%	n.d.	n.d.
Median rent	$43.00	$82.00	90.70%	$197.00	140.24%	$400.50	103.30%	$734.00	83.27%

Source: U.S. Census

146

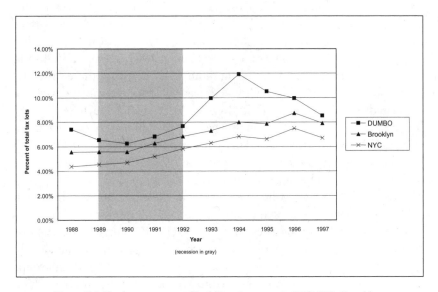

Figure 7.9: Yearly percentage of buildings in arrears in DUMBO, Brooklyn, and New York City, 1988–1997

Source: NYC Dept. of Finance

and his plan was revived. The first renovated building, aptly named the Walentas Building, was completed in 1998, and unit renovations involving several thousand apartments are currently underway. Expensive restaurants and upscale storefronts are increasingly common replacements for the machine shops and working studios that peppered the neighborhood only ten years ago. DUMBO was characterized as one of the most rapidly gentrifying neighborhoods in the city during the late 1990s (Ennen 1999; Trebay 1999; Weir 1999; Dunlap 1998; Garbarine 1998). Though its aggregate tax arrearage was still higher than the city's in 1997, the reversal of disinvestment in 1994 is unmistakable (see figure 7.9). Much of the subsequent reinvestment is associated with Walentas's property and the buildings containing a large number of resident and working artists.

Informal changes in the stance of City Hall toward developers like Walentas have been an important component of the process. During the 1970s and 1980s, Walentas had difficulty getting City Hall to support his project largely because he was unable to find finance capital on his own. Requiring developers to achieve funding in the private market was once a common litmus test for state involvement in New York, but in the 1990s an increasing amount of public sector support has gone to developers who could not otherwise find lenders for their projects. City Hall has made important zoning decisions and given Walentas uncontested approval to redevelop the waterfront despite public opposition (Finder 1999; Sengupta 1999) and mixed signals from the lending community. By removing these obstacles (and its previous litmus test), City Hall has also removed much of the risk associated with gentrifying DUMBO. Walentas had a much easier time convincing lenders after the support from City Hall had materialized.

As in Clinton and Long Island City, gentrification resistance in DUMBO is also more reserved than opposition in earlier waves, but the reasons are slightly different. The most active source of resistance to Walentas's gentrification of the neighborhood comes from the residents who had been part of the small-scale gentrification of the 1980s. Opposition to the Walentas Project is being spearheaded by the DUMBO Neighborhood Association (a small group of resident artists) and assisted by the nearby Brooklyn Heights Neighborhood Association (Ennen 1999). Both groups have been most concerned with Walentas's plan for the waterfront, which includes a movie theater, a shopping mall, and several hundred parking spaces. Like LIC, the DUMBO Neighborhood Association has organized to oppose the scale of development rather than the threat of displacement that it poses per se. However, most residents who are critical of current gentrification in DUMBO live there illegally in converted lofts, so their position is more precarious than normal. Because of the famous scarcity of housing in New York, City Hall rarely enforced the loft laws in certain key locations until very recently. Beginning in the mid-1990s, DUMBO residents complained about more regular visits by city officials to investigate which buildings in DUMBO were being used for residence (Richardson 1995). This has undermined the already lukewarm efforts to oppose gentrification because residents fear retaliation from a City Hall that has made its support for Walentas clear (see Ennen 1999; Garbarine 1998). Undergirding this fear have been several high-profile loft-building evictions elsewhere in the city, including one that was executed days before Christmas of 1999 in Williamsburg, a gentrifying neighborhood to the north. When combined with DUMBO's palpable lack of a rich history of gentrification resistance, the threat of eviction has undermined the potential of effective opposition.

Neoliberal Gentrification

Since recession of the early 1990s, gentrification has expanded in virtually every city in the advanced capitalist world, but in a form that often does not resemble earlier manifestations of the process. Some of these changes appear to be continuations of earlier patterns, while others seem to be wholly new. Overall, gentrification is now more corporate, more state-facilitated, and less resisted than ever before. The combination of these changes has encouraged gentrification so as to fundamentally alter the inner city land economics of the last thirty years. That said, it would be a mistake to conclude that such changes were somehow internal to the workings of ostensibly autonomous urban and regional economies in the United States and elsewhere. To the contrary, recent changes to the process suggest a closer linkage than ever before between the happenings of local real estate investment and neoliberalism. It could be said, in fact, that gentrification is the knife-edge neighborhood-based manifestation of neoliberalism. Not only has it created a profit opportunity for real estate capital, but it has also created a high-profile ideological opportunity to replace physically Keynesian managerialist landscapes of old—represented by public housing, public space, and so on—with the entrepreneurial privatized landscapes of the present. But gentrification is not the only form of inner city real estate investment, much less the only one intimately connected to neoliberal urbanization. As the next chapter attempts to show, commercial mega-projects have also become a material manifestation of neoliberalism at the local scale.

Chapter 8

Mega-Projects in the Urban Core

Bread or Circus?

In Michael Moore's classic film *Roger and Me*, the Rouse Corporation's now-defunct Autoworld was used to show the often desperate lengths to which city officials will go to return people and investment to downtown. Autoworld was a public-private response to the crushing economic travails that have plagued Flint, Michigan, since the late 1970s (but particularly since the early 1980s, when GM closed its largest plant there). Federal, state, and local money was provided to create an almost risk-free atmosphere for Rouse to come in and revitalize downtown. Like many other of its developments, including Boston's Faneuil Hall, Baltimore's Harborplace, and New York's South Street Seaport, Rouse attempted to draw on a local niche in its development in Flint. The project was paralleled by enormous subsidies to bring a luxury Hyatt Hotel to the downtown, presumably to handle all of the visitors who were expected to come to Autoworld. But as Moore points out in his film, the physical paean to an industry that had just deserted Flint was doomed from the start. It produced very few jobs, attracted very few visitors, and was eventually demolished in the 1990s.

While humorous in its details, Autoworld was not anomalous in the annals of city government in the 1980s or 1990s. Efforts to revitalize commercial areas (usually some combination of retail and office space) were replicated in hundreds of cities throughout the United States in the 1980s and 1990s. Many of these developments met a similar fate to Autoworld, but many others were able to attract visitors to consume the "essence" of a city. Much of this redevelopment effort focused on the immediate central business district (CBD), largely because, as Crilley has argued, it provided a very high-profile "circus" to distract from the absence of "bread" being produced by the local economy (1993). It also provided for a high-profile billboard to advertise a city's willingness to promote a business-friendly atmosphere, no matter how risky or counter to the real needs of a particular region.

Because they are such a crucial part of post-1970s city politics in the United States, major commercial redevelopment efforts can usefully be seen as windows into wider-scale restructuring. It is somewhat of a paradox that such small physical spaces can be so firmly connected to wider-scale politico-economic changes—such as the lurch toward neoliberalism—but it is nonetheless the case that commercial redevelopments in places as diverse as Phoenix, Arizona, and New York City were motivated and prodded by similar politico-economic changes happening at a broader scale. These factors include structural changes in finance, the widespread adoption of urban entrepreneurialism, and the secular shift toward a service economy in the advanced capitalist world. Such efforts can be considered neoliberal not least because they entail a turn toward the market to solve social problems in particular regions, and because they often involve a significant privatization of publicly held land or resources to reach completion. This chapter details the development of four commercial projects in the Phoenix metropolitan area in order to clarify and describe this response to economic changes since the 1970s.

The Downtown Redevelopment Fix

Commercial property redevelopment in American downtowns was very common during the 1980s and 1990s. Festival marketplaces, shimmering office complexes, and indoor sports arenas were constructed at an astonishing rate during this period in downtowns across the United States. But while the actual construction of these developments took place during the 1980s, they are rooted in a much deeper history of investment, disinvestment, and reinvestment in American CBDs.

Prior to the 1930s, the prototypical America city was a fairly tight unit of industrial production peppered with relatively homogeneous residential enclaves. With the Great Depression suppressing much of the industrial capital invested in the central city, a "spatial fix" was necessary for capital to grow its way out of the crisis (chapter 5). Prior to World War II, the spatial fix remained more or less within the same metropolitan area as suburbanization, and the New Deal temporarily solved the capital crisis (Walker 1977). After World War II, capital made an even wider leap to the conurbations of the American South and West where land was cheap, labor tame, and regulations lax. Midwestern and northeastern inner cities, once a symbol of might for the industrial mode of production, were forced to cede an increasing amount of power to both the suburbs within their own metropolitan areas and the "sunbelt" cities as well. The elite residential communities of the central city were the first to leave, followed by department stores in the 1950s and offices in the 1960s and 1970s. Many central cities went on a binge of slum clearance during the 1960s in order to spark a reversal of the dispersion of investment, but most were unsuccessful at returning meaningful investment. Municipalities became ever more desperate to return vitality to the core. The stage was set for a wave of entrepreneurial redevelopment schemes by cities during the 1970s and 1980s (Harvey 1989b). Tax abatements, land giveaways, and lax or nonexistent zoning became the modus operandi for cities across the United States. The downtown was by far the most active intra-urban theater of such activity.

In 1973, the first major recession in the U.S. economy since World War II once again suppressed capital invested in industrial production. With American dollars still heavily committed in the industrial sector, the crisis was severe. Investors scrambled to find more productive outlets for their capital. It is little surprise that this period prompted a tremendous switch of capital to the secondary circuit, of which the commercial built environment is one significant part (Harvey 1989a). As industrial sector decline had been in place for several decades prior to 1973, it made little sense to swim upstream, as it were, by reinvesting in the American industrial infrastructure. The most profitable returns were to be made in the commercial property market. With the commercial real estate growth in the suburbs (shopping malls) beginning to taper off by the 1970s, the blighted downtown suddenly became an attractive investment possibility (Frieden and Sagalyn 1990). A switch from the industrial infrastructure of the primary circuit to the downtown commercial real estate of the secondary circuit ensued with vigor. The older urban cores of the industrial Northeast were the first to experience the state-assisted return of capital in the form of festival marketplaces and, later, office complexes. Boston's Faneuil Hall, Baltimore's Harborplace, and New York's South Street Seaport are early examples of the capital switch "back to the city."

This switch was assisted by the neoliberal turn at the national level. Beginning with the Nixon administration, the federal government began to assume a distinctly laissez-faire urban policy posture. Fiscal outlays to cities were slashed during the Nixon and Reagan eras as the federal government slowly withdrew from its role in solving the "urban problem." This only exacerbated the erosion of power that municipalities were experiencing by constricting the flow of much-needed federal dollars, especially for social service provision. With conservative legislation also loosening up restrictions on thrifts, commercial banks, and pension funds during this period, the switch of capital was accelerated even further (Logan 1993). The deregulation during this period also indirectly led to concentration in the real estate development industry. Mainly during the 1980s, property development moved from being a primarily local enterprise to being a national, even global affair. The Rouse Corporation, Melvin Simon and Associates, Olympia and York, and the Trammel Crow Corporation are but a few examples of large corporate land development organizations that were able to dominate local markets (especially downtowns) across the United States. Although these companies did erect many useful buildings during the 1970s and 1980s, their political influence and sheer fiscal power led in no small way to the overbuilding of the urban landscape during this period (Fainstein 2001). They were more able to bankroll long development processes for controversial projects and to capitalize on desperate city governments than the property developer of earlier decades, who was typically local or regional in stature. If suburban house builders like the Levitts were iconic facilitators of the Keynesian spatial fix, large commercial developers like Rouse are the iconic facilitators of the neoliberal spatial fix. The commercial mega-projects that they build have utterly transformed the physical landscape of cities while also serving as symbols of a new form of urban governance. This chapter explores the development of four such projects in the Phoenix metropolitan area.

Phoenix Area Redevelopment

The Phoenix metropolitan area (see figure 8.1) is composed of twenty-five separate municipalities, which are collectively home to about 2.5 million people. Phoenix proper is the seventh-largest city in the United States, with over one million residents sparsely peppered over more than 420 square miles. Although settlement in the area is thought to have been initiated as early as 300 A.D. by the Hohokam, the present conurbation is barely a hundred years old (Sargent 1983). True to its namesake, the Phoenix area rose from the ashes of the earlier settlement that mysteriously

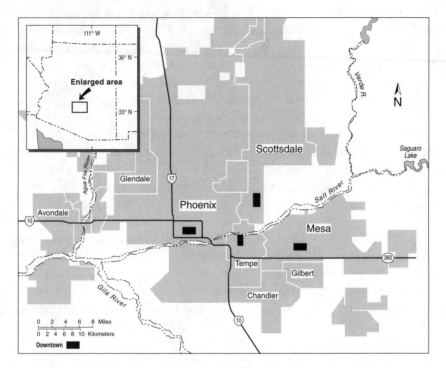

Figure 8.1: Municipal boundaries and major downtowns, Phoenix metropolitan area

vacated the Salt River Valley about five hundred years prior to Anglo occupation.

For most of the early twentieth century, the Phoenix area was an agricultural production complex supplying oranges, alfalfa, and cotton to other parts of Arizona and to growing metropolises elsewhere like Los Angeles. During these early years, the cities and towns of the valley were relatively tight spatial units with a large percentage of the area population living either in or adjacent to the downtowns. After World War II, however, the population exploded in size and extent as the region began to assume its present-day sprawling form. This growth was aided by the placement of two large Air Force bases (Luke and Williams) in the valley by the federal government during World War II. The diffusion of air-conditioning technology and the aforementioned geographical capital switch were also important to the area's growth. Unlike many major conurbations in the Southwest, Phoenix-area growth has not been seriously inhibited by its wa-

ter supply. During the early years of the twentieth century, the federal government subsidized the creation of a series of reservoirs to the east and
north of the valley to support the agriculture economy and to protect
against floods. Named the "Salt River Project," this impressive system of
water provision keeps water bills at an astonishingly low level in the area
and does not seriously inhibit growth in most of the valley's cities. The
overwhelming tendency toward suburban sprawl seriously eroded several
valley downtowns after World War II. Downtown Phoenix and Tempe
were hit particularly hard, while Scottsdale fared only slightly better during this period (Russell 1986; Schmandt 1991). Simply put, the sprawl had
even diluted the cores of the suburbs.

The flight of department stores from downtown Phoenix in the 1950s
was followed by offices as the central core ceded increasing power to its
satellite municipalities. With an underdeveloped expressway system restricting auto access to central Phoenix, the core became an increasingly
inefficient location for all but a few banks and government services. In an
effort to reverse the fortune of its downtown, Phoenix declared its core a
redevelopment zone in 1979, clearing the way for property condemnation
(Schmandt 1995).

Downtown Redevelopment in Phoenix

The core area of Phoenix has experienced phenomenal growth in recent
years. One telling indication of this growth has been the decline in the
number of blocks associated with redevelopment.[1] In its first 110 years of
existence, the seventy-four–block Phoenix downtown was reduced by only
eight blocks. Between 1980 and 1995, the number has been reduced by
twenty-four blocks, a testament to the restlessness of the landscape. Recent
developments continue to rework the urban palimpsest in the core, including the Bank One Ballpark (1996), the Arizona Science Center (1996),
and the Phoenix Newspapers Incorporated Building (1996). This wave of
redevelopment was preceded by an equally prolific wave that included the
new Municipal Hall (1993), the America West Arena (1993), Renaissance
Square (1990), the Arizona Center (1990), and the Mercado (1989). Most
of these structures are located in the eastern frame of the downtown "zone

1. I am referring here to block assemblages associated with redevelopment. The absolute size
of the downtown has remained the same while internal assemblages have reduced the number
of freestanding blocks.

of assimilation" (Ford 1994), which has been the prominent direction of core growth for several years.[2]

The review process that a given land use project in Phoenix must undergo varies depending upon its size and location. For small projects outside of the core area, a proposal goes through the eleven-step site plan evaluation process carried out by the development services department (McKinley 1996). Here, a project coordination manager is assigned; he or she becomes the developer's contact with the city. In most cases, the developer must correspond with this person regarding every aspect of their proposed structure, from zoning to design review. Ideally, this process (which alone can consume six months) is the full extent to which the developer must deal with the city.

For the large developer wishing to build in the core, however, the development protocol becomes more nebulous. Most large-scale developers wishing to build in downtown begin the development process by notifying a high-level official in either the economic development or planning departments (Hatmaker 1996). Depending upon the extent and nature of the project, advisory teams are usually assembled from pertinent city departments who work with the developer to create an acceptable plan for review. This process includes, at the very least, a staff member from development services, but it often involves an official from the planning, economic development, zoning, law, and finance departments. Once negotiation at this level has been completed, the developer typically takes the proposal to the planning commission, which hears the case and makes a recommendation to the city council, which has the final say. The planning commission is a council-appointed board of citizens to which city staff must report with recommendations. If negotiations with city staff go well, the developer's plan will probably get approval. If, on the other hand, a compromise cannot be made with city staff, it is likely that the development will be stalled indefinitely or perhaps canceled outright. It is the policy of the city council to accept the recommendations of the planning commission and the board of adjustment (Hatmaker 1996), so any attempt to appeal the lower board's decision is not likely to be successful. In effect, then, the initial negotiation with the city is enormously important for the developer wishing to build in downtown Phoenix.

2. Ford has argued that the spine of office buildings emanating from the north of downtown Phoenix along Central Avenue is the zone of assimilation for Phoenix (1994). While I agree that during the 1970s this was clearly the direction of core growth, in recent years (mid-1980s to the present), redevelopment on the eastern edge of the core has redefined the zone of assimilation for the city.

The actions of the city's staff and boards are motivated by a planning exercise that occurred during the late 1970s and early 1980s (City of Phoenix 1985). The area was designated a redevelopment zone in a 1979 plan resulting from extensive input from local landholders. The designation enhanced the city's ability to condemn needed property in the area through eminent domain. Property condemnation was necessary in one of the developments (the Arizona Center) that will be discussed later, but not in the other (the Mercado) because the city already owned the site. A 1985 follow-up general plan for the entire city attached more specific zoning changes to the core district (City of Phoenix 1985). The most pertinent of these changes were those that encouraged higher density and paved the way for generous land-use variance offers. More recently, a twenty-five–year "vision" plan for the downtown area was ratified by the city council in 1991 that was based upon the earlier exercises (City of Phoenix 1991). It is worth following some projects through this land use review protocol in order to show how the actual development process plays itself out within these constraints.

The Arizona Center Development Process

The Arizona Center is a Rouse Corporation development that started in 1987. The 18.5-acre site is home to two large office buildings ("One Arizona Center" and "Two Arizona Center") totaling over 800,000 square feet and a retail structure of 150,000 square feet. A 2,700-car parking garage and a three-acre garden are also found on the site.[3] The sheer mass of built form dwarfs what was there prior to construction—the megastructures that now occupy the property were preceded by modest traditional and modern structures a mere fraction of their size. Historically, the site served as part of the Churchill Addition (one of the first residential subdivisions in Phoenix) and the St. Mary's Hospital; after World War II there were many blighted residences in the site. Immediately prior to redevelopment, the site was characterized by the semi-public uses of the nearby St. Mary's High School, the commercial office uses of the local newspaper, and the vacant land in the northern portion of the site.

In 1984 (see figure 8.2), the Phoenix Community Alliance (PCA), a local growth machine coalition, began working with the city to develop what was then referred to as the "Superblock" (Herold 1990). The PCA is com-

---

3. The long-term Arizona Center plan calls for a large hotel, a movie theater, more parking, and at least one new office building.

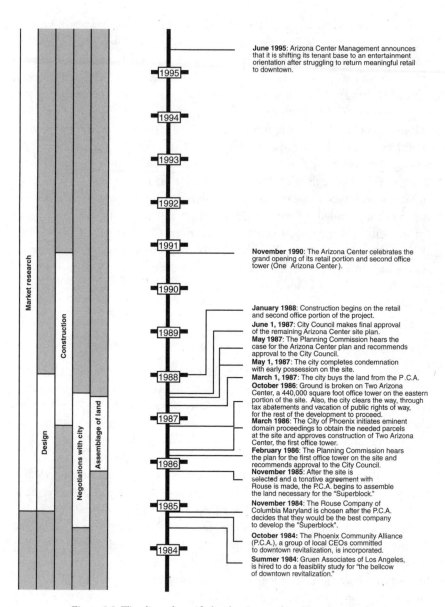

Figure 8.2: Timeline of specific local actions and construction phases, Arizona center development process

Source: City of Phoenix 1987; Deters 1995; Dragos 1989; and Schmandt 1995

158

posed of chief executive officers from local corporations, several of which now consume the majority of Arizona Center office space. The PCA's purpose was to build a vibrant, mixed-use facility in downtown Phoenix—a "bellcow" of core revitalization (Dragos 1989). In the summer of 1984, the PCA hired Gruen Associates of Los Angeles to do a feasibility study for their idea. In only a few months, they had identified several possible locations in the frame of the downtown area. It was decided that the present site, north of Van Buren between Fifth and Third Streets, would be the easiest to acquire and the best to develop. The first task was to find an appropriate developer for the project. The Rouse Corporation, so famous for its past accomplishments, was chosen from a pool of three developers. Within a year, the developer had compiled a detailed project proposal; it was to be their biggest development to date (Cook 1990). Meanwhile, the PCA had begun assembling the needed land with their own money. In early 1986, the city of Phoenix aided this process by condemning the few needed parcels of land at the site (Dragos 1989). The city later bought the land from the organization for $13 million (City of Phoenix 1987). In addition to assembling the land for Rouse, the city also gave them $40 million in tax incentives. Not surprisingly, Rouse had little problem dealing with city regulations and began construction of their first office tower in October 1986. The future profitability of this building was fairly certain, as the chief executive officer of Pinnacle West, a PCA member, agreed to move his company into the facility; the company virtually filled the structure. While the initial tower was being constructed, Rouse conducted extensive market research and designed the remaining retail and office portions. By June 1987, the site had been completely rezoned to the needs of Rouse's plan. Construction on the retail portion began only six months later, in January 1988 (Phoenix Community Alliance 1988). The first phase of the project cost $200 million, with the long-term plan for the site estimated at $515 million.

Rouse's aggressive marketing campaign for the Arizona Center was extensive in scope. Regular press releases gave the local papers abundant material to script a narrative of "renewal" in the urban core. Local newspaper articles ranged from technical details of the development itself to the vacation habits of Rouse executives. Many felt that this project could finally push Phoenix to the next level of national urban prominence. Financing for the project was obtained with little problem from Citicorp, aided no doubt by the Rouse Corporation's reputation for success. The development's first phase of two office towers (including the one already built), a retail center, a parking garage, and a three-acre garden was rapidly constructed in a year and a half. In November 1990, after the project had officially become the

"Arizona Center," the retail portion of the complex opened. The ceremony was attended by hundreds and was accompanied by a marching band hired to help kick off the rebirth of retailing in downtown Phoenix, Rouse style. Scarcely a decade after its opening, however, Rouse was forced to redefine the role of the Arizona Center from a retail magnet to an entertainment node for the valley (Deters 1995). This was in response to market research surveys in which local residents viewed the Arizona Center as more of an entertainment facility than as a legitimate shopping center. Rouse altered the tenant mix to meet this perception, with some success.

The Mercado Development Process

While the Arizona Center development process was characterized by expedient financing and significant private leadership, the nearby Mercado functioned as a tangible symbol of financial misconduct and mismanagement by its developer, J. Fife Symington, who later became governor of Arizona (and later still a convicted felon[4]). While this development was also within the 1979 redevelopment district, it is much smaller, both financially and spatially, than the Arizona Center. Encompassing two original city blocks, the Mercado is composed of 72,000 square feet of boutique retail and 45,000 square feet of office space. The $15.3 million redevelopment took approximately a year and a half to build. The design is a postmodern interpretation of Spanish mission revival architecture. Six separate buildings surround a courtyard to form a rendition of a festive Spanish town square. Prior to construction, the city-owned, four-acre site was being used as a parking lot for nearby municipal facilities. Since its construction, the Mercado has been a failure, eventually leading to Symington's bankruptcy and legal problems.

The development process for the Mercado (see figure 8.3) was initiated when the developer—Symington, in partnership with a local nonprofit organization Chicanos Por La Causa[5]—approached the city with a proposal for a mixed-use redevelopment in downtown with a Hispanic theme. A plot of land at the southwest corner of the intersection at Seventh Street and Van Buren Street was identified for the project (Trost 1988). In May 1986, planning permission was granted to build the facility with the stipulation that it be financed by July 17, 1987 (City of Phoenix 1988). As an incentive, the city council offered the developer a $1.3 million tax break. The fi-

---

4. Symington was eventually pardoned by President Clinton.
5. The role of Chicanos Por La Causa in the development of the Mercado was quite limited.

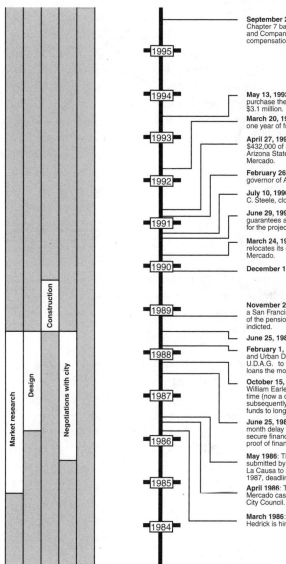

September 20, 1995: Symington files for Chapter 7 bankruptcy protection after McMorgan and Company make it very clear that they want compensation for the failed project.

May 13, 1993: Union pension trust funds purchase the Mercado at a trustee sale for $3.1 million.

March 20, 1992: Mercado merchants request one year of free rent after plummeting sales.

April 27, 1991: Symington appropriates $432,000 of State money to Arizona State University's annual lease in the Mercado.

February 26, 1991: Symington becomes governor of Arizona.

July 10, 1990: The first failed retail tenant, C. Steele, closes its doors.

June 29, 1990: Symington personally guarantees a $10 million long-term loan for the project.

March 24, 1990: Arizona State University relocates its downtown campus to the Mercado.

December 1, 1989: The Mercado opens.

November 23, 1988: McMorgan and Company, a San Francisco investment group, assumes control of the pension fund money invested after Miller is indicted.

June 25, 1988: Construction begins.

February 1, 1988: The U.S. Dept. of Housing and Urban Development approves a $2.7 million U.D.A.G. to the City of Phoenix, which subsequently loans the money to the Mercado Partnership.

October 15, 1987: The Mercado Partnership pays William Earle Miller, an investment manager at the time (now a convicted felon) $10,000. Miller subsequently commits $11.1 million in pension funds to long-term financing for the Mercado.

June 25, 1987: The Phoenix City Council approves an eight-month delay to allow the Mercado developers to secure financing. Symington promises to show proof of financing agreement by July 17, 1987.

May 1986: The Phoenix City Council approves a plan submitted by the Symington Company and Chicanos Por La Causa to build the Mercado. They set a July 1, 1987, deadline for J. Fife Symington III to secure financing.

April 1986: The Planning Commission hears the Mercado case and recommends approval to the City Council.

March 1986: Local architectural firm Cornyer Hedrick is hired to begin designing the Mercado.

Figure 8.3: Timeline of specific local actions and construction phases, Mercado development process

Source: City of Phoenix 1988; Dougherty 1995; Hemphill 1994; and Jarman 1995.

161

nancing stipulation was a difficult one to fulfill, as the Mercado was a risky, self-enclosed retail center located barely within walking distance of the Phoenix office core. On June 25, 1987, the city agreed to extend the financing deadline eight months after Symington had failed to corral the requisite funding in time (City of Phoenix 1988). With the city applying pressure to build, the Symington Company became ever more desperate to find a long-term financier. First Interstate Bank of Arizona decided to take the risk by loaning the developer $10 million for construction, but only on the (very routine) condition that a long-term financier be found elsewhere. Symington paid $10,000 to local investment fund manager William Earle Miller as a loan processing fee, "a fee that [was] later alleged to be illegal" (Dougherty 1995, p. 10). Miller subsequently agreed to commit $11.1 million of the Arizona Laborers, Teamsters, and the Cement Masons Local 395 pension trust to the Mercado (ibid.). The final piece in the funding package was a federal Urban Development Action Grant to the city for $2.7 million that was, in turn, loaned to the Mercado Partnership. Construction began on June 25, 1988. The investment manager was fired shortly thereafter by the pension fund participants after an unrelated criminal indictment; the San Francisco–based McMorgan and Company was contracted to fill in as the new pension fund manager.

The Mercado finally opened in December 1989, just before the Christmas season (*Phoenix Gazette* 1989). In large part, the deal was secured because the developer personally guaranteed the loan. McMorgan and Company forced him to do so after they assumed responsibility for the pension fund money. Without the guarantee, the financing probably would have fallen through. In these beginning stages, the Mercado boasted a respectable occupancy rate (70 percent) but mostly in its retail space (Novotny 1989). On March 24, 1990, Arizona State University (ASU) decided to relocate its downtown campus into the empty Mercado office space. Shortly thereafter, the developer became governor of Arizona and subsequently approved $483,000 in state money for ASU's annual $598,000 Mercado lease (Dougherty 1995). In the end, however, not even Symington's prominent position could revive the moribund facility.

Several years after completion, the Mercado sat virtually empty, its developer bankrupt and convicted for federal offenses related to the project. After an attempt by Symington to get the city to purchase the Mercado, McMorgan and Company finally bought the land from the city for $800,000 and the governor's share for just over $3 million, a fraction of his defaulted obligation (Hemphill 1994). McMorgan and Company reinvested in the Mercado hoping to capitalize on spillovers from several recent core redevelopments like the Bank One Ballpark and the Arizona Science Center, both within walking distance. Like Rouse with the Arizona Center, McMorgan and Company tried to reorient the character of the development from retail to entertainment by signing several new restaurants to fill some of its 45,000 square feet of space (Jarman 1994).

The development processes in Phoenix can be characterized by their generous municipal tax incentive packages and general willingness to accommodate land developers. The strategy proved successful for the Arizona Center, while the Mercado incentives have done little more than delay the decline of a project fated for death anyway. The major theme of the processes is that returning traditional retail activity to the core is easier said than done, at least in downtown Phoenix. Both facilities have redesigned their purpose to serve more as entertainment meccas than shopping centers. The latter use, it seems, is still firmly planted in the shopping malls of the suburbs, like Scottsdale.

Downtown Redevelopment in Scottsdale

Downtown Scottsdale is a 1.2-square-mile district tightly coalesced around its main arterial, Scottsdale Road. In addition to its two major shopping malls, the Fashion Square and the now-empty Galleria, the city has four specialty retail districts: Old Town, West Main, Craftsman Court/Marshall Way, and the Fifth Avenue area (City of Scottsdale 1993). Combined, these six areas account for 2.8 million square feet of retail space in the downtown area alone, the majority of which is located in the two developments to be described later, the Fashion Square and Galleria (City of Scottsdale 1993).

At the time of the two redevelopments in question, the city's land use review protocol was a bit different than it is today (Roe 1996), so its character in the late 1980s will be the focus here. Like Phoenix, the quantity and quality of interaction that a developer might have with the city varied considerably, depending upon a project's magnitude and location. For the small-scale developer, the city's "one-stop shop"—Scottsdale's equivalent to the development services department in Phoenix—was the only office with which they were required to interact. Here, the developer was assigned a case manager who guided them through the process. The case manager worked to get the developer's plans to merge with the city's general objectives and made recommendations to the development review board (DRB) regarding the plan. If the project was over 200,000 square feet, two hearings with the DRB were required—one to discuss issues of density and another to review architectural style (Roe 1996).

Massive redevelopment projects like the ones described here required a more complex protocol. With very large downtown projects, the city assembled an interdepartmental team to negotiate with the developer. Typically, this team included officials from Scottsdale's planning and economic development departments who dealt with long-range general planning issues and an official from the community development department who dealt with zoning ordinance issues. The planning commission and board of adjustment were only advisory boards to the city council. The development review board has some decision-making autonomy, but all of their decisions were ultimately appealable to the city council (Roe 1996). In the cases considered here, the large-scale developers needed only to deal with the planning commission and the development review board. The city staff from the two departments made recommendations to these council-appointed boards during the hearings.

The city's stance on development in the downtown area was driven primarily by its existing plan, which was approved in 1984 (City of Scottsdale 1984) and amended in 1986 (City of Scottsdale 1986). It was based on several years of citizen participation in the late 1970s. Although the problems facing downtown Scottsdale were nowhere near as severe as the problems facing the central core in Phoenix, by the 1970s the Scottsdale core had also become a casualty of sprawl. It had lost some of its original vitality, so the citizenry made a concerted effort to refocus attention on the downtown area. The most prevalent issues at the citizen forums dealt with relieving congestion on Scottsdale Road and keeping a small-town atmosphere, should redevelopment pressures intensify. The plan called for the creation of a "couplet street system" to divert traffic around the congested Scottsdale Road through the core area. Retail intensity was to be highest within the confines of the two couplets (Roe 1996), and buildings were supposed to retain the small-scale western flair that had given the city its vernacular identity. Given their relatively strong negotiating stance with developers, the city was able to get most of the couplet street system constructed with private money and little risk. In both of the cases (Fashion Square and Galleria) described here, the city required the developers to construct the couplet street adjacent to their property if they wanted to get the project approved (Roe 1996). The city only provided a subsidy if, after construction, the mall was successful at generating sales tax. If not, as in the case of the Galleria, the developer was forced to absorb the loss. With the Fashion Square, however, the city later paid the developer for work done on the western couplet (Goldwater Boulevard), as the development has been successful at generating revenue.

The Scottsdale Fashion Square Development Process

The Scottsdale Fashion Square, an immensely successful mixed-use redevelopment located on the northwest corner of the intersection at Scottsdale and Camelback Roads, was transformed from a basic outdoor shopping mall in the early 1980s into the largest enclosed mall of its kind in the state of Arizona by the early 1990s. The multi-staged development process (see figure 8.4) culminated in the joining of this mall with the adjacent Camelview Plaza, itself a 500,000-square-foot structure (Jarman 1995). Together, the enclosed mall contains over 1.4 million square feet of retail and specialty retail space in addition to an office tower containing 120,000 square feet. In all, the $150 million project consumes fifty-seven acres of downtown space, by far the largest of the projects being examined in this chapter. Westcor, the developer and current owner, acquired the property from a pension trust organized by Coldwell Banker in 1984 (James 1996). Westcor, like Rouse, is known for its success in retail development, although mostly on a regional basis. Westcor controlled over ten million square feet of shopping mall space in the valley at the time of development (Fickess 1994). Their market specialty is the suburban shopping mall, and they do not often stray from this niche.

Once Westcor had acquired the property where the Fashion Square now sits, they went about the task of redeveloping it. Their initial plans were very modest, as they wanted only to refurbish the existing mall. However, after long negotiations, a team of planners and economic development officials from the city persuaded Westcor to "think big" with their plans for the property (Roe 1996). Such requests were possible because of the city's relative ease in attracting development in the mid-1980s. As a result, they were able to take a much more aggressive stance on this and other land-use issues than Phoenix could.

After a few years of planning and further negotiation, Westcor unveiled a three-phase plan to redevelop the property into the largest mall in the state. The first step was to construct a controversial office tower on the southeast corner of the site (the northwest corner of the intersection at Scottsdale and Camelback Roads). Its 100–foot height exceeds the city's height limit by 35 feet; its variance was allowed by a legal loophole that has since been closed. Sam Campana, a Scottsdale councilperson (now the city's mayor), was publicly castigated by other council members for asking

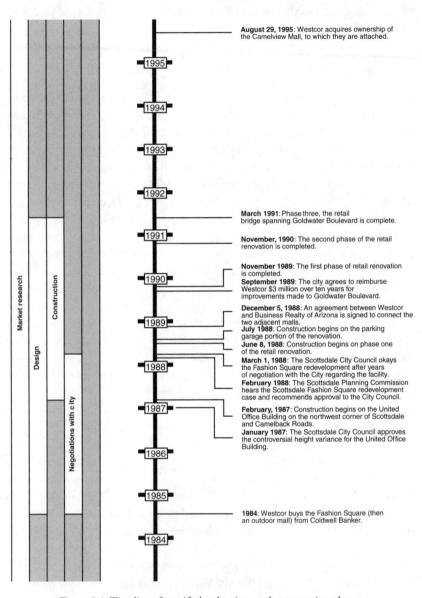

August 29, 1995: Westcor acquires ownership of the Camelview Mall, to which they are attached.

1995

1994

1993

1992

March 1991: Phase three, the retail bridge spanning Goldwater Boulevard is complete.

1991

November, 1990: The second phase of the retail renovation is completed.

November 1989: The first phase of retail renovation is completed.

1990

September 1989: The city agrees to reimburse Westcor $3 million over ten years for improvements made to Goldwater Boulevard.

December 5, 1988: An agreement between Westcor and Business Realty of Arizona is signed to connect the two adjacent malls.

1989

July 1988: Construction begins on the parking garage portion of the renovation.

June 8, 1988: Construction begins on phase one of the retail renovation.

March 1, 1988: The Scottsdale City Council okays the Fashion Square redevelopment after years of negotiation with the City regarding the facility.

1988

February 1988: The Scottsdale Planning Commission hears the Scottsdale Fashion Square redevelopment case and recommends approval to the City Council.

1987

February, 1987: Construction begins on the United Office Building on the northwest corner of Scottsdale and Camelback Roads.

January 1987: The Scottsdale City Council approves the controversial height variance for the United Office Building.

1986

1985

1984: Westcor buys the Fashion Square (then an outdoor mall) from Coldwell Banker.

1984

Market research

Design

Construction

Negotiations with city

Figure 8.4: Timeline of specific local actions and construction phases, Fashion Square development process

Source: Arizona Republic 1988; James 1996; Jarman 1995; Meyhill 1996, and Roe 1996

166

Westcor to offer the city something in return for the variance (*Arizona Republic* 1988).[6] Nevertheless, construction on the retail portion of the plan began on June 8, 1988 (James 1996). Later, Westcor did receive an indirect incentive when the city gave one of their tenants, Niemann-Marcus, a $3 million sales tax abatement—an act that was next to unheard of for the city of Scottsdale at the time. All land costs, taxes (except for the aforementioned abatement), and infrastructure financing were handled by the developer.

Westcor's reputation helped them to obtain financing easily. The construction loan was arranged through Citibank. The long-term financing was a combination of an internally arranged real estate investment trust (REIT) and a pension fund (Meyhill 1996). In all, the construction loan was as high as $180 million, but the mall was sold to the long-term investment groups for just over $100 million (ibid.). The remainder of the debt was absorbed internally by Westcor and offset by the city's reimbursement for alterations made to the couplet street system.

Today, Westcor still manages the mall and the United Office Building on its southeast corner. They recently acquired the Camelview Plaza, the adjacent mall, after years of trying to do so (James 1996). Opinions are mixed about the design of the Fashion Square and the process that created it, but no one can deny the success that the facility has had in the intensely competitive Scottsdale retail market. The management at the Fashion Square now boasts an occupancy rate of 99 percent—an astonishing figure considering the tenancy problems faced by regional malls throughout the Valley's overbuilt retail landscape (Fickess 1994).

The Scottsdale Galleria Development Process

Even though the Scottsdale Galleria was developed under a similar public planning scenario and private market context to the Fashion Square, it was a miserable failure during its short tenure in the early 1990s. The 427,000-square-foot boutique retail mall was built in the late 1980s for about $115 million. Unlike the other three projects being examined in this chapter, the Galleria is strictly retail; no office space exists on the site. Altogether, the redevelopment spans seven acres—two original city blocks—in downtown Scottsdale.

The Galleria development process (see figure 8.5) began with the part-

6. It should be noted in fairness that while Campana was publicly ridiculed for this behavior, it is very routine for the local state to negotiate with developers within a neoliberal political atmosphere.

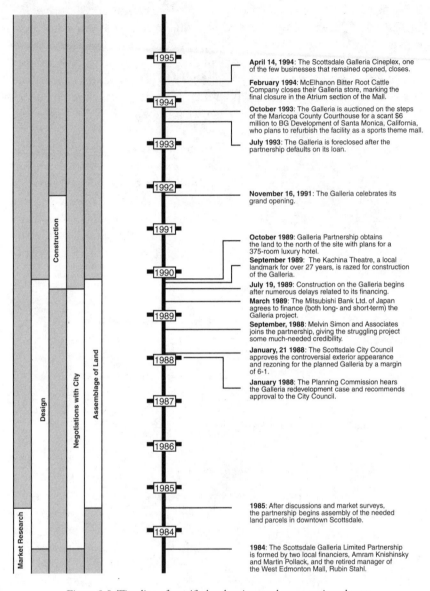

Figure 8.5: Timeline of specific local actions and construction phases,
Galleria development process

Source: Arizona Republic 1989; Morrell 1988; Roe 1996; *Scottsdale Scene* 1988

nership of local financial and real estate figures Amram Knishinsky, Rubin Stahl, and Martin Pollack in 1984 (*Scottsdale Scene* 1988). The association was named the Scottsdale Galleria Limited Partnership. In September of 1988, the partnership was joined by the renowned shopping mall developer Melvin Simon and Associates, the third-largest shopping center owner in the United States at the time. Once the partnership was established, the first task was to select a site. The chosen site required the assembly of thirteen parcels of land, but they were eventually able to obtain only twelve of these parcels (the design was modified to accommodate the smaller lot). At several junctures in the development process, city officials tried to convince the partnership that their plans were a bit too extravagant (Roe 1996), but the developers kept pushing their plan (backed with the financial resources to do so) for the "largest mall in the world without an anchor tenant." In order to justify its size to skeptical banks and city officials, the partnership made hyperbolic claims that the Galleria would attract a market base as far away as Los Angeles, Las Vegas, and Tucson (*Scottsdale Scene* 1988).

The land acquisition—a privately funded event—began in 1985 and was paralleled by an aggressive marketing regime that depicted the Galleria as "Arizona's answer to Rodeo Drive" (Morrell 1988). The partnership eagerly began to sign up tenants in the late 1980s before they had even secured financing for the land. At one point before the complex was built or the land even acquired, the partnership had signed intent contracts for almost 75 percent of the space within the facility; actual opening day occupancy only reached 50 percent (McDonnell 1990). Despite the promising early numbers, banks were not convinced; several times the project nearly buckled because it lacked adequate financing. Like the Mercado development process, the developers of the Galleria had to return to the city for reapproval after long delays in arranging financing. A Japanese firm, the Mitsubishi Bank, finally put up most of the money for both construction and long-term finance. Their share of the $123 million facility was nearly $100 million (*Arizona Republic* 1989). Once construction began in July 1989, the building was completed in just under two and a half years.

It did not take long for the Galleria to confirm the worst nightmares of those closely involved with the project, especially the city officials who had tried to get the partnership to curtail it from the start. Only three years after the investment, the Mitsubishi Bank was forced to auction the foreclosed facility to B. G. Development of Santa Monica, California, for a scant $6 million. After several attempts to refurbish the facility under a different theme, the massive structure now sits empty, save for one restaurant and an IMAX movie theater.

The two Scottsdale redevelopments are characterized by developer-led processes, as opposed to those in Phoenix that had to be pulled along by the city government. Much of the zeal to invest in Scottsdale was prompted by an early 1980s study that characterized the Scottsdale retail core as servicing one of the fastest-growing and affluent populations in the country (Gruen Gruen and Associates 1982). The amount of planned retail space that was subsequently brought to the city of Scottsdale exceeded the amount that retailers could successfully fill. This put the city in an advantageous negotiating position, which allowed them to make demands of developers that would be virtually unthinkable in development-desperate Phoenix. Their strict control did not, however, always translate into success, as the case of the Galleria illustrates.

Redeveloping commercial spaces in central business districts has become arguably the most high-profile form of economic development for cities in the United States since the 1970s. Though the spaces in question are typically small in size, their development often entails the commitment of enormous resources by the state at various scales to offset risks posed to real estate capital. But while commercial redevelopment is highly popular, there are serious questions about its larger success on a variety of dimensions. First, as the cases here (and certainly elsewhere) show, there is no guarantee of success even when an experienced developer is offered considerable public resources to assist their endeavors. Selling the urban core to outsiders cannot by itself reverse the fortunes of a struggling regional economy. Second, commercial redevelopment often entails a diminution of public space (see Mitchell 2003). Though many commercial redevelopments are publicly funded or supported, most are regulated and policed by the private sector. Third, while some of these developments have produced jobs for local residents, they are often of a much different sort than those that preceded the development. Despite recent organizing successes, most service employees are still non-unionized, and entry-level work in the retail and hotel sectors tends to be poorly paid, often on a part time basis, and without serious opportunity for advancement. With this record, there are serious questions as to why cities continue to choose this path of economic development. Perhaps the largest reason for the reluctance to abandon this path has to do with the discourse of inevitability that accompanies neoliberalism (see chapter 10). Transforming the local state into a more aggressive vehicle for business and selling the cultural assets of a particular place are increasingly seen as the only option for struggling regions. Many city officials see such efforts as a "natural" response to the broader structural changes discussed earlier. It allows them to promote business, downsize government, and privatize resources on high-profile spaces in their urban cores. The commercial core has become the billboard of neoliberal governance in American cities, mega-projects the featured product.

PART 3

CONTESTING THE NEOLIBERAL CITY

This book is about the influence of neoliberalism on the process of urbanization. One of the central arguments is that there is an urban geography to neoliberalism, and that the practices associated with it is sometimes at odds with theoretical neoliberalism. Urbanization occurs in actual places with their own cultures, histories, economic structures, and institutions, and of course they affect how any generalized ideological influence like neoliberalism actually works in practice. But while the spatial contingency of neoliberal urbanism is evident, it is just as clear that there are some of the changes happening to cities appear to be independent of locality. Neoliberal urbanism is characterized by a departure from managerialist governance and a different form of wildly uneven development. Beneath these abstractions lie palpable changes—many of them negative—for real people in real cities. Those people have been removed from welfare rolls, public housing, and unionized jobs in the direct—more often, indirect—name of neoliberalism. Some of these people have begun to organize a resistance movement to these changes.

The final section of this book looks at various efforts to alter or even reverse the course of neoliberal urbanism. Such struggles are a crucial part of understanding neoliberal urbanism, even though they have yet to impede its progress meaningfully. The section is organized inductively, first with a consideration of a very specific struggle by public housing tenants to contest the liberalization of housing policy in the United States (chapter 9), followed by a more general discussion of the material and discursive obstacles to challenging neoliberal urbanization and its consequences (chapter 10). The latter draws on the rich body of critical literature on social movements that may be useful at devising alternatives to the neoliberal city. The story of anti-neoliberal activism is, of necessity, the most incomplete one of this book, because meaningful resistance to neoliberal urbanism is only now developing, and it is taking place in a highly fragmented way. This section attempts to glue some of these fragments together and to frame questions for future inquiry.

Chapter 9

Social Struggle in a Neoliberal Policy Landscape

Neoliberal urbanism is highly segmented and far from complete. Public housing, social welfare, and other Keynesian artifacts still exist, and their destruction is neither inevitable nor complete. But while the segmented and contradictory nature of implemented neoliberalism has been made abundantly clear by a variety of scholars, the difficulties of political organizing within this context have received less notice (for notable exceptions, see Gilbert 2001; Glassman 2001). This chapter attempts to begin this discussion by exploring efforts to retain public housing in the United States. It uses such efforts to explore whether the fight for basic necessities (adequate food, housing, and so on) is fundamentally the same as it was under Keynesianism or whether the extremely uneven and segmented policy landscape of neoliberalism has had an analogously fragmenting effect on such struggles. Is it more difficult for movements to retain public housing under a neoliberal policy regime than it was under a Keynesian system? Furthermore, given neoliberalism's spatial contingency, is it more difficult to retain public housing in a relatively socially progressive city like New York City than it is in, say, Atlanta? And above all, what can we learn from these difficulties to guide future struggles?

The basic theses of this chapter—and the section overall—is that neoliberal social policy has had a fragmenting effect on progressive activism and that there are important lessons to be learned from current activist projects attempting to operate within a neoliberal context. In particular, efforts to "jump scale"—conceived here as the ability to widen individual social struggles into a broader movement (see N. Smith 1992a)—are powerfully inhibited by the fragmented policy landscape that undergirds public housing in the United States. The first section of this chapter provides some general background on the U.S. public housing system in order to situate the subsequent case study more precisely. The second section describes three central obstacles facing activists and tenants endeavoring to retain the public housing stock. The conclusion uses this case study to think about the wider implications of progressive political organizing within a neoliberal context.

Opposing the Destruction of Public Housing in the United States

As discussed in chapter 3, public housing is a marginalized institution within the already marginal welfare state in the United States. It has remained smaller in size than in other advanced capitalist nations, and it has never enjoyed a strong constituency. Despite this, it was not until the HOPE VI program of the 1990s (and beyond) that a systematic policy was developed to remove public housing outright. Not surprisingly, there have been many battles to prevent or even reverse the destruction of public housing throughout the United States, but so far they have remained local in their orientation. Such struggles are often initiated by tenant leaders (usually elected to a tenant council) and assisted by outside activists, particularly lawyers who donate their time to assist tenant groups but also members of local groups like the Seattle Displacement Coalition or national groups like the Association of Organizations for Community Reform Now (ACORN) who assist with rallies, alternative redevelopment proposals, and tenant rights counseling. Thus far, despite the national scale of the program, such local efforts have failed to spread into a wider movement for public housing. The following case study attempts to address why this has been the case by engaging in discussions with public housing agency (PHA) officials, residents, and community leaders at 54 HOPE VI awardee sites.[1] Additionally, the Housing Research Foundation's online HOPE VI archive was used to identify major litigation and tenant complaints across the United States. The intent was to identify the key inhibitors to larger-scale activism growth in this context.

Based on these sources, it appears that there are at least three broad rea-

1. There are 164 HOPE VI implementation grant recipients in total.

sons that a wider social movement for tenants has thus far been elusive. First, the details of HOPE VI implementation often include a physical dispersal of tenants who do not qualify for a redeveloped housing unit. The geographic dispersal of these tenants has undermined activism by making it physically harder to organize than was the case when tenants were closer to one another. Second, litigation has been the preferred method of anti–HOPE VI activism. Because such an approach requires a narrowing of tenant issues to correspond with relevant case law, activists have been less able to widen the message of such movements in many circumstances. Finally, and perhaps most important, the discursive framing of HOPE VI cleverly situated the policy as "progressive" and those who disagree as "resistant to change."

The Impact of Implementation

Within the HOPE VI policy framework, there is a conspicuous lack of regulation governing how housing authorities choose tenants for redeveloped communities. This is no accident, as one raison d'être for the program was to return power to PHAs in the governance of their tenants (see U.S. HUD 1995). One central consequence is that tenants often lack a clear understanding of how to receive a better housing unit once redevelopment is complete. In certain locations, the process resembles a lottery, with a lucky few receiving units, while in others it more closely resembles a competition based on a variety of factors including the tenant's credit history, past behavior, or participation in any activism against the PHA. Those who "lose" this competition are often given Section 8 vouchers, if not removed from the public housing system entirely. There are two pertinent consequences to the highly variable way that HOPE VI units are meted out. First, the competition ethos fostered by the process of unit allocation makes it difficult to enlist tenants in critical activism because many feel that their chances of receiving a redeveloped unit will be significantly undermined by participating in such activity. Second, the dispersal of tenants through Section 8 makes it logistically more difficult for activists to organize tenants.

Most tenant groups dealing with HOPE VI have expressed some concern about displacement resulting from the implementation of the policy in individual complexes. In some cases, such as New York City in the mid-1990s, the fear of displacement was sufficient to organize tenants against the HOPE VI program. Tenant groups were successful at limiting the PHA's efforts in this case. The New York City Housing Authority pursued and won only two HOPE VI grants since the program's inception; in both cases it pursued a strategy of full unit retention. In most cases, however, tenant groups have neither the level of organization nor the wider political support enjoyed by activists in New York, so their protests are less critical and often less successful. More often, tenant groups protest an aspect of the HOPE VI process early on in the planning stages. These protests have taken many forms (rallies, litigation, and so on) but are often undermined by the very process they are contesting. That is, because a certain percentage will receive a redeveloped housing unit, tenants are often faced with the de facto choice of trying to receive such a unit or fighting against the program in general. The PHA typically offers tenants the opportunity to "participate" in the formal planning process (for a critical description of this process, see Keating 2000), and many realize that this could enhance their chances of receiving a redeveloped unit. Conversely, many also realize that participating in any activism antagonistic to the overall plan or the PHA could undermine their chances of receiving a redeveloped housing unit. In Miami's Carver Housing Complex, for example, tenants were initially unified in their opposition to the HOPE VI program. But as the planning process continued and began to appear inevitable, self-interest started to cleave tenant organizing. Families that the PHA had no apparent interest in housing remained active against the plan (see Robinson 2001), but many others began to do everything in their power to put themselves in a favorable light with the PHA. When asked why she was participating in the HOPE VI planning process given that much of her constituency did not support her in doing so, Carver Tenants Association President Lottie Hines remarked, "HOPE VI is here. There's a new development coming. Let me be part of it and get what I can out of it" (quoted in Robinson 2001). This sentiment, replicated in many HOPE VI implementations, can be devastating to unified activism when the PHA has no intention of providing all affected tenants with a housing unit.

The actual method of dispersal also has the effect of undermining activist efforts. Dispersing tenants through the device of Section 8 vouchers often does not produce the intended result of deconcentration or desegregation (Hartung and Henig 1997), but it is the most common method of removing tenants from the original housing complex. Often, such tenants are forced to move into neighborhoods as poor and segregated as the public housing complex from which they were displaced, and sometimes it can even translate into a de facto eviction from the city (because of a lack of Section 8 units). Much of this is because landlords are not legally required to accept tenants with Section 8 vouchers, so tenants are not actually "free to choose"[2] any, or even most, housing in the private market. Some land-lords who are willing to accept vouchers contract with HUD for an ex-tended period of time (usually forty years) to have their entire development dominated or entirely composed of voucher recipients. Such landowners typically have difficulty in siting complexes of this sort in all but poor neighborhoods. Residents of more powerful neighborhoods in the United States have consistently and successfully resisted the siting of almost any form of public housing. Those that do not contract with HUD on a formal basis are often either the owners of large multi-family developments or the owners of property in poor communities who derive some benefit from their participation. In many large cities, existing opportunities for Section 8 redemption had already largely been filled before HOPE VI was even im-plemented. In cities like Chicago, for example, as many as 30 percent of the tenants awarded vouchers as part of the HOPE VI program must either re-turn the voucher within a few years or move to another city where such units do exist (Fischer 1999). In short, allocating Section 8 vouchers as a method of dispersal is plagued with well-documented problems (for a fuller discussion, see Hartung and Henig 1997). This issue is revisited here only to underscore the point that Section 8 voucher recipients in HOPE VI plans often do not receive a better, or even less segregated, residential en-vironment. Because such tenants are removed from the public housing de-velopment site (even if they are not "dispersed"), the likelihood of their participation in activism over the development of that site decreases. Once displacement has taken place, it is much harder for tenants to organize be-cause many of the most likely participants have already been removed. To be sure, tenants who have been "vouchered out" face an array of problems that are conducive to activism, but they are often different from those sur-rounding the HOPE VI development site itself.

Anti–HOPE VI Litigation

Litigation and the filing of formal complaints by tenant groups against PHAs and HUD has arguably been the most common form of protest against the HOPE VI program.[3] The litigation approach, however, was

2. The paternalistic notion that public housing authorities were doing tenants a favor by award-ing them vouchers was rife throughout HUD's promotional material for HOPE VI, and it was also common in my discussions with HOPE VI award complex managers.
3. This is not to deny the significance of activist litigation that was very much in line with the goals of HOPE VI in the early 1990s. Inequitable demolition plans in at least thirteen Ameri-can cities were the ironic result of settlements of well-intended lawsuits filed on behalf of ten-

largely unsuccessful at broadening individual struggles or even at achieving gains within the frame of the judiciary. Most court cases take enormous resources to pursue properly and, more importantly, require tenant groups to atomize their grievances into separate and locationally specific issues. This section describes several examples of anti–HOPE VI litigation to illustrate the point. Three anti–HOPE VI litigation strategies have emerged: (1) highlighting the issue of displacement; (2) noting violations of due process; and (3) pointing out improprieties in the procurement of private developers for the complex.

Highlighting displacement was one of the most common strategies of anti–HOPE VI litigators. Litigation of this sort focused on the unreasonable nature of tenant screening, "broken promises" by the PHA, and civil rights violations made during the development process. The complaint that tenant screening grew too punitive under the HOPE VI program was voiced by activists in Seattle, San Francisco, Miami, and New Brunswick, New Jersey, among other places. Much of the criticism focused on the unreasonable credit screening, housekeeping checks, and security procedures to which those who receive rehabilitated housing units are subjected. The sharpest criticism was reserved for HUD's "One Strike and You're Out" policy described earlier. Activists argue that the policy is being used as a way to "weed out" many of the tenants waiting for better housing units.

A second strategy used by activist lawyers is to highlight a "broken promise" or accuse a PHA of negotiating in "bad faith" after the number of public housing units fails to live up to the number promised. This approach was used by the United Public Housing Residents (UPHR) of Washington, D.C., who filed a formal protest petition against HUD in the spring of 2001 for what they considered "bad faith" negotiations by the District of Columbia PHA in the Arthur Capper–Carrollsburg HOPE VI application process (DeVault 2001). The petition, signed by 67 percent of the tenants in the complex, protested the overwhelming use of Section 8 vouchers in a housing market like that of the Washington, D.C., area. They argued that the use of Section 8 vouchers was not a legitimate way for the PHA to deal with the needs of tenants, because there are not enough eligible units in the D.C. area, and those that do exist are predominately located in neighborhoods that have the same problems of income and racial segregation that beset many public housing complexes. Using vouchers as

---

ants to deconcentrate urban poverty by demolishing public housing complexes. But as the details of these settlements emerged in the mid-1990s, the overwhelming emphasis of tenant litigation has been directed against the HOPE VI program and its methods.

a method to house the extremely poor, the UPHR argues, was thus a flawed, or even disingenuous, policy instrument of the PHA (ibid.). Little resulted from their action, however, as the HOPE VI implementation process at Arthur Capper–Carrollsburg continued. Other groups using this strategy have met a similar fate.

In another case, residents of the Desire Housing Complex in New Orleans filed a lawsuit in October 2001 against the PHA and its former director, Michael Kelly, for negotiating in "bad faith" and conspiring to displace thousands of impoverished tenants to make way for middle-class residents (ibid.). The New Orleans Housing Authority received a $44.3 million HOPE VI award in 1994 to demolish 1,832 units in the complex. In their place, the PHA promised to build 575 housing units, 280 of which would be public rentals. The remaining tenants were promised housing vouchers or some other form of housing within the remaining New Orleans public system. As the development process progressed, however, tenants began to complain not only that the number of replacement units was too small but also that the PHA had not properly negotiated with them about the development in the first place (ibid.). Furthermore, as with many other HOPE VI development plans, the public units were the first portion of the proposal to be discarded by PHA officials when development costs proved unexpectedly high.

Another strategy used by tenant activists is to assert that civil rights violations have been committed or to highlight the disproportionate impact that the HOPE VI program inflicts on certain groups. In St. Louis, for example, tenant groups filed a lawsuit against their PHA because its $44.7 million HOPE VI plan for the Darst-Webbe Housing Complex displaced African Americans at a disproportionately high rate (Housing Research Foundation 2003). The 1995 plan called for the demolition of 1,206 public housing rental units, to be replaced by only 576 units of a similar type. The remaining residents were forced out of the complex, mostly with Section 8 vouchers. In December 2001, a U.S. District Court judge found in favor of the PHA, and the HOPE VI process is now proceeding as planned (ibid.).

This has not, however, deterred other activists or housing attorneys from attempting to highlight the impact of HOPE VI plans on certain groups. In Miami, for example, the Florida Justice Institute assisted former residents of the James E. Scott and Carver Homes Complex in highlighting the disproportionate impact of a 1990s HOPE VI grant on large families. In a lawsuit filed in September 2001, tenants argued that the Miami-Dade Housing Agency illegally conspired to displace thousands of tenants, particularly large families, by refusing to build enough apartments with more than two bedrooms (Robinson 2001). As part of their 1999 HOPE VI award for $35 million, the Housing Agency promised to replace 215 of the 850 units that they would demolish in the two complexes. As elsewhere, most relocated tenants would be given Section 8 vouchers. But as the lawsuit asserted, the Housing Agency was not serious about serving all residents, since only ten of the planned public rental units would contain more than two bedrooms and there is a well-known paucity of large (over two bedrooms) Section 8 apartments in the county (ibid.). The legal action taken by the tenants was not successful at getting more large units built.

Arguing a violation of due process is a another broad litigation strategy currently being employed by anti–HOPE VI activists. A number of tenant groups involved in a HOPE VI application process assert that PHAs have not properly included their participation. In one case, Octavia Anderson, the former president of the Scott Homes Resident Council in Miami, filed a suit against the Miami-Dade Housing Agency for refusing to recognize her as the tenants' representative after she made her disapproval of their HOPE VI plan evident (Housing Research Foundation 2003; Robinson 2001). She survived an effort by the PHA to remove her (after a favorable court decision) but was unable to stop a highly market rate–oriented HOPE VI plan, despite widespread tenant feeling for her and against the plan. In another case, residents from Cincinnati's Lincoln Homes Complex complained that the PHA disregarded their input during a planning process that culminated in a $31.1 million HOPE VI award in 1998 (Housing Research Foundation 2003). Former tenants filed suit against the Cincinnati Housing Authority in 1999, alleging that it had not properly followed HUD's participation requirements. The case was later dismissed by a Judge Sandra Beckwith, who found that there was no federal law requiring such consultation with tenants.

The final legal strategy that aims to disrupt the HOPE VI program in individual cities has been to highlight improprieties in the procurement of developers for the housing complexes in question. In many cases, there have been serious conflicts of interest where, for example, a PHA director uses his or her influence to obtain a construction contract for a company on whose board of directors he or she sits. The aforementioned case of the New Orleans Desire Complex is one such example. Tenants there argued that former PHA director Michael Kelly improperly channeled a contract for development of the complex to a nonprofit organization called New Orleans Works that he had previously established (DeVault 2001). Though probably successful at embarrassing Kelly, their strategy was unsuccessful at derailing the HOPE VI implementation there. In another case, the Seattle Displacement Coalition (SDC) charged a local developer involved in the city's Holly Park HOPE VI Complex, Bruce Lorig, with violating HUD's conflict of interest rules (Bush 1999). Lorig, the chosen developer for the complex, allegedly used his position of influence to divert a $1.9 million contract to an architectural firm with which he had business ties. The allegation was serious enough to prompt an investigation by HUD. But while auditors ultimately agreed with the SDC's complaint, they only asked that the Seattle Housing Authority implement a better strategy for dealing with such complaints in the future (Baca 2000). The legal strategy neither slowed the development process nor impeded the involvement of the private developer in question.

In general, litigation against the HOPE VI program has not been favorable for tenant groups. Though legally successful on a few issues, litigation has thus far been unable to derail a single HOPE VI plan or any of the policies supporting it. More important, the experience demonstrates that this approach, for all of its potential at remedying short-term conflicts, can atomize and decontextualize (whether intentional or not) individual tenant grievances if pursued in isolation from a wider movement for change.

Discourses of "HOPE"

The legal system is not the only means through which the conflict in public housing has been articulated. The "official" policy discourse of the HOPE VI program, as it was conveyed by the media, PHA officials, planners, and housing scholars, effectively silenced dissent for the program by generating a narrative that situates the program as an "inevitable" and even "progressive" intervention by the state to "empower" tenants. Displacement has been obscured in the prevailing narrative of HOPE VI, changing even tenant conceptions of the process. Though the discourse and justification of HOPE VI have a variety of intellectual and political sources, one of the recurrent themes of this discourse has been public housing's inferior physical design. It is worth exploring this particular theme to shed light on the larger effect of such discourses on current activist efforts.

Improving the architectural design of public housing is a central justification for the HOPE VI program. The program mostly targets prototypical high-rise public housing "projects," encouraging PHAs to replace such structures with garden apartments and townhouses scattered throughout the city. The underlying discourse focuses on how the physical design of most public housing (1) stigmatizes tenants, by forcing them to live in dwellings that stand out from the rest of the housing stock; (2) makes crime prevention nearly impossible; and (3) makes activities like child care all but impossible. The idea of pointing out the flaws and improving the architectural design of public housing has a long history in the field of urban studies and architecture. Oscar Newman (1995; 1972) and Jane Jacobs (1961) are two of the original scholars who argued this point. Newman continues to be outspoken in this regard, suggesting that public housing's design fosters crime and discourages nearby real estate investment because it lacks "defensible space"—areas over which tenants feel a sense of ownership and can properly surveil. The work of both thinkers has influenced ongoing academic literatures in geography (for instance, Coleman 1985), architecture (Schnee 1998), and urban planning (Varady and Preiser 1998), which attempt, through various means, to evaluate how better-designed housing can influence tenants' attitudes, integration with the wider community, and chances for social advancement. The "failed architecture" argument has also been harshly criticized by a group of housing scholars who argue that the overwhelming focus on design obscures more important causes of "failure," such as congressional funding levels, federally imposed design restrictions, and pressure from homebuilding lobbyists to make public housing "stand out" (Marcuse 1998; Stockyard 1998; Bristol 1991; Bratt 1990).

The point of mentioning this literature here is less to engage with the debate itself than to note that only one side was co-opted by the HOPE VI policy discourse. The notion that public housing problems are reducible to a series of design mistakes is now popular among many housing planners, PHA officials, and increasingly, tenants. It is used not only to justify the current state intervention in public housing but also to frame such intervention as a progressive, self-correcting response to one of the "most serious" problems of public housing. Obscured in this discourse is, of course, any mention of either the copious amount of scholarship contesting this notion or the displacement that this intervention is causing.

The "failed architecture" theme was repeated in media accounts of both the HOPE VI program and general critiques of the public housing system during the 1990s. Almost every mainstream media portrayal of new public housing focused on the improved design of HOPE VI replacement housing. Critical discussion by lawmakers and tenant activists was obscured by the imagery of new garden apartments that HUD successfully promoted through such outlets as *CNN*, *20/20*, and the *New York Times*. One of the more in-depth media discussions of public housing design took place in the

Chicago Tribune in 1995, the year that the federal government took control of the Chicago Housing Authority (Kamin 1995a, b, c). Like other journalistic representations of the problem, this discussion focused predominately on public housing's physical design and on the pronounced need for an alternative (see also Vergara 1989). The language of "defensible space" and "failed architecture" is rife throughout this and many other media accounts of both the HOPE VI program and public housing in general.

Policy designers at the federal level frequently deploy the discourse of "failed architecture" as well. Henry Cisneros, former HUD director and key promoter of the HOPE VI program in the mid-1990s, very directly deployed the discourse on a number of occasions (see Cisneros 1995a, b; U.S. HUD 1995). In one of his speeches on the subject, for example, he explains that,

> We are replacing the worst of the housing units . . . that have, for too long, been the settings for our children's urban nightmares. . . . Instead of the super blocks of Cabrini-Green, grids of traditional streets are being designed. Instead of mammoth apartment buildings, small-scale, townhouse-style housing is being constructed. (1995b, p. 30)

The theme of "failed architecture" continued to be central to the HOPE VI program even after the departure of Cisneros. HUD, for example, sponsored three workshops in 2000 to educate HOPE VI recipients on better architectural design (Housing Research Foundation 2003). The workshops were organized by the Congress for New Urbanism and the American Institute of Architects, key promoters of neotraditional design in public housing. Attendees were to come away from the meeting with a series of "best practices"—all of which focused, as the sessions promised, on physical design, not on how to ensure that most of the existing tenants have access. Though the conference organizers never promised anything other than a focus on design, the choice by HUD to devote such attention to this topic itself illuminates the importance of this theme within the HOPE VI policy discourse.

The discourse of improved design has also been deployed locally in the HOPE VI planning process itself. Tenant involvement in this process often consists of a series of design charrettes in which architects, planners, and PHA officials gauge tenant feelings about design by displaying professionally drawn images of the apartments that will be built. Not surprisingly, many tenants are very pleased by the idea of moving into better-designed apartments. That many will not have the opportunity to live in such structures is seldom emphasized. A documentary film by Ronit Bezalel and Antonio Ferrera entitled *Voices of Cabrini* (2000) provides excellent footage of this process in Chicago, where PHA officials were very open to discussing what the housing would look like but refused to explain who exactly would receive this improved housing. Discussions with residents and PHA officials elsewhere conducted as part of this study suggest a similar pattern in other cities.

How does the discourse of "failed architecture" or any other pro–HOPE VI narrative serve to undermine activism? Political organizing is, at a minimum, about scripting a version of reality that differs from the one being used to suppress, distract, or confuse the reality of those affected. In the case of HOPE VI, the prevalent discourse is one that, on the surface, enjoys almost universal agreement, even (perhaps especially) among tenants. By deploying the language of design, policymakers are able to frame the federal government as a "savior" of sorts, who finally "decided" to improve the lives of tenants by improving the design of their dwellings. Situating the problem and solution as such has the effect not only of obscuring the regressive impact of the state's intervention but also of allowing for a "solution" that is relatively easy for policymakers to achieve (unlike the more complicated solutions to urban poverty). The very legitimate arguments that have countered (or repositioned) this discourse and the reality of displacement following HOPE VI implementation are both obscured. Tenant activists have more difficulty linking the issue of displacement to a wider set of principles, not least because the prevailing discourse has so successfully obscured the fact that displacement even took place.

The individual travails of public housing tenants in a variety of American cities are not entirely local but rather part of a larger restructuring of public housing policy, which is itself part of the larger neoliberal policy regime. The supply of affordable units in the public housing stock is decreasing rapidly, and conditions for tenants everywhere are becoming more punitive and less redistributive. Despite this, it has been extremely difficult to generate a movement or consciousness that links together the struggles of tenants in each affected city. Rather, the activism has remained focused on the local details of injustices occurring at particular housing developments. In this case, at least three specific factors inhibit such struggles from emerging as a wider movement for public housing retention in the United States. First, HOPE VI plans, like other manifestations of post-Keynesian welfare (for example, workfare), foster an ethos of competition among residents wishing to obtain better opportunities—in this case, a redeveloped housing unit. Many tenants realize that their chances of receiving such a unit will be undermined by participating in activism that is antagonistic to the PHA and, conversely, enhanced by their support of the "inevitable" plan. Moreover, once demolition does take place, most residents are permanently removed from the site and surrounding neighborhood, further undermining the potential for geographically focused activism. Second, the overwhelming focus on litigation as a strategy serves to narrow the issue at hand, in part because the judiciary requires its participants to link their claims to the existing legal framework, which is often not conducive to "jumping scale." Finally, the state successfully promoted a discourse that situates this particular intervention as a progressive one, not least by co-opting only superficial arguments about the problems of public housing.

Though it is difficult to tell how applicable these factors are to other activist efforts, cases such as this can be useful for understanding neoliberalism as it actually exists. A few generalizations emerge. First, in parallel with the larger Keynesian landscape under neoliberalism, political organizing designed to motivate redistribution within the current context is highly uneven and fragmented. Numerous relics from the Keynesian era (such as public housing, but also various forms of income redistribution and Keynesianesque labor regulations) still exist, and they are plainly worth fighting for. But often, the fight for such artifacts entails a time-consuming localization of the struggle. It is very difficult to motivate a larger struggle, in other words, when there are very specific (and apparently achievable) local objectives in mind. A related second point is that this case demonstrates not only that the evolution of neoliberalism is far from linear, but also that, more importantly, the rollback/destruction is not nearly as complete as it is often framed to be in the United States. Though constantly under attack, Keynesian artifacts still shape the lives of many people, including but not limited to public housing tenants. The enduring presence of such institutions obviously affects how redistributive social struggles take place. Finally, this case helps to underline the fact that neoliberalism can at once be both a unified meta-concept *and* a locally contingent, actually existing set of policies that contradict one another. The ideas underlying neoliberalism are relatively unified and reproduced by a specific set of institutions (IMF, bond rating agencies, Washington consensus, etc.), but at the same time the geography of neoliberal implementation is much more complicated. This poses an obvious problem for redistributive activism (the aforementioned problem of fragmentation), but it also poses an opportunity, as the complicated geography of implementation exposes a series of fissures, not only in the logic of neoliberalism but also in the scope of its enforcement.

Chapter 10

Alternative Futures at the End of History

In 1989, scarcely months before the Berlin Wall fell, a little-known U.S. State Department policy planner, Francis Fukuyama, wrote an essay entitled "The End of History?" (1989). In it, he surmised that the battle of ideologies was over; that rationalism had defeated tribalism; that capitalism had defeated communism; that democracy had finally overcome aristocracy and fascism. All we had left to fear was centuries of boredom, and an occasional pre-historical ideology causing a regional skirmish now and again. Western liberal democracy was set to spread uncontested across the globe, as all major pre-historical challenges had been defeated. His provocative essay drew much attention from social scientists and commentators. Some deemed it a seminal document in the proliferation of global neoliberalism. Many others were highly critical, but in retrospect it does appear that his idea was eerily prescient. The Berlin Wall would fall a few months later, soon followed by the Soviet empire, and the 1990s saw the most rapid spread of neoliberalism in history. It is now difficult to imagine a serious, desirable, and systemic counter-ideology to neoliberal capitalism.

Curiously, though, enormous effort is still spent by the neoliberal right, countering a left that apparently (according to Fukuyama) does not exist. Peter Saunders, a prominent neoliberal urbanist intellectual, has even lamented that

> Capitalism has . . . created a class of opinion leaders who no longer believe in or endorse the traditional bourgeois values of hard work,

individual effort, family responsibility and Christian charity. The influence of this class, not only on the masses but even on the bourgeoisie itself, is pernicious and profound, for even the capitalist class is losing faith in its own creed. (1995, pp. 116–17)

A strange sentiment from a member of the supposed winning team of history, but he is apparently not alone in his fear that this class of "opinion leaders" might return us to a history where liberal capitalism is contestable. The massive pecuniary contributions made to neoliberal think tanks, the aggressive purchase and cooptation of media outlets, and the funneling of cash to sympathetic politicians is curious in a time when all serious challenges to neoliberal capitalism are said to have been dissolved. An entire cadre of its supporters are furiously working to keep its image intact and to counter a set of "opinion leaders" who dare to challenge its power—to spin the contradictions of neoliberalism as either inevitable, completely expected, or desirable, when they are none of the above.

How might this be explained? Could it be that we have returned to history? Or could it be that western neoliberal capitalism is neither natural nor functional for everyone and that, as such, sympathetic institutions and people must actively work to maintain its credibility? These are not easy questions to answer, but they are certainly important to consider at a time when the terrain of ideological conflict has shifted so much. This chapter briefly explores some of the challenges to neoliberal urbanism with such an intent in mind. It details some of the strategies, rationales, and mindsets being used to counter neoliberal urbanism. What follows, however, is not a quixotic road map for "replacing" neoliberal urbanism. Much of the discussion focuses on the challenges (internal and external) facing activists who are trying to forge a more progressive form of urbanization.

Though cities have historically been both the most active centers of incipient ideologies like neoliberalism, they have also been the most active breeding grounds for alternative visions. A critical exploration of the discursive and material challenges to a systematic counter-ideology to neoliberal urbanism is thus a starting point for a much wider discussion of a systematic counter-ideology to neoliberal capitalism in general. This chapter is necessarily the most speculative, incomplete, and hopeful of the book, as the project of neoliberal urbanism and its discontents is very much a story in progress.

Existing Threads of Resistance

There are at least five overlapping threads of resistance that offer some hope of change and that are useful to consider in this context. Each is concerned with either protesting one of neoliberalism's impacts through direct action or bypassing it altogether to form progressive alternatives. Though none has thus far coalesced into a systematic challenge to neoliberal urbanism, they are all useful to consider.

One set of movements aims to protect or preserve gains made under the Keynesian managerialist state (see chapter 9 for an example). Within American cities, the fight to save public housing, space, welfare, hospitals, child care, and the like have been the most conspicuous activity of this "neo-Keynesian" sort. As Gilbert (2001) points out, such struggles are actually not new with, for example, a set of welfare rights institutions active since the 1960s. They have, however, become much more conspicuous since the mid-1990s, when the federal government so effectively dismantled welfare and public housing "as we knew it." Success among groups with this approach has been highly limited, as they have been marginalized by a neoliberal and neoconservative right (Kristol 1995). The former has decried the "inefficiency" and "lack of choice" within the public sector, while the latter has used racialized stereotypes—"welfare queens" being the most famous—to marginalize recipients of aid as lazy or unintelligent.[1] But while the neo-Keynesian variant of anti-neoliberalism has achieved little success and sometimes appears reactive, if not quixotic, the actual participants of these struggles are literally and figuratively on the front lines for those adversely affected by neoliberal urbanism. In a sense, theirs is the most purely anti-neoliberal urbanist struggle currently afoot, and much can be learned form their efforts, successful or not.

The "anti-globalization" movement is a second struggle worth considering (see, among others, Glassman 2001). I use this label with caution, though, because Klein (2002), among others, has argued that this label is mainstream media-imposed and misleading; the target of such organizing has not been globalization per se but rather the corporate-led, neoliberally inspired centralization of global resources in a small number of institutions and individuals. But coming up with an alternative or appropriate label for this movement is no easy task—even for sympathizers—because it is, by design, an extremely diffuse amalgam of sub-movements, NGOs, activists,

---

1. See in particular Murray (1994; 1984) for an extended version of the neoconservative viewpoint.

and labor unions—each with a slightly different raison d'être. The internal diversity—and division—within this movement is certainly remarkable, but most of its participants are primarily concerned with disrupting the wheels of neoliberal globalization. This involves direct action against the mechanisms and methods of neoliberal globalization, including the quasi-state institutions (IMF, WTO, G-8) that promulgate and perpetuate its vision. Unfortunately, as Defilippis (2003) has argued, the efforts of most anticorporate globalization activists have thus far remained limited to such global institutions alone. This approach has generally failed to "localize," either by linking up with the more mundane problem-specific struggles occurring daily in cities or by considering the systematic linkages between global and local neoliberal policies. However, they provide the most direct ideological attack on neoliberalism—despite the comparative lack of focus on cities in particular.

A third set of struggles have coalesced around the goal of economic justice, particularly the right to a living wage. They tend to be the least openly ideological and the most pragmatic of the three threads of resistance considered, but they have garnered important attention from the socialist left (Merrifield 2002; Soja 2000). Such struggles are organized in an Alinsky-esque (1971) fashion of agitating to improve the economic (or social) plight of a particular group in response to a particular injustice. Labor unions form a core of this struggle, if not *the* core, but it would be mistake to confuse it as a simple extension of the racially exclusive and nationalist American union movement of the mid–twentieth century (see Ranney 2003 for a discussion of this). First, the economic justice movement is neither union- nor industry-specific, but rather an amalgam of the disenfranchised—service workers, welfare recipients, the unemployed. Second, the movement is less parochial than "traditional" U.S. unions. It is characterized by a wider variety of affected industries and sectors, and the most common source of new participants are poor immigrants to the United States—not disaffected unionists from big industries that have fallen on hard times. Though the activities of economic justice advocates have drawn criticism for their parochialism and "unimaginative pragmatism" (Klein 2002, p. 27) from others on the left, their efforts are worthy of consideration here not least because their collectivist strategies provide a direct challenge to the neoliberal notion that individual autonomy (and responsibility) is normatively ideal no matter how much it adversely affects individuals.

A fourth group of movements worth considering includes those centered around the private real estate development in cities. As argued earlier, inequitable real estate development in cities is the knife-edge of neoliberal urbanism, reflecting a wider shift toward a more individualist and market-driven political economy in cities. Gentrification, publicly funded projects for private benefit, and the demolition of affordable housing are all part of this knife-edge, and all of these are occurring in very different locales. Yet while the geographical scope of such events seems clear, it has been much more difficult to link such struggles together on a systemic basis. Most struggles of this sort tend to be rather small in size and to concentrate on the gentrification of a particular neighborhood or even the development (or demolition) of a single building. Because such struggles are so intrinsically local, it is often difficult to widen the struggle beyond the issue at hand. The narrowness of focus is often paralleled by an equally narrow, or at least equally pragmatic, ideological foundation. Though such struggles are often assisted and even organized by openly political groups, much of their support comes from individuals who are concerned about a particular development and its implications for their day-to-day life. They are also often beset with a plurality of class interests that can end up in conflict. The development of a sports stadium in a mixed-income neighborhood, for example, is disruptive to everyone living there and, as such, could inspire a relatively general protest. With time, though, it becomes clear that the development affects various people differently. Small business owners, homeowners, wealthy renters, and poor renters, for example, have different interests, each of which is not necessarily compatible with challenging the neoliberal ideology underlying development in cities—or even with one another. These differences often inhibit a wider alliance against such development, but these struggles (no matter how factional in nature) tend to be the most "urban" and worthy of consideration here.

A fifth strategy that has emerged to counter neoliberal urbanism has been the collective ownership of various aspects of life that have been affected by neoliberalism. Defilippis provides perhaps the most comprehensive portrait of these efforts in his recent book *Unmaking Goliath* (2003), in which he notes that various communities across the United States have decided that collectivizing various resources is the most effective way to counter a neoliberal globalization that has typically left their neighborhoods with poor housing, few jobs, and a general lack of investment. Collectives of various sorts have existed in the United States since at least the nineteenth century, but are now being used to combat footloose capital and the forms of neoliberal individualistic governance that often follow in its wake. Defilippis argues that we can divide these movements into at least three categories. First, the collectivization of money involves communities that have either started printing their own currency or have opened banks that try to lend or pool money locally for the community. Second, the collectivization of work has taken place in a variety of locations where workers either purchase their existing workplace from a global corporation or start producing their own goods. Third, the collectivization of housing has taken the form of housing cooperatives and land banking practices that attempt to preserve affordable apartment buildings by removing them from the market and maintaining them for community (rather than individual) consumption. In all of these efforts, the underlying theme is to keep as much capital as local as possible and to replace individualist property rights with collectivist ones. Most of these efforts have emerged in situations of economic deprivation, but they hold great potential for rethinking the way that cities are "handed" neoliberalism "from above." Of course, it is not a given that such methods will always go toward progressive ends, and the numerical impact of such strategies has thus far been limited. But as Defilippis argues, it is not the raw number, size, or influence of such institutions that matters. "Their potential," he argues, "lies in what they represent, and the potential for greater local autonomy that is possible, rather than in what they are actually able to achieve given their limited size and capacity at this time" (2003, p. 12). To this extent, they offer a possible antidote to neoliberal urbanism that is useful to consider here.

Though comparatively small in scope, these five threads of resistance provide the most acute ideological opposition to neoliberal urbanism. But there are obvious and not-so-obvious obstacles to their expansion that activist scholars are just beginning to understand. What follows is a brief exploration of some of the challenges that transect these overlapping counter-ideologies to neoliberalism.

Obstacles to Challenging Neoliberal Urbanism

Each of the movement styles mentioned has struggled to generalize or expand beyond a narrow base. Though many localized obstacles to such an expansion no doubt exist, a number of scholars have pointed to more systemic obstacles that are worth considering. One of the most vexing challenges to an explicitly anti-neoliberal movement is that liberalism, particularly egalitarian liberalism, has a number of desirable features for progressives (see Katznelson 1997). As Mitchell (2003) points out, the issue of social rights for individuals (so common within neoliberal discourses) is a difficult one for the activist, particularly socialist, left to confront. Though many on the left, including Marx himself (1996, p. 172), have dismissed social rights as a thinly veiled concession by the state to avoid granting serious economic rights, most contemporary leftists are deeply conflicted about the issue. While it is clear that neoliberals have disingenuously co-opted social rights, it is difficult to attack this agenda directly. Neo-Marxists and egalitarian liberals have tried to deal with this issue by arguing that economic rights are a prerequisite for the meaningful experience of social rights, but they have had less success at pushing this subtle point than neoliberals have had at promoting their (ostensibly broader) notion of rights. Expanding the right to public space, for example, is certainly not going to solve homelessness in American cities, but it is difficult to argue against the idea that homeless people should have the right to sleep in public places (Mitchell 2003). In short, a deep and understandable ambivalence exists among the erstwhile challengers—both intellectuals and on-the-ground activists—to neoliberal urbanism because so much of it is couched in the language of individual rights. It is difficult to build a spirited resistance on such ambivalence. Moreover, contemporary activist intellectuals have proven far less effective than their egalitarian liberal counterparts of the late nineteenth and early twentieth centuries at separating the normatively positive attributes of neoliberalism from the normatively negative attributes. Neoliberalism and its proponents are able historically to claim—without much resistance—social rights as "their territory," in part because the left is ambivalent about the importance of social rights to a non-neoliberal alternative.

The notion of diffuse governance also serves to complicate challenges to neoliberalism more generally. As it is with social rights, the left is quite divided internally on the issue of diffuse governance. Some have agitated for a strong centralized regulatory state, while others argue for a diffuse model that is difficult to distinguish from ideal-type neoliberalism. Lake, for example, laments the decline of the large activist Keynesian state, especially its regulatory and redistributory potential. He argues that a return to "big government" is a necessary condition for future progressive social policy. The neoliberal penchant for diffuse governance is simply a red herring, according to this view, designed to shield a set of "business-friendly" policies that actually use a highly centralized state apparatus to assist capital (2002; see also Polanyi 1944). Others on the left are less inclined to favor "big government," progressive or not, because they feel that the concentration of power itself is the key inhibitor of social change. This view argues that the American state is already big and centralized, as are the key institutions that regulate this and other governments around the world—

rating agencies, currency traders, the IMF, and the like. Klein has been a most prominent articulator of this viewpoint. Her critique draws on a long line of leftist thought—particularly coming from anarchist corners—that argues that diffuse governance is a key to a more progressive future. She proudly describes the current anticorporate globalization movement as lacking a singular vision and describes recent attempts to create one as at best folly, at worst a replication of the centralization of power and ideology that allows corporations and neoliberal governments to wield so much power in the first place. Any resistance movement, she and others suggest, must be built on the principles of diffuse governance that respects individual perspectives. "One of the great strengths of this model of laissez-faire organizing," she argues, "is that it has proven extraordinarily difficult to control, largely because it is so different from the organizing principles of the institutions and corporations that it targets" (2002, p. 21).

The left is clearly not unified on the normative geography of power, but this is more than just an insular struggle. Not only do these ideological disagreements provide an additional source of dissent among erstwhile anti-neoliberals, they also paradoxically produce a confusing set of commonalities with the neoliberal right. This too, as discussed above, becomes an organizing hurdle when one of the key attributes of one's opposition (diffusion of governance à la Hayek and Friedman) is oddly similar to one's own ostensibly different vision (diffusion of governance à la Klein). It softens, or at least confuses, the terms of the debate, making anti-neoliberalism a more difficult project to build, even though neoliberalism is the stated target of many such activists.

The difficulties are not limited to ambivalence about ideology. A series of tactical differences have also inhibited a unified anti-neoliberalism from developing. Within the activist intelligentsia, arguably the most prominent of these differences is the split between what might be called discursive and direct action resistance. Discursive activism is rooted in the idea that neoliberal capitalism is itself a powerful discourse (in addition to being a set of material practices) that is often followed blindly. Neoliberal capitalism is often framed as natural, inevitable, or tending toward some higher-order equilibrium (Marcuse and van Kempen 2000). It is difficult to contest such a process without disrupting this set of beliefs. Providing images, narratives, and other writings that illustrate neoliberal capitalism's poor fit with is any of the above provides a meaningful challenge to its expansion (for a contemporary example, see Aune 2001).

Activist scholars have attempted to denaturalize neoliberalism by exposing its contradictions or demonstrating its weaknesses—much as the neoliberal right has done more successfully through think tanks and scholarship to discredit socialist or egalitarian alternatives. This line of thought has at least two historico-intellectual roots. First, there is the politics and scholarship of deconstruction, particularly the work of Jacques Derrida and Michel Foucault. They argued that all of the concepts that we use to understand society are themselves socially and politically constructed. We should abandon any hope of understanding and contesting a socially independent reality through traditional research means. Rather, we should explore the political history of the language used to describe and understand various concepts. Recent scholarship has argued that we can view capitalism, and our struggles against it, in a similar fashion. Gibson-Graham (1996) has argued that the prevailing narrative of anticapitalism, Marxism, suffers from its own debilitating conceptualization of capitalism (see also Gibson and Cameron 2001). They argue that any anticapitalism has to begin with a reconstruction of our understanding of capitalism itself, in particular an understanding that views capitalism as a porous system that can be exploited at the edges, rather than a monolith that must be attacked with force.

The second source of such activist thought is much older, dating back to the critical realism of political scholarship and art in the late nineteenth and early twentieth centuries. This work has a variety of sources, including Charles Dickens, Friedrich Engels, and Jacob Riis, but was relatively united around the goal of challenging (or disrupting) the hegemonic view of industrial capitalism by exposing to the common public its excesses, injustices, and inconsistencies. Contemporary forms range from the critical academic urbanism of Harvey, Smith, and Davis to the populist filmmaking of Michael Moore. Such efforts are actually not fairly similar in approach to the work done by neoliberal think tanks to discredit or denaturalize socialist or egalitarian alternatives. But the right has been vastly more successful at organizing around such work than the left.

Though few on the left would challenge such critical urban scholarship as irrelevant or normatively negative, some have challenged it as less important than either direct action organizing (see Merrifield 2002; Castells 1983, among others) or the formation of collectivist alternatives (see Defilippis 2003). Some activist academics have also dismissed such work as analytically weak, further undermining its ability to generate consensus against neoliberalism. Whereas the neoliberal (and, increasingly, the neoconservative) right enjoys a relatively cohesive relationship between its discursive wing (think tanks, right-wing journalists, and so on) and its direct action wing (elected politicians, conservative organizers, and so on), the anti-neoliberal left is beset with internal division on this dimension.

Why is this the case? Part (though not all) of the challenge is rooted in the obscurity of linkages between global-scale neoliberal institutions and the everyday processes that negatively affect the urban poor. It tends to be easier to organize the disenfranchised urban poor to reject the prevailing general ideology when there are particular negative outcomes to reject (Piven and Cloward 1977; Fainstein and Fainstein 1974). There are thousands of disparate struggles to resist or reject one of neoliberalism's manifestations—the erosion of public housing, public space, welfare, labor laws, and so on—but there is no unified struggle against the global forces causing these injustices, in part because the linkages between the former and the latter are not always clear or, at least, are not always *made* clear by activist intellectuals. The connection that globally neoliberal institutions—think tanks, rating agencies, and the like—have to cities tends to be too obscure to organize against effectively, so almost by necessity the power of a potential resistance is split into hundreds of local struggles in a variety of cities.

The difficulty of melding these struggles is compounded by an even deeper set of differences that have long beset the left. In his 1996 book *Justice, Nature and the Geography of Difference*, David Harvey recounts an experience of encountering a group of Christian fundamentalists who happened to be meeting at a conference next to one that he was attending. Curious, he roamed into the meeting rooms and conference halls of the fundamentalist conference and was struck immediately by the unity of purpose and message, despite the internal diversity of both. He left wondering why such unity has been so elusive for the activist and intellectual left. It may seem strange to begin a book about nature and difference with such a vignette, but Harvey does so to illustrate what he sees as a fundamental inability of the left to unite on a general set of issues. Rather, following from Raymond Williams, he suggests that the left is composed of various factions that have seized upon "militant particularisms" unwilling to build an ideological coalition with other disenfranchised ideas or peoples. Harvey's vignette is instructive here as well. Writers and activists trying to forge an alternative to neoliberal urbanism are far less able to unify around a set of principles than either the neoconservative or neoliberal right.

There are several understandable and historically rooted reasons for this difficulty. First, the various political challenges to neoliberalism in general, and to neoliberal urbanism in particular, come from a much more diverse set of sources than do the promoters of such ideas themselves. Anti-neoliberal activists are motivated by feminism, anarchism, Marxism, Keynes-ianism, poststructuralism, and environmentalism, among other ideologies, while the intellectual motivation of neoliberals tends to be more limited (see chapter 1). One particularly salient division to consider here is the split between the "New" and "Old" Left during the late 1960s (Levy 1994). Prior to this point, class reigned supreme as the organizing principle of the left, often at the direct expense of "other" injustices, like sexism, rac-ism, and colonialism (see N. Smith 2000; Levy 1994). Many anti-sexists, anti-racists, and anti-colonialists abandoned the "orthodox" left after it proved incapable of framing such injustices as anything but part of a thinly veiled "superstructure." The civil rights movement, the women's move-ment, and the anti–Vietnam War movement of the 1960s and 1970s pro-vided more successful vehicles for social change, so many scholars and activists simply abandoned Marxism, and with it the Old Left, in favor of the New Left.

These divisions were, of course, much more than esoteric matters of the-oretical interpretation. In one of the more iconic events in this transition (Old Left–inspired), construction workers in New York City physically at-tacked a group of (New Left–inspired) antiwar protesters in 1973 (Levy 1994). The workers saw their struggle as one that was so different from that of the protestors that it was worth a romp of roguish violence to prove it. The division between the interests of the Old Left and the New Left reached a symbolic apex in this event, but it was paralleled by a more sub-tle lack of interest in—indeed, sometimes outright rejection of—class among progressives in the United States (N. Smith 2000; Harvey 2000). This division is useful to bring up in this context because it complicates a "unity of purpose" among those trying to carve out an alternate urban re-ality. Proponents of neoliberal urbanism have a very specific and well-organized set of "economic" reasons for why this ideology should be in place, while the potential dissent is more fragmented and internally di-vided. Recent years have seen a rediscovery of class and more generally a more meaningful union between what Harvey deems "militant particu-larisms" and economic injustice, but these alliances are very far from solid at this point (N. Smith 2000). Class—or at least generalized disenfran-chisement—has returned to the social justice agenda, but it remains to be seen how well it confronts neoliberal urbanism.

The final obstacle to countering neoliberal urbanism is arguably the most challenging. It deals with the sometimes disingenuous way that ne-oliberalism is deployed by its promoters. Some argue that neoliberalism is simply a more popular packaging for the true agenda of its supporters, so it is used to mask neoconservatism—either a desire to retain the status quo or something more sinister like the demonization of urban minorities. This has both intellectual and organizing implications for the left. Intellectually, it makes ideal-type neoliberalism a more difficult idea to critique. Exposing the internally contradictions of neoliberalism, whether in its abstract form or in real life, has become common on both the right (Gray 1989; Kristol 1995) and the left (Brenner and Theodore 2002; Gough 2002; Kekes 1997). Scholars have, for example, seized on the contradictions posed by the simultaneous necessity of centralized power and diffuse governance within neoliberal thought, not to mention the hundreds of ways that idealized neoliberalism fails to live up to the outcomes it actually produces—public housing is *not* more diffusely organized, nor is real estate investment more rationally and equitably distributed. In short, there are many examples of actually existing neoliberalism contradicting its idealized roots. A more difficult issue is how to critique such ideas when they are used in a disingenuous way. Simply put, how does one critique neoliberalism when its proponents are merely using the ideas of neoliberalism as political cover for some other usually antisocial motivation or policy?[2] If the ideas of neoliberalism are simply a veneer to mask a much deeper cultural antipathy for a specific group or issue—the minority poor, taxes, regulations, and so on—then the project of critiquing them becomes rather onerous.

This obviously creates a problem for on-the-ground activists as well. As Alinsky would frequently argue, it is much more difficult to organize the disenfranchised around an abstract set of ideas than it is to organize them around its pernicious outcomes (1971). If neoliberalism is little more than red herring to distract attention from another policy, then it is not only difficult to organize against neoliberalism, it is also strategically questionable. The actual motivation or its actual outcome become logical targets for activists in this context, not the language of neoliberalism that is used so sanctimoniously. For example, organizing against the neoliberalization of public housing is superseded by fighting specific evictions; organizing against the ideal of neoliberal governance is elided by the fight against specific social service cutbacks for "welfare queens"; organizing against the uneven development unleashed by neoliberalism takes a back seat to fighting against reductions in affordable housing for minorities. This tendency

2. Polanyi (1944) is famous for making a similar argument about nineteenth-century economic liberals. He persuasively argued that their desire for a noninterventionist state was at best hypocritical and at worst demagogic, given the aggressive state actions necessary to impose this vision and the number of state policies that were directly designed to aid capitalists.

to disregard the general premise in favor of a particular event, policy, or outcome is especially pronounced in this case, because neoliberalism is so often used to justify a set of policies that are counter to its professed ideal. Reduced zoning regulations, real estate taxes, and subsidies for public housing are framed in neoliberal discourses about enhancing competition and choice when they are simply naked attempts to provide fewer impediments for a certain segment of society to accumulate wealth. It is not so much that neoliberalism is internally contradictory—although it is also that (see Gray 1989)—but rather that its proponents often use it disingenuously to promote a set of policies that are anything but liberal (whether classical, egalitarian, or neo-). It is difficult to stay focused or unified against neoliberalism when the ideology is widely seen as a cover for something else.

All told, the internal and external obstacles to building a desirable counter to neoliberal urbanism are substantial. Some are rooted in existing fissures among the left, while others are the product of more recent developments. Some, moreover, are tactical, while others are ideological. None, however, are natural or intrinsically insurmountable, and several movements have already arisen to contest neoliberalism in one form or another. That story is ongoing—but still worth exploring no matter how incomplete.

Curing the TINA Syndrome

Marcuse and van Kempen (2000) have persuasively argued that the success of neoliberalism is built on the widespread belief that "there is no alternative" (TINA) to such policies. The TINA syndrome is built on the discursive naturalization of neoliberalism. Neoliberalism gets transformed from a political movement into something that is natural, democratically chosen, or completely predictable. In this narrative, "socialism fails" not because of a concerted attack by monetarists but because its ideas were "unsustainable" or "against human nature" from the start. "History ends" not because of political reasons, but because humanity has realized its destiny. What other choice is there? After all, "there is no alternative," right? The bravado of this discourse would seem more absurd if the ideology of TINA was not been so successful. In many ways, TINA's success vindicates Fukuyama—not, of course, for Hegelian reasons but more simply because it creates a self-fulfilling prophecy. For the first time in history, there appears to be no significant challenge to the idea of unregulated liberal capitalism. If there is one necessary condition for challenging neoliberal urbanism and creating a more progressive urban realm, it lies in the rejection of TINA. Neoliberalism is hegemonic not because it "won" in a democratic, intellectual, or moral sense. It "won" because its powerful institutions and individual proponents organized enough people and interests to believe that there is no alternative; as with all hegemonic orders, its "victory" is always incomplete, contestable, and in flux.

It would be arrogant and naïve of this author to suggest a simple antidote to the prevailing TINA syndrome, but there are, I argue, hopeful lessons that can be learned from the experience of activists currently trying to replace neoliberalism with something fundamentally more progressive or even just a bit more compassionate. None of these movements has been successful at replacing neoliberalism outright, but they each have offered a model and alternative that future activists should heed. These movements offer potential antidotes to the TINA syndrome, and intellectuals on the left have much to learn from them, no matter how local or applied they may seem.

Merrifield (2002) describes one such movement—the struggle for a living wage—in his fantastic book on recent urban social movements in the United States (see also Soja 2000). He recounts in particular the activities of the HERE (Hotel Employees and Restaurant Employees) Local 100 Union in Los Angeles during the mid-1990s and their eventual success at procuring a living wage for a segment of society much broader than their immediate constituency. Before 1989, Merrifield notes, "the local was nothing more than a corrupt, top-down, white, old guard irrelevance" (2002, p. 78), but things began to change when Maria-Elana Durazo was elected as head of the union. She led the union on a more creative and militant path. Immediately, the union engaged in mass boycotts, protests, and mailing campaigns. Significantly, they also broadened their focus beyond a particular hotel, or even industry, by allying with different labor unions and community groups to form the Los Angeles Living Wage Coalition. They did meticulous research on other living wage campaigns in Baltimore and on the organizational layout of the industries that they were hoping to unionize.

Their efforts were impressive at reaching an agreement with all but one downtown hotel (the Bonaventure) to pay employees $8.15 an hour in 1997, to be increased to $11.05 after six years. This was $3 per hour more than the prevailing national minimum wage at the time and marked an impressive success for HERE Local 100, but they were not content to stop there. The union lobbied the city council to widen the benefits to a larger number of poor people in the city, and in March 1997 the L.A. City Council enacted a living wage ordinance (LWO) that required all employers receiving government contracts of over $25,000 to pay their employees at least $7.39 per hour ($8.64 without health insurance). The pro-business mayor vetoed the ordinance but was subsequently overruled by the council, so Los Angeles officially joined the ten cities that had LWOs of some sort or another at the time. There are now 130 municipal living wage laws in the United States (Living Wage Resource Center 2005), suggesting that this is more than a simple parochial struggle specific to L.A.

A second struggle worth considering here formed in response to mid-1990s cutbacks to welfare. One group that has received a great deal of attention is the Kensington Welfare Rights Union (KWRU) of North Philadelphia. They formed in 1991 under the umbrella of the National Welfare Rights Union (which formed in 1987 and has since grown). Based in the poorest neighborhood in Pennsylvania—Kensington, in North Philadelphia—the KWRU began as a specific response to Governor Robert Casey's proposal to reduce welfare expenditures to poor people in the state. The organization was (and still is) run by those actually affected by such cuts. The KWRU soon began to broaden its focus as the members drew connections between what was happening to them and poor people in other cities. As their promotional material suggests, after their initial direct action campaigns against the Casey cuts, they broadened their goals: "1. Speak to the issues which directly affect our lives; 2. Help each other, and all poor people get what we need to survive; 3. Organize a broad-based movement to end poverty" (KWRU 2005). Theirs was not a struggle to maintain a romanticized Keynesian status quo.

In 1996, the organization (along with its sister organizations in other cities) gained new relevance as the U.S. federal government enacted welfare reform under the "Personal Responsibility and Work Opportunity Reconciliation Act." It cut funding for welfare programs, implemented time limits on eligibility for welfare and public housing clients, and established work requirements for receiving existing benefits. Closer to home, KWRU members were also reeling from a proposal by Governor Tom Ridge (elected in 1994) to cut medical benefits to the poor in Pennsylvania. The KWRU reacted to these developments by organizing the "March For Our Lives"—a 140–mile trek to the state capital of Harrisburg to set up a tent city and protest these changes. The state legislature enacted laws prohibiting them from sleeping in the Capitol Complex or even to set up tents, so they began a walking campaign to protest the changes. They then joined forces with fifty-six other organizations around the country under the umbrella of the National Economic Rights Campaign to create a bus tour of the United States that would culminate at the United Nations in New York, where members testified that the United States was in violation of basic economic rights as set forth by the Universal Declaration of Human Rights.

Though similar in appearance to earlier welfare rights organizations—namely the National Welfare Rights Organization of the 1960s—Gilbert argues that KWRU and organizations like it are very different from their troubled predecessors (2001). First, it is led by people who are actually affected by poverty rather than middle-class professionals. Gilbert points out that earlier groups of this sort were often led by a benevolent but not impoverished class whose ideas and interests were often at odds with those in the movement. Second, the group is explicitly multi-racial. It has an intrinsic class identity, but it does not dismiss the influence of race and gender in the creation of poverty, unlike earlier movements that focused more on a particular dimension of inequality. Third, it aims not to ally with Democrats or Republicans but rather with the Labor Party, because this is the only group that is openly fighting for a living wage for its constituency. This effort has also brought the KWRU together with labor unions, who now see the group's interests as more compatible than before. Finally, the KWRU, while locally based, is constantly trying both to ally with other poverty and economic rights groups and to think outside of existing institutional boxes. Its efforts at the United Nations are a sharp and creative departure from earlier modes of protest.

What can we learn from both of these ongoing movements? These movements, moments, and actions teach us several things. First, they show us that any movement to counter neoliberalism must be broader than one housing project, neighborhood, urban redevelopment project, or policy change. It needs to link commonly affected people together in different cities. As Alinsky famously argued, it is much easier to organize people who are affected by a common action, event, or policy change, but as the KWRU and living wage movements show us, there needs to be a broader theoretical basis around which to organize. These movements also teach us that any resistance to neoliberalism must be grassroots in nature. It needs to be composed of and led by those who are most affected in order to be sustainable. It also should not be orthodox in either its activities or its composition, and it should be multi-racial and employ creative tactics.

Finally, and most importantly, any solution needs to be political—one that combats the TINA syndrome and that recognizes that neoliberalism itself is a political (rather than natural) process. Above all, we can learn from these movements that the neoliberal city is as discursive as it is material. It is a set of ideas rooted in a very selective reading of classical liberalism, on the one hand, and a set of material practices that have yet to be fully implemented on the other. It is an experiment that has not been completed, and efforts to replace it are neither doomed to failure amidst "the lack of alternatives" nor naturally fated for some Hegelian absorption by the state at some later date. Any resolution, alternative, or counter to neoliberalism must by necessity be a contested political one, and the crucial first step is winning the discursive right to claim that viable and progressive alternatives are possible.

REFERENCES

ABT Associates. 1996. *An Historical and Baseline Assessment of H.O.P.E. VI.* Volume 1. Washington, D.C.: HUD.

Abu-Lughod, J. 1994. "Introduction." In *From Urban Village to East Village: The Battle for New York's Lower East Side*, edited by J. Abu-Lughod. Cambridge: Blackwell Publishing.

Adams, C. T. 1987. "The Politics of Privatization." In *Between State and Market: Housing in the Post-Industrial Era*, edited by B. Turner, J. Kemeny, and L. Lundqvist. Stockholm: Almqvist and Wiksell.

———. 1990. "The Decentralization of Housing: Introduction." In *Government and Housing: Developments in Seven Countries*, edited by W. van Vliet and J. van Weesep. Newbury Park, CA: Sage Publishing.

———. 1991. "Philadelphia: The Slide toward Municipal Bankruptcy." In *Big City Politics in Transition*, edited by H. Savitch and J. Thomas. Newbury Park, CA: Sage Publishing.

Alinsky, S. 1971. *Rules for Radicals: A Pragmatic Primer for Realistic Radicals.* New York: Vintage.

Anderson, P. 2000. "Renewals." *New Left Review* 1:17.

Arizona Republic. 1988. "2 on Scottsdale Council Label Move 'Extortion,' Decry Member's Proposal on Developer." March 3, B2.

———. 1989. "Galleria near $100 Million, Sigh of Relief: Japanese Bank Weighs Bulk of Financing." March 19, E1.

Atkinson, R. 2000. "Measuring Gentrification and Displacement in Greater London." *Urban Studies* 37 (1):149–65.

Aune, J. Arnt. 2001. *Selling the Free Market: The Rhetoric of Economic Correctness.* New York: Guilford Press.

Baca, F. 2000. Unpublished memorandum on the audit of the Seattle Housing Authority. Housing and Urban Development. www.hud.gov/oig/ig001801.pdf. Accessed January 15, 2000.

Badcock, B. 1993. "Notwithstanding the Exaggerated Claims, Residential Revitalization Really Is Changing the Form of Some Western Cities: A Response to Bourne." *Urban Studies* 30:191–95.

——. 1995. "Building on the Foundations of Gentrification: Inner-City Housing Development in Australia in the 1990s." *Urban Geography* 16:70–90.

Bagli, C. 1991. "'De-Gentrification' Can Hit when Boom Goes Bust." *New York Observer*, August 5–12.

Ball, M. 1994. "The 1980s Property Boom." *Environment and Planning A* 26:671–95.

Beauregard, R. 1993. "The Turbulence of Housing Markets: Investment, Disinvestment, and Reinvestment in Philadelphia, 1963–1986." In *The Restless Urban Landscape*, edited by P. Knox. Englewood Cliffs, NJ: Prentice Hall.

Beauregard, R., and B. Holcomb. 1984. "New Brunswick," *Cities*, February, pp. 215–20.

Berlin, I. 1969. *Four Essays on Liberty*. New York: Oxford University Press.

Berry, B. 1985. "Islands of Renewal in Seas of Decay." In *The New Urban Reality*, edited by J. Peterson. Washington, D.C.: Brookings Institution.

Bezalel, R., and A. Ferrera. 2000. *Voices of Cabrini: Remaking Chicago's Public Housing*. Video recording. Chicago, IL: Facets Video.

Bondi, L. 1999. "Between the Woof and the Weft: A Response to Loretta Lees." *Environment and Planning D* 17:253–55.

Bourne, L. 1993a. "The Demise of Gentrification? A Commentary and Prospective View." *Urban Geography* 14:95–107.

——. 1993b. "The Myth and Reality of Gentrification: A Commentary on Emerging Urban Forms." *Urban Studies* 30:183–89.

Bowden, C. 2003. "Little Big Man." *Mother Jones*, November/December.

Box, R. 1999. "Running Government like a Business: Implications for Public Administration Theory and Practice." *American Review of Public Administration* 29:19–43.

Bratt, R. 1986. "Public Housing: The Controversy and Contribution." In *Critical Perspectives on Housing*, edited by R. Bratt, C. Hartman, and A. Meyerson. Philadelphia, PA: Temple University Press.

——. 1990. "Public Housing: Introduction." In *Government and Housing: Developments in Seven Countries*, edited by W. van Vliet and J. van Weesep. Newbury Park, CA: Sage Publishing.

Bratt, R., and W. D. Keating. 1993. "Federal Housing Policy and HUD: Past Problems and Future Prospects of a Beleaguered Bureaucracy." *Urban Affairs Quarterly* 29:3–27.

Brenner, N., and N. Theodore. 2002. "Cities and the Geographies of 'Actually Existing Neoliberalism.'" *Antipode* 34:349–79.

Bristol, K. 1991. "The Pruitt-Igoe Myth." *Journal of Architectural Education* 44:163–71.

Brown, M. 1992. "The Possibility of Local Autonomy." *Urban Geography* 13:257–79.

——. 1999. "Reconceptualizing Public and Private in Urban Regime Theory: Governance in AIDS Politics." *International Journal of Urban and Regional Research* 23:70–87.

Bunting, T., P. Filion, and H. Priston. 2000a. "Changing Patterns of Residential Centrality: Population and Household Shift in Large Canadian CMAs, 1971–1996." *Cahiers de géographie du Québec* 44:341–61.

———. 2000b. "Density Gradients in Canadian Metropolitan Regions, 1971–96: Differential Patterns of Central Area and Suburban Growth and Change." *Urban Studies* 39:2531–52.

Bush, J. 1999. "Prickly Holly: Activists Charge Conflict of Interest in the Most Expensive Housing Project in Seattle's History." *Seattle Weekly*, March 11–17.

Cahill, J. 2002. "New Brunswick State of the City Address 2002." www.cityofnew brunswick.org/mayorsoffice/stateofthecity2002.asp. Accessed January 15, 2002.

Campbell, R., C. Ghosh, and C. Sirmans. 1998. "The Great REIT Consolidation: Fact or Fancy?" *Real Estate Finance* 15:45–54.

Canterbery, E. R. 1995. *The Literate Economist*. New York: Harper Collins.

Cantor, R., and F. Packer. 1995. "The Credit Rating Industry." *Journal of Fixed Income* 5:10–34.

Caris, P. 1996. *Declining Suburbs: Disinvestment in the Inner Suburbs of Camden County, New Jersey*. Ph.D. dissertation. Department of Geography, Rutgers University.

Caro, R. 1975. *The Power Broker: Robert Moses and the Fall of New York*. New York: Vintage.

Castells, M. 1983. *The City and the Grassroots: A Cross-Cultural Theory of Urban Social Movements*. Berkeley: University of California Press.

———. 1989. *The Informational City: Information, Technology, Economic Restructuring and the Urban-Regional Process*. Cambridge, MA: Blackwell Publishing.

———. 1996. *The Rise of the Network Society*. Cambridge, MA: Blackwell Publishing.

Caulfield, J. 1994. *City Form and Everyday Life: Toronto's Gentrification and Critical Social Practice*. Toronto: University of Toronto Press.

Cawley, J. 1995. "New York Community Boiling over Name Change." *Chicago Tribune*, January 15, p. 17.

Chandrashekaran, V., and M. Young. 1999. "Industry Concentration: The Case of Real Estate Investment Trusts." *Real Estate Finance*, Fall, 27–35.

Chang, H. 1997. "The Economics and Politics of Regulation." *Cambridge Journal of Economics* 21:703–28.

Checkoway, B. 1980. "Large Builders, Federal Housing Programmes, and Postwar Suburbanization." *International Journal of Urban and Regional Research* 4:21–45.

Cisneros, H. 1995a. *Defensible Space: Deterring Crime and Building Community*. Washington, D.C.: U.S. Government Printing Office.

———. 1995b. "The Public Interest, the Greater Good: How Government Should Work." *Journal of Housing and Community Development*, March/April, 27–33.

City Limits. 1999, "Bed-Stuy Brawl Puts Contract out on Housing Group." March 22, p. 168.

City of Phoenix. 1985. *General Plan for Phoenix: 1985–2000*. City of Phoenix.

———. 1987. "Status Report for the Rouse Corporation Superblock Project." Unpublished report to the city council signed by George Flores, director of economic development.

———. 1988. "Status Report for the Mercado Project." Unpublished report to the city council signed by Denny Maus, development director.

———. 1991. *Downtown Phoenix: A 25-Year Vision*. Phoenix, AZ.

City of Scottsdale. 1984. *Downtown Plan*. Scottsdale, AZ.

——. 1986. *Downtown Plan*. Scottsdale, AZ.

——. 1993. "Scottsdale." Unpublished information sheet compiled by the City Planning Department.

Clark, E. 1995. "The Rent Gap Re-examined." *Urban Studies* 32:1489–1503.

Clark, G. 1984. "A Theory of Local Autonomy." *Annals of the Association of American Geographers* 74:195–208.

Clark, G., and M. Dear. 1981. "The State in Capitalism and the Capitalist State." In *Urbanization and Urban Planning in Capitalist Society*, edited by M. Dear and A. Scott. London: Methuen.

Clarke, J. 1997a. Interview by the author with the executive director of the New Brunswick Housing Authority. August 25.

——. 1997b. Interview by the author with the executive director of the New Brunswick Housing Authority. December 12.

Clarke, S., and A. Kirby. 1990. "In Search of the Corpse: The Mysterious Case of Local Politics." *Urban Affairs Quarterly* 25:389–412.

Coakley, J. 1994. "The Integration of Property and Financial Markets." *Environment and Planning A* 26:697–713.

Cohen, J. 1996. "Big Plans for a Sliver of Long Island City: Queens West Project Will Play Gulliver to the Brownstones." *New York Times*, December 29, RE1.

Coleman, A. 1985. *Utopia on Trial: Vision and Reality in Planned Housing*. London: Hillary Shipman.

Cook, J. 1990. "$515 Million Buys 'Energy' for Downtown." *Arizona Republic*, October 25, E1.

Courchene, T. 1995. "Glocalization: The Regional/International Interface." *Canadian Journal of Regional Science* 18:1–20.

Cox, K. 1993. "The Local and the Global in the New Urban Politics: A Critical View." *Environment and Planning D* 11:433–48.

Cox, K., and A. Mair. 1988. "Locality and Community in the Politics of Local Economic Development." *Annals of the Association of American Geographers* 78:307–25.

Crilley, D. 1993. "Megastructures and Urban Changes: Aesthetics, Ideology and Design." In *The Restless Urban Landscape*, edited by P. Knox. Englewood Cliffs, NJ: Prentice Hall.

Dahl, R. 1961. *Who Governs?* New Haven, CT: Yale University Press.

Dear, M., and S. Flusty. 1998. "Postmodern Urbanism." *Annals of the Association of American Geographers* 88:50–72.

deCourcy Hinds, M. 1992a. "Philadelphia Getting Credit for Reversing a Fiscal Fall." *New York Times*, May 21.

——. 1992b. "Philadelphia Mayor Proposes Bailout." *New York Times*, February 21.

——. 1993. "Philadelphia Climbs Out of Fiscal Depths and Builds by Sharing Sacrifices." *New York Times*, April 6.

Defilippis, J. 1999. "Alternatives to the 'New Urban Politics': Finding Locality and Autonomy in Local Economic Development." *Political Geography* 18:973–90.

——. 2003. *Unmaking Goliath: Community Control in the Face of Global Capital*. New York: Routledge.

Deters, B. 1995. "Arizona Center's Changes Shift to More Nightlife, New Tenant Mix Stirs Turmoil." *Arizona Republic*, June 30, E1.

Deutsch, C. 1996. "In Hell's Kitchen, Retail Is on the Front Burner." *New York Times,* May 5.

DeVault, J. 2001. "HOPE VI Suit Names Kelly." *The Common Denominator,* www .thecommondenominator.com. Accessed March 15.

Dougherty, J. 1995. "Paying the Piper: A Kickback Raises New Questions about Symington and the Mercado." *New Times,* 26–40.

Dragos, S. 1989. Unpublished personal letter to Steven Lampier.

Dunlap, D. 1998. "Community Seeks End to Redevelopment Ban." *New York Times,* January 10.

Dworkin, R. 1985. *A Matter of Principle.* Cambridge, MA: Harvard University Press.

Economist. 1993. "Detroit's Mayor: A Job Fit for Heroes." August 28.

——. 1994. "Recalled to Life: A Survey of International Banking." April 30.

——. 1996a. "Aaaargh! Credit-Rating Agencies." April 6.

——. 1996b. "The Use and Abuse of Reputation." April 6.

Eisinger, P. 1998. "City Politics in an Era of Federal Devolution." *Urban Affairs Review* 33:308–25.

Elkin, S. 1987. *City and Regime in the American Republic.* Chicago, IL: University of Chicago Press.

Ennen, M. 1999. "An Immodest Proposal." *Brooklyn Bridge Magazine,* January, pp. 48–53.

Fainstein, N., and S. Fainstein. 1974. *Urban Political Movements: The Search for Power by Minority Groups in American Cities.* Englewood Cliffs, NJ: Prentice-Hall.

——. 1983. "Regime Strategies, Communal Resistance, and Economic Forces." In *Restructuring the City: The political economy of urban redevelopment,* edited by S. Fainstein, N. Fainstein, R. C. Hill, D. Judd, and M. P. Smith. New York: Longman.

——. 1985. "Is State Planning Necessary for Capital? The U.S. Case." *International Journal of Urban and Regional Research* 9 (4):485–507.

——. 1987. "Economic Restructuring and the Politics of Land Use Planning in New York City." *Journal of the American Planning Association* 53:237–48.

——. 1989. "New York City: The Manhattan Business District, 1945–1988." In *Unequal Partnerships,* edited by G. Squires. New Brunswick, NJ: Rutgers University Press.

Fainstein, S. 1992. "The Second New York Fiscal Crisis." *International Journal of Urban and Regional Research* 16:129–38.

——. 1995. "Politics, Economics, and Planning: Why Urban Regimes Matter." *Planning Theory* 14:34–41.

——. 2001. *City Builders: Property Development in New York and London, 1980–2000.* Second edition, revised. Lawrence: University of Kansas Press.

Fainstein, S., I. Gordon, and M. Harloe, eds. 1992. *Divided Cities.* Oxford, UK: Blackwell Publishing.

Fazzi, R. 1990. "City Sets Sights on Housing Sites." *Home News and Tribune,* December 12, A1–A2.

Feldman, M. 1997. "Spatial Structures of Regulation and Urban Regimes." In *Reconstructing Urban Regime Theory: Regulating Urban Politics in a Global Era,* edited by M. Lauria. Thousand Oaks, CA: Sage Publishing.

Feldman, M., and R. Florida R. 1990. "Economic Restructuring and the Changing

Role of the State in U.S. Housing." In *Government and Housing: Developments in Seven Countries*, edited by W. van Vliet and J. van Weesep. Newbury Park, CA: Sage Publishing.

Fickess, J. 1994. "The Present State of Shopping Development: Giant Westcor Sets Pace as Power Centers Proliferate." *Arizona Business Gazette*, March 31, p. 16.

Finder, A. 1999. "Long View from the Waterfront: Developer Has Pursued a Brooklyn Dream for 20 Years." *New York Today*, June 24, p. 1.

Finotti, J. 1995. "Clinton: Hell's Kitchen Recipe: A Tangy Diversity." *New York Times*, April 9, RE1.

Fischer, P. 1999. "Section 8 and the Public Housing Revolution: Where Will the Families Go?" Metropolitan Planning Council, www.metroplanning.org/resources/101intro.asp. Accessed February 15.

Fitch, R. 1993. *The Assassination of New York*. New York: Verso.

Fitch IBCA Investors Corporation. 2000. Fitch Ratings, www.fitchibca.com.

Florida, R. 1986. "The Political Economy of Financial Deregulation and the Reorganization of Housing Finance in the United States." *International Journal of Urban and Regional Research* 10:207–31.

Florida, R., and M. Feldman. 1988. "Housing in U.S. Fordism." *International Journal of Urban and Regional Research* 12:187–210.

Ford, L. 1994. *Cities and Buildings: Skyscrapers, Skid Rows, and Suburbs*. Baltimore, MD: Johns Hopkins University Press.

Forrest, R., and A. Murie. 1988. *Selling the Welfare State*. London: Routledge.

Frieden, B., and L. Sagalyn. 1990. *Downtown Inc.: How America Rebuilds Cities*. Cambridge, MA: MIT Press.

Friedman, M. 1962. *Capitalism and Freedom*. Chicago, IL: University of Chicago Press.

——. 1984. *Market or Plan? An Exposition of the Case for the Market*. London: Centre for Research into Communist Economies.

Fukuyama, F. 1989. "The End of History?" *National History*, Summer.

Gaffakin, F., and B. Warf. 1993. "Urban Policy and the Post-Keynesian State in the United Kingdom and United States." *International Journal of Urban and Regional Research* 17:67–84.

Garbarine, R. 1998. "A Neighborhood Called Dumbo has High Hopes." *New York Times*, August 7, B1.

Gibson, K., and J. Cameron. 2001. "Transforming Communities: Towards a Research Agenda." *Urban Policy and Research* 19 (1):7–24.

Gibson-Graham, J. K. 1996. *The End Of Capitalism (As We Knew It): A Feminist Critique of Political Economy*. Oxford, UK: Blackwell Publishing.

Gilbert, M. 2001. "From the 'Walk for Adequate Welfare' to the 'March for Our Lives': Welfare Rights Organizing in the 1960s and 1990s." *Urban Geography* 22:440–56.

Gill, S. 1995. "Globalisation, Market Civilization, and Disciplinary Neoliberalism." *Millennium: Journal of International Studies* 24:399 423.

Gillespie, E., and B. Schellhas, eds. 1994. *Contract with America: The Bold Plan by Rep. Newt Gingrich, Rep. Dick Armey, and the House Republicans to Change the Nation*. New York: Times Books.

Gilmore, R. 1998. "Globalisation and U.S. Prison Growth: From Military Keynesianism to Post-Keynesian Militarism." *Race and Class* 40:171–88.

Girvetz, H. 1963. *The Evolution of Liberalism.* New York: Collier.

Glasberg, D. 1988. "The Political Economic Power of Finance Capital and the Urban Fiscal Crisis: Cleveland's Default, 1978." *Journal of Urban Affairs* 10:63–76.

Glassman, J. 2001. "From Seattle (and Ubon) to Bangkok: The Scales of Resistance to Corporate Globalization." *Environment and Planning D* 19:513–33.

Goetz, E., and S. Clarke, eds. 1993. *The New Localism: Comparative Urban Politics in a Global Era.* Newbury Park, CA: Sage Publishing.

Goodwin, M., and J. Painter. 1996. "Local Governance, the Crises of Fordism and the Changing Geographies of Regulation." *Transactions of the Institute of British Geographers* 21:635–48.

Goonewardena, K. 2003. "The Future of Planning at the 'End of History.'" *Planning Theory* 2:183–224.

Gottdiener, M., ed. 1986. *Cities in Stress: A New Look at the Urban Crisis.* Newbury Park, CA: Sage Publishing.

——. 1987. *The Decline of Urban Politics: Political Theory and the Crisis of the Local State.* Newbury Park, CA: Sage Publishing.

Gough, J. 2002. "Neoliberalism and Socialisation in the Contemporary City: Opposites, Complements, and Instabilities." *Antipode* 34:405–26.

Gray, J. 1989. *Liberalisms.* London: Routledge.

Gruen Gruen and Associates. 1982. *An Economic and Market Analysis of Downtown Scottsdale.* San Francisco, CA: Gruen Gruen and Associates.

Gwertzmann, M. 1997. *Keeping the "Kitchen" in Clinton: Community Efforts to Resist Gentrification.* New York: Hell's Kitchen Neighborhood Alliance.

Hackworth, J. 2000. "State Devolution, Urban Regimes, and the Production of Geographic Scale: The Case of New Brunswick, NJ." *Urban Geography* 21:450–58.

——. 2002. "Local Autonomy, Bond-Rating Agencies, and Neoliberal Urbanism in the U.S." *International Journal of Urban and Regional Research* 26:707–25.

——. 2003. "Public Housing and the Re-scaling of Regulation in the U.S." *Environment and Planning A* 35:531–49.

——. 2005. "Emergent Urban Forms, or Emergent Post-Modernisms? A Comparison of Large U.S. Metropolitan Areas." *Urban Geography* 26(6):484–519.

Hackworth, J., and N. Smith. 2001. "The Changing State of Gentrification." *Tijdschrift voor Economische en Sociale Geografie* 92:464–77.

Hall, T. 2000. "Discovering Bed-Stuy's Brownstones." *New York Times,* May 21, RE1, RE10.

Hall, T., and P. Hubbard. 1996. "The Entrepreneurial City: New Urban Politics, New Urban Geographies." *Progress in Human Geography* 20:153–74.

——. 1999. *The Entrepreneurial City: Geographies of Politics, Regime, and Representation.* New York: John Wiley and Sons.

Hammel, D. 1999. "Gentrification and Land Rent: A Historical View of the Rent Gap in Minneapolis." *Urban Geography* 20:116–45.

Hamnett, C. 1973. "Improvement Grants as an Indicator of Gentrification in Inner London." *Area* 5:252–61.

Harloe, M. 1995. *The People's Home: Social Rented Housing in Europe and America.* London: Blackwell Publishing.

Harmes, A. 1998. "Institutional Investors and the Reproduction of Neoliberalism." *Review of International Political Economy* 5:92–121.

Hartshorn, T. 1992. *Interpreting the City: An Urban Geography.* New York: John Wiley and Sons.

Hartung, J., and J. Henig. 1997. "Housing Vouchers and Certificates as a Vehicle for Deconcentrating the Poor: Evidence from the Washington D.C. Metropolitan Area." *Urban Affairs Review* 323:403–19.

Harvey, D. 1978. "The Urban Process under Capitalism: A Framework for Analysis." *International Journal of Urban and Regional Research* 2:101–31.

———. 1982. *The Limits to Capital.* Chicago: University of Chicago Press.

———. 1985. *The Urbanization of Capital: Studies in the History and Theory of Capitalist Urbanization.* Baltimore: The Johns Hopkins University Press.

———. 1989a. *The Condition of Postmodernity.* Oxford, UK: Blackwell Publishing.

———. 1989b. "From Managerialism to Entrepreneurialism: The Transformation of Urban Governance in Late Capitalism." *Geografiska Annaler* 71:3–17.

———. 1996. *Justice, Nature, and the Geography of Difference.* Oxford, UK: Blackwell Publishing.

Hatmaker, J. 1996. Interview by the author with the Phoenix central city planner.

Hayek, F. 1944. *The Road to Serfdom.* Chicago: University of Chicago Press.

———. 1960. *The Constitution of Liberty.* Chicago: University of Chicago Press.

Hayllar, B. 1999. "Addressing Unfunded Pension Liability: Pension Bonds in the City of Philadelphia." *Government Finance Review,* December, pp. 31–33.

Hemphill, R. 1994. "The Troubled Mercado." *Phoenix Gazette,* August 2, B1.

Herold, S. 1990. "Heart of City Hopes for Downtown Ride on Arizona Center." *Phoenix Gazette,* October 30, p. 1.

Hewson, M., and T. Sinclair, eds. 1999. *Approaches to Global Governance Theory.* Albany: State University of New York Press.

HKNA. 2000. Hell's Kitchen Online, www.hellskitchen.net.

Hoch, I., and P. Waddell. 1993. "Apartment Rents: Another Challenge to the Monocentric Model." *Geographical Analysis* 25:20–34.

Holcomb, B. 1997. "New Brunswick Walk." Unpublished notes. Department of Urban Studies, Rutgers University.

Horan, C. 1991. "Beyond Governing Coalitions: Analyzing Urban Regimes in the 1990s." *Journal of Urban Affairs* 13:119–35.

Housing Research Foundation. 2003. HOPE VI press clippings, www.housingresearch.org. Accessed August 15.

Hoyt, H. 1933. *One Hundred Years of Land Values in Chicago.* Chicago: University of Chicago Press.

———. 1939. *The Structure and Growth of Residential Neighborhoods in American Cities.* Washington, D.C.: U.S. Federal Housing Administration.

———. 1966. *Where the Rich and the Poor People Live.* Washington, D.C.: Urban Land Institute.

HPCC. 1996. *The View: Newsletter of the Hunter's Point Community Coalition* 3(5).

Jacobs, A. 1998. "A New Spell for Alphabet City." *New York Times,* August 9, p. 1.

Jacobs, J. 1961. *The Death and Life of Great American Cities.* London: Peregrine Books.

James, J. 1996. Interview by the author with Scottsdale Fashion Square manager.

Jarman, M. 1994. "Restaurant-Bars Seek Mercado Space, Center's Focus Changes to Food, Entertainment." *Arizona Business Gazette*, August 18, p. 23.

———. 1995. "Bullock's Space Question: Sears, Penney's, Macy's Interested?" *Arizona Business Gazette*, April 20, p. 3.

Jessop, B. 2002. "Liberalism, Neoliberalism, and Urban Governance: A State-Theoretical Perspective." *Antipode* 34:452–72.

Jessop, B., J. Peck, and A. Tickell. 1999. "Retooling the Machine: Economic Crisis, State Restructuring, and Urban Politics." In *The Urban Growth Machine: Critical Perspectives Two Decades Later,* edited by A. E. G. Jonas and D. Wilson. Albany: State University of New York Press.

Jones, B., and L. Bachelor. 1993. *The Sustaining Hand: Community Leadership and Corporate Power.* Lawrence: University of Kansas Press.

Kamin, B. 1995a. "Building a Sense of Security: Fences, Individual Front Doors and Porches Can Create Safe Spaces that Free Residents from Being Virtual Prisoners of Drug Dealers and Prostitutes." *Chicago Tribune*, June 21.

———. 1995b. "An Elusive Blend: Redesigned Development Can Bring Different Groups Together, But It Can't Prevent Class, Racial Tensions." *Chicago Tribune*, June 20.

———. 1995c. "Myth Must Be Exploded: Stereotyping Ignores Factors that Make Livable Buildings or Monumental Eyesores." *Chicago Tribune*, June 22.

Katznelson, I. 1997. "Social Justice, Liberalism and the City: Considerations on David Harvey, John Rawls and Karl Polanyi." In *The Urbanization of Injustice*, edited by A. Merrifield and E. Swyngedouw. New York: New York University Press.

Keating, L. 2000. "Redeveloping Public Housing: Relearning Urban Renewal's Immutable Lessons." *Journal of the American Planning Association* 66:384–97.

Kekes, J. 1997. *Against Liberalism.* Ithaca: Cornell University Press.

Kennedy, M. 1984. "The Fiscal Crisis of the City." In *Cities in Transformation*, edited by M. P. Smith. Thousand Oaks, CA: Sage Publishing.

Kensington Welfare Rights Union (KWRU). 2005. www.kwru.org/kwru/abtkwru .html.

Kerner Commission. 1968. *Report of the National Advisory Commission on Civil Disorders.* Washington, D.C.: U.S. Government Printing Office.

Keyes, L., A. Schwartz, A. Vidal, and R. Bratt. 1996. "Forum: Networks and Nonprofits: Opportunities and Challenges in an Era of Federal Devolution." *Housing Policy Debate* 7:201–29.

Keynes, J. M. 1926. *Laissez-Faire and Communism.* New York: New Republic Press.

———. 1936. *The General Theory of Employment, Interest, and Money.* New York: Harcourt, Brace and World.

Klein, N. 2002. *Fences and Windows.* Toronto: Vintage Canada.

Kodras, J. 1997. "Restructuring the State: Devolution, Privatization, and the Geographic Redistribution of Power and Capacity in Governance." In *State Devolution in America: Implications for a diverse society*, edited by L. Staeheli, J. Kodras, and C. Flint. Thousand Oaks, CA: Sage Publishing.

Kristol, I. 1995. *Neoconservatism: The Autobiography of an Idea.* New York: The Free Press.

Lake, R. 1979. *Real Estate Tax Delinquency: Private Disinvestment and Public Response.* Piscataway, NJ: Center for Urban Policy Research, Rutgers University.

——. 1994. "Negotiating Local Autonomy." *Political Geography* 13:423–42.

——. 1995. "Spatial Fix 2: The Sequel." *Urban Geography* 16:189–91.

——. 1997. "State Restructuring, Political Opportunism, and Capital Mobility." In *State Devolution in America*, edited by L. Staeheli, J. Kodras, and C. Flint. Thousand Oaks, CA: Sage Publishing.

——. 2002. "Bring Back Big Government." *International Journal of Urban and Regional Research* 26:815–22.

Lamb, R., Rappaport S. 1987. *Municipal Bonds.* New York: McGraw Hill.

Lang, R. 2003. *Edgeless Cities.* Washington, D.C.: Brookings Institution Press.

Larner, W. 2000. "Neo-Liberalism: Policy, Ideology, Governmentality." *Studies in Political Economy* 63:5–25.

——. 2003. "Neoliberalism?" *Environment and Planning D* 21:509–12.

Laska, S., and D. Spain, eds. 1980. *Back to the City: Issues in Neighborhood Renovation.* New York: Pergamon.

Lauria, M., ed. 1997a. *Reconstructing Urban Regime Theory: Regulating Urban Politics in a Global Era.* Thousand Oaks, CA: Sage Publishing.

——. 1997b. "Introduction." In *Reconstructing Urban Regime Theory: Regulating Urban Politics in a Global Era*, edited by M. Lauria. Thousand Oaks, CA: Sage Publishing.

——. 1997c. "Regulating Urban Regimes: Reconstruction or Impasse?" In *Reconstructing Urban Regime Theory: Regulating urban politics in a global era*, edited by M. Lauria. Thousand Oaks, CA: Sage Publishing.

Lees, L. 2000. "A Re-appraisal of Gentrification: Towards a 'Geography of Gentrification.'" *Progress in Human Geography* 24 (3):389–408.

Leitner, H. 1990. "Cities in Pursuit of Economic Growth: The Local State as Entrepreneur." *Political Geography Quarterly* 9:146–70.

Levy, P. 1994. *The New Left and Labor in the 1960s.* Urbana, IL: University of Illinois Press.

Lewis, P. 1983. "The Galactic Metropolis." In *Beyond the Urban Fringe*, edited by R. Platt and G. Macinko. Minneapolis: University of Minnesota Press.

Ley, D. 1992. "Gentrification in Recession: Social Change in Six Canadian Inner Cities, 1981–1986." *Urban Geography* 13:220–56.

——. 1996. *The New Middle Class and the Remaking of the Central City.* Oxford, UK: Oxford University Press.

Lichten, E. 1986. *Class, Power, and Austerity: The New York City Fiscal Crisis.* South Hadley, MA: Bergin & Garvey Publishers.

Lilley W. 1980. "The Homebuilders' Lobby." In *Housing in Urban America*, edited by J. Pynoos, R. Schafer, and C. W. Hartman. New York: Aldine.

Linneman, P. 1997. "Changing Real Estate Forever." *Journal of Real Estate Investment Trusts* 2:3–8.

Lipnick, L., Y. Rattner, and L. Ebrahim. 1999. "The Determinants of Municipal Credit Quality." *Government Finance Review* 15:35–41.

Litvack, D. 1999. "Measuring Municipal Default Risk." *Government Finance Review* 15:19–21.

Living Wage Resource Center. 2005. www.livingwagecampaign.org.

Lobbia, J. 1998. "Hell's Kitchen Is Burning." *Village Voice*, September 8, 47–51.

Logan, J. 1993. "Cycles and Trends in the Globalization of Real Estate." In *The Restless Urban Landscape,* edited by P. Knox. Englewood Cliffs, NJ: Prentice Hall.

Logan, J., and H. Molotch. 1987. *Urban Fortunes: The Political Economy of Place.* Berkeley: University of California Press.

Lueck, T. 1991. "Prices Decline as Gentrification Ebbs." *New York Times,* September 29, p. 1.

Lundqvist, L. 1988. "Privatization: Towards a Concept for Comparative Policy Analysis." *Journal of Public Policy* 8:1–19.

MacKinnon, D. 2001. "Regulating Regional Spaces: State Agencies and the Production of Governance in the Scottish Highlands." *Environment and Planning A* 33: 823–44.

MacLeod, G., and M. Goodwin. 1999. "Space, Scale and State Strategy: Rethinking Urban and Regional Governance." *Progress in Human Geography* 23 (4):503–27.

Marcuse, P. 1986. "Abandonment, Gentrification, and Displacement: The Linkages in New York City." In *Gentrification of the City,* edited by N. Smith and P. Williams. Boston, MA: Allen and Unwin.

——. 1998. "Mainstreaming Public Housing: A Proposal to a Comprehensive Approach to Housing Policy." In *New Directions in Urban Public Housing,* edited by D. Varady, D. W. Preiser, and F. Russell. New Brunswick, NJ: Center for Urban Policy Research Press.

Marcuse, P., and R. van Kempen. 2000. "Conclusion: A Changed Spatial Order." In *Globalizing Cities: A new spatial order?* edited by P. Marcuse and R. van Kempen. Oxford, UK: Blackwell Publishing.

Marx, K. 1996. *Capital Volume I.* London: Lawrence and Wishart.

McDonald, T., and S. Ward, eds. 1984. *The Politics of Urban Fiscal Policy.* Beverly Hills, CA: Sage Publishing.

McDonnell, T. 1990. "Scottsdale Galleria Adds Five-Star Hotel Omni, Developer Reported Close to Deal." *Arizona Business Gazette,* October 19, p. 1.

McKinley, D. 1996. Interview by the author with the Development Services Deputy Director for the City of Phoenix.

Meier, G. 1993. "The New Political Economy and Policy Reform." *Journal of International Development* 54:381–89.

Merrifield, A. 2002. *Dialectical Urbanism: Social Struggles in the Capitalist City.* New York: Monthly Review Press.

Meyhill, B. 1996. Interview by the author with Westcor's chief financial officer.

Miliband, R. 1969. *The State in Capitalist Society.* New York: Basic Books.

Mills, E. 1987. "Non-Urban Policies as Urban Policies." *Urban Studies* 24:561–69.

Mitchell, D. 2003. *The Right to the City: Social Justice and the Fight for Public Space.* New York: Guilford Press.

Mitchell, K. 2001. "Transnationalism, Neo-Liberalism, and the Rise of the Shadow State." *Economy and Society* 30:165–89.

Mollenkopf, J., and M. Castells, eds. 1991. *Dual City.* New York: Russell Sage.

Molotch, H. L. 1976. "The City as a Growth Machine: Toward a Political Economy of Place." *American Journal of Sociology* 82:309–30.

Monkkonen, E. 1995. *The Local State: Public Money and American Cities.* Stanford, CA: Stanford University Press.

Moody, K. 1997. *Workers in a Lean World*. New York: Verso.

Moody's Investors Service. 1999. *Credit Report for Detroit*. December, New York, New York.

———. 2000a. *Credit Report for New York City*. September, New York, New York.

———. 2000b. *Credit Report for Philadelphia*. July, New York, New York.

———. 2004. www.moodys.com.

Morrell, L. 1988. "Beverly Hills of Arizona': Scottsdale Shops Aim High." *Arizona Republic*, October 9, p. E1.

Moss, M. 1990. "Pinpointing Conflicts in Queen's Development: Hunter's Point Proposals Put Mayor's Pledge to Test." *Newsday*, April 26.

Murray, C. 1984. *Losing Ground: American Social Policy, 1950–1980*. New York: Basic Books.

———. 1994. *The Bell Curve*. New York: Free Press.

Nagel, T. 1978. *The Possibility of Altruism*. Princeton, NJ: Princeton University Press.

National Housing Law Project. 2000. Unpublished memorandum. National Housing Law Project, www.nhlp.org/html/pubhsg/onestrike.htm. Accessed August 15, 2003.

New Brunswick Housing Authority [NBHA]. 1996. "HOPE VI Application," An unpublished funding proposal submitted to the Department of Housing and Urban Development in September of 1996.

New York City Department of Finance. 1998. *Tax Arrears and Sales Price Data for New York City*. New York, New York.

Newman, O. 1972. *Defensible Space*. New York: The Macmillan Company.

———. 1995. "Defensible Space: A New Physical Planning Tool for Urban Revitalization." *Journal of the American Planning Association*, Spring, 149–55.

Nijman, J. 2000. "The Paradigmatic City." *Annals of the Association of American Geographers* 90:135–45.

Noble, B. 1992. "A Downgraded Detroit Cries Foul." *New York Times*, November 3.

Novotny, J. 1989. "Mercado Attracting Interest but Doesn't Open until Mid-October." *Arizona Republic*, September 14, D1.

O'Barr, W., and J. Conley. 1992. "Managing Relationships: The Culture of Institutional Investing." *Financial Analysts Journal*, September/October, 21–27.

O'Cleireacain, C. 1997. "The Private Economy and the Public Budget of New York City." In *The City and the World: New York's Global Future*, edited by M. E. Crahan and A. Vourvoulias-Bush. New York: Council on Foreign Relations.

O'Connor, J. 1973. *The Fiscal Crisis of the State*. New York: St. Martins Press.

Parisi, P., and B. Holcomb. 1995. "Symbolizing Place: Journalistic Narratives of the City." *Urban Geography* 15:379–94.

Passell, P. 1996. "Pioneers Wanted; East River Views: Innovative Financing—and $25,000 Average Prices—Are Lures at First Queens West Building." *New York Times*, October 6, RE1.

Patterson, G. 1997. Interview by the author with the Head of New Brunswick Community Planning Department, 12 December.

Peck, J. 2001a. *Workfare States*. New York: Guilford Press.

———. 2001b. "Neoliberalizing States: Thin Policies/Hard Outcomes." *Progress in Human Geography* 253:445–55.

Peck, J., and A. Tickell. 2002. "Neoliberalizing Space." *Antipode* 34:380–404.

Peterson, P. 1981. *City Limits*. Chicago, IL: University of Chicago Press.

Phoenix Community Alliance, 1988, "Superblock Timeline." Unpublished information sheet on the Arizona Center.

Phoenix Gazette. 1989. "The Mercado: It's Here!" December 2, A12.

Piven, F. and R. Cloward. 1977. *Poor People's Movements: Why They Succeed, How They Fail*. New York: Pantheon Books.

Plotkin, S. 1987. *Keep Out: The Struggle for Land Use Control*. Berkeley, CA: University of California Press.

Plunz, R. 1990. *A History of Housing in New York City: Dwelling Type and Social Change in the American Metropolis*. New York: Columbia University Press.

Polanyi, K. 1944. *The Great Transformation*. Boston: Beacon Press.

Port Authority. 2000. The Port Authority of New York and New Jersey, www.panynj.gov.

Poulantzas, N. 1969. "The Problem of the Capitalist State." *New Left Review* 58:67–78.

Pugh, C. 1991a. "The Globalization of Finance Capital and the Changing Relationships between Property and Finance: Part 1." *Journal of Property Finance* 2:211–15.

——. 1991b. "The Globalization of Finance Capital and the Changing Relationships between Property and Finance: Part 2." *Journal of Property Finance* 2:369–79.

Ranney, D. 2003. *Global Decisions, Local Collisions*. Philadelphia: Temple University Press.

Rawls, J. 1971. *A Theory of Justice*. Cambridge, MA: Harvard University Press.

——. 1993. *Political Liberalism*. New York: Columbia University Press.

Rich, W. 1991. "Detroit: From Motor City to Service Hub." In *Big City Politics in Transition*, edited by H. Savitch and J. Thomas. Newbury Park, CA: Sage Publishing.

Richardson, L. 1995. "Amid Old Brooklyn Factories, a Shrinking Canvas: Artists Priced out of SoHo Fear Fate in 'DUMBO.'" *New York Times*, July 24, B1.

Robertson, R. 1995. "Glocalization: Time-Space and Homogeneity-Heterogeneity." In *Global Modernities*, edited by M. Featherstone, S. Lash, and R. Robertson. London: Sage Publishing.

Robinson, A. 2001. "Confrontation and Lawsuit Fuel Debate on Housing Plan." *South Florida Community Development Coalition Newsletter*, www.floridacdc.org. Accessed March 17.

Robinson, T. 1995. "Gentrification and Grassroots Resistance in San Francisco's Tenderloin." *Urban Affairs Review* 30:483–513.

Roe, G. 1996. Interview by the author with the City of Scottsdale director of planning.

Rubin, H. 1990. "Memorial Homes Fate Murky." *Home News and Tribune*, February 14, A1, A8.

Russell, P. 1986. "Downtown's Downturn: A Historical Geography of the Phoenix, Arizona, Central Business District, 1890–1986." Master's thesis. Department of Geography, Arizona State University.

Sally, R. 1998. *Classical Liberalism and International Economic Order*. London: Routledge.

Sargent, C. 1983. "Evolution of Metro Phoenix." In *A Guide to the Architecture of Metro Phoenix*, edited by J. W. Elmore. Phoenix, AZ: Phoenix Publishing.

Sassen, S. 1991. *The Global City: New York, London, Tokyo.* Princeton, NJ: Princeton University Press.

——. 1996. *Losing Control? Sovereignty in an Age of Globalization.* New York: Columbia University Press.

Saunders, P. 1995. *Capitalism: A Social Audit.* Buckingham, UK: Open University Press.

Sbragia, A. 1983. "Politics, Local Government, and the Municipal Bond Market." In *The Municipal Money Chase: The Politics of Local Governmental Finance,* edited by A. Sbragia. Boulder, CO: Westview Press.

——. 1996. *Debt Wish: Entrepreneurial Cities, U.S. Federalism, and Economic Development.* Pittsburgh: University of Pittsburgh Press.

Schaeffer, R., and N. Smith. 1986. "The Gentrification of Harlem?" *Annals of the Association of American Geographers* 76:347–65.

Schefter, M. 1992. *Political Crisis, Fiscal Crisis: The Collapse and Revival of New York City.* New York: Columbia University Press.

Schlosser, E. 1998. "The Prison-Industrial Complex." *Atlantic Monthly* 282:51–77.

Schnee, D. 1998. "An Evaluation of Robert Pitts Plaza: A Post-Occupancy Evaluation of New Public Housing in San Francisco." In *New Directions in Urban Public Housing,* edited by D. Varady, D. Preiser, and F. Russell. New Brunswick, NJ: Center for Urban Policy Research Press.

Schmandt, M. 1991. *Local Government Decisions and Landscape Change: Downtown Tempe, 1972–1991.* Master's thesis. Department of Geography, Arizona State University.

——. 1995. *Postmodernism in the Southwestern Urban Landscape.* Ph.D. dissertation. Department of Geography, Arizona State University.

Sclar, E. 1993. "Analysis of the Special Clinton District." Unpublished report prepared for Community Board no. 4, New York, New York.

Scottsdale Scene. 1988. "Scottsdale Galleria: An Arizona Happening." *Scottsdale Scene,* 12 2.

Sengupta, S. 1999. "A Neighborhood Identity Crisis: Transformation Brings Anxiety in Brooklyn's DUMBO." *New York Times,* June 9, B1.

Silver, H. 1990. "Privatization Self-Help and Public Housing Homeownership in the United States." In *Government and Housing: Developments in Seven Countries,* edited by W. van Vliet and J. van Weesep. Newbury Park, CA: Sage Publishing.

Sinclair, T. 1994a. "Between State and Market: Hegemony and Institutions of Collective Action under Conditions of International Capital Mobility." *Policy Sciences* 27:447–66.

——. 1994b. "Passing Judgment: Credit Rating Processes as Regulatory Mechanisms of Governance in the Emerging World Order." *Review of International Political Economy* 1:133–59.

——. 1999. "Synchronic Global Governance and the International Political Economy of the Commonplace." In *Approaches to Global Governance Theory,* edited by M. Hewson and T. Sinclair. Albany: State University of New York Press.

Smith, J. 2000. "The Space of Local Control in the Devolution of U.S. Public Housing Policy." *Geografiska Annaler Series B* 82:221–33.

Smith, N. 1979a. "Gentrification and Capital: Theory, Practice, and Ideology in Society Hill." *Antipode* 11:24–35.

——. 1979b. "Toward a Theory of Gentrification: A Back to the City Movement by Capital, Not People." *Journal of the American Planning Association* 45:538–48.

——. 1982. "Gentrification and Uneven Development." *Economic Geography* 58:139–55.

——. 1990. *Uneven Development: Nature, Capital, and the Production of Space.* Oxford, UK: Blackwell Publishing.

——. 1992a. "Contours of a Spatialized Politics: Homeless Vehicles and the Production of Geographical Scale." *Social Text* 33:54–81.

——. 1992b. "New City, New Frontier: Lower East Side as Wild, Wild West." In *Variations on a Theme Park*, edited by M. Sorkin. New York: Hill and Yang.

——. 1996. *The New Urban Frontier: Gentrification and the Revanchist City.* New York: Routledge.

——. 1999. "Which New Urbanism? New York City and the Revanchist 1990s." In *The Urban Moment: Cosmopolitan Essays on the Late-20th Century City*, edited by R. Beauregard and S. Body-Gendrot. Thousand Oaks, CA: Sage Publishing.

——. 2000. "What Happened to Class?" *Environment and Planning A* 32:1011–32.

——. 2002. "New Globalism, New Urbanism: Gentrification as Global Urban Strategy." *Antipode* 34:427–50.

Smith, N., P. Caris, and E. Wyly. 2001. "The 'Camden Syndrome' and the Menace of Suburban Decline: Residential Disinvestment and Its Discontents in Camden County, New Jersey." *Urban Affairs Review* 36:497–531.

Smith, N., and J. Defilippis. 1999. "The Reassertion of Economics: 1990s Gentrification in the Lower East Side." *International Journal of Urban and Regional Research* 23:638–53.

Smith, N., B. Duncan, and L. Reid. 1989. "From Disinvestment to Reinvestment: Tax Arrears and Turning Points in the East Village." *Housing Studies* 4:238–52.

Soja, E. 2000. *Postmetropolis: Critical Studies of Cities and Regions.* Oxford, UK: Blackwell Publishing.

Squires, G. 1992. "Community Reinvestment: An Emerging Social Movement." In *From Redlining to Reinvestment: Community Responses to Urban Disinvestment*, edited by G. Squires. Philadelphia: Temple University Press.

Staeheli, L., J. Kodras, and C. Flint, eds. 1997. *State Devolution in America: Implications for a Diverse Society.* Thousand Oaks, CA: Sage Publishing.

Standard and Poor's. 2000. www.standardandpoor.com.

Stockyard, J. 1998. "Epilogue: Public Housing—The Next Sixty Years." In *New Directions in Urban Public Housing*, edited by D. Varady, D. Preiser, and F. Russell. New Brunswick, NJ: Center for Urban Policy Research Press.

Stoker, G. 1995. "Regime Theory and Urban Politics." In *Theories of Urban Politics*, edited by D. Judge, G. Stoker, and H. Wolman. London: Sage Publishing.

Stone, C. 1989. *Regime Politics: Governing Atlanta, 1946–1988.* Lawrence: University of Kansas Press.

——. 1993. "Urban Regimes and the Capacity to Govern: A Political Economy Approach." *Journal of Urban Affairs* 15:1–28.

Stout, D. 2002. "Supreme Court Approves Public Housing Drug Ban." *New York Times*, March 26.

Sudjic, D. 1993. *The 100 Mile City.* New York: Harcourt Brace and Company.

Swann, D. 1988. *The Retreat of the State: Deregulation and Privatization in the U.K. and U.S.* Ann Arbor: University of Michigan Press.

Swanson, R., and R. Vogel. 1986. "Rating American Cities—Credit Risk, Urban Distress, and the Quality of Life." *Journal of Urban Affairs* 8:67–84.

Swyngedouw, E. 1997. "Neither Global nor Local: 'Glocalization' and the Politics of Scale." In *Spaces of Globalization: Reasserting the Power of the Local,* edited by K. Cox. New York: Guilford Press.

Tabb, W. 1982. *The Long Default: New York City and the Urban Fiscal Crisis.* New York: Monthly Review Press.

Texas Low Income Housing Information Service. 2002. www.texashousing.org, accessed February 2002.

Tickell, A., and J. Peck. 1995. "Social Regulation after Fordism: Regulation Theory Neo-Liberalism and the Global-Local Nexus." *Economy and Society* 243:357–86.

Todd, S. 1989. "Uneasy Wait for New Homes." *Home News and Tribune,* September 17, A1, A6.

Trebay, G. 1998. "Out of the Garret: A New Study Examines the Economic Life of Artists." *Village Voice,* October 21.

Trost, T. 1988. "Public, Private Projects Remake Face of Phoenix." *Arizona Business Gazette,* August 22, p. 8.

U.N. Habitat. 2001. *Cities in a Globalizing World: Global Report on Human Settlements.* New York: Earthscan Publications.

U.S. Bureau of the Census. 1960. *Census of Population and Housing.* Washington, D.C.

——. 1970. *Census of Population and Housing.* Washington, D.C.

——. 1980. *Census of Population and Housing.* Washington, D.C.

——. 1990. *Census of Population and Housing.* Washington, D.C.

——. 2000. *Census of Population and Housing.* Washington, D.C.

U.S. Department of Housing and Urban Development [HUD]. 1995. *HUD Reinvention: From Blueprint to Action.* Washington, D.C.: HUD.

——. 2002. www.hud.gov. Accessed February 2002.

——. 2003. "Quality Housing and Work Reform Act Background Material," www.hud.gov. Accessed July.

U.S. Department of Housing and Urban Development, Office of Public Housing Investments [OPHI]. 2001. "Unpublished Data on HOPE VI Grantees, 1993–2000." Washington, D.C.: HUD.

U.S. Department of Justice. 1998. "DOJ Urges SEC to Increase Competition for Securities Ratings Agencies." U.S. Department of Justice, www.usdoj.gov/atr/public/press_releases/1998/1596.htm.

Useem, M. 1996. *Investor Capitalism: How Money Managers are Changing the Face of Corporate America.* New York: Basic Books.

Vale, L. 2000. *From the Puritans to the Projects: Public Housing and Public Neighbors.* Cambridge, MA: Harvard University Press.

van Vliet, W. 1990. "The Privatization and Decentralization of Housing." In *Government and Housing: Developments in Seven Countries,* edited by W. van Vliet and J. van Weesep. Newbury Park, CA: Sage Publishing.

Varady, D., and W. Preiser. 1998. "Scattered-Site Public Housing and Housing Satisfaction: Implications for the New Public Housing Program." *Journal of the American Planning Association* 64:189–207.

Varady, D., and J. Raffel. 1995. *Selling Cities: Attracting Homebuyers through Schools and Housing Programs.* Albany: State University of New York Press.

Vergara, C. 1989. "Hell in a Very Tall Place." *Atlantic Monthly*, September, pp. 72–78.

Waddell, P. 1994. "Dallas: Will Suburban Dispersion Ever Cease?" *Built Environment* 20:25–39.

Waddell, P., and V. Shakla. 1993. "Employment Dynamics, Spatial Restructuring, and the Business Cycle." *Geographical Analysis* 25:35–52.

Walker, R. 1977. *The Suburban Solution.* Ph.D Dissertation. Department of Geography, Johns Hopkins University.

Wall Street Journal. 1996a. "Bond-Rating Agencies May Be Required to Disclose when Work Is Unsolicited." July 11.

——. 1996b. "Triple-A Dispute: Unsolicited Ratings from Moody's Upset Some Bond Issuers." May 2.

Wallace, E. 1990. "Riverwatch Plans Aired: Project Touted as City's New 'Gateway.'" *Home News and Tribune*, February 14, A1, A9.

Wallis, J., and B. Dollery. 1999. *Market Failure, Government Failure, Leadership, and Public Policy.* New York: St Martin's Press.

Warf, B. 1988. "The Port Authority of New York–New Jersey." *Professional Geographer* 40:287–97.

——. 1999. "The Hypermobility of Capital and the Collapse of the Keynesian State." In *Money and the Space Economy*, edited by R. Martin. London: John Wiley and Sons.

Weir, R. 1999. "Why Long Island City Hasn't Happened." *New York Times*, November 7, p. 1.

Wilson, D., and D. Grammenos. 2000. "Spatiality and Urban Redevelopment Movements." *Urban Geography* 21:361–70.

Wilson, W. 1987. *The Truly Disadvantaged: The Inner City, the Underclass, and Public Policy.* Chicago: University of Chicago Press.

Wyly, E., and D. Hammel. 1999. "Islands of Decay in Seas of Renewal: Urban Policy and Resurgence of Gentrification." *Housing Policy Debate* 10 (4):711–71.

——. 2000. "Cities and the Reinvestment Wave: Underserved Markets and the Gentrification of Housing Policy." *Housing Facts and Findings* 2 (1):11–15.

Yaro, R., and T. Hiss. 1996. *Region at Risk: The Third Regional Plan for the New York–New Jersey–Connecticut Metropolitan Area.* Washington, D.C.: Island Press.

Zukin, S. 1982. *Loft Living: Culture and Capital in Urban Change.* Baltimore: Johns Hopkins University Press.

INDEX